The Kindness
of Strangers

Issues in Academic Ethics
Series Editor: Steven M. Cahn

The Kindness of Strangers

Philanthropy and Higher Education

Deni Elliott

ROWMAN & LITTLEFIELD PUBLISHERS, INC.
Lanham • Boulder • New York • Toronto • Oxford

ROWMAN & LITTLEFIELD PUBLISHERS, INC.

Published in the United States of America
by Rowman & Littlefield Publishers, Inc.
A wholly owned subsidiary of The Rowman & Littlefield Publishing Group, Inc.
4501 Forbes Boulevard, Suite 200, Lanham, Maryland 20706
www.rowmanlittlefield.com

PO Box 317
Oxford
OX2 9RU, UK

Copyright © 2006 by Rowman & Littlefield Publishers, Inc.

British Library Cataloguing in Publication Information Available
Library of Congress Cataloging-in-Publication Data

Elliott, Deni.
    The kindness of strangers : philanthropy and higher education / Deni Elliott.
        p. cm.
    Includes bibliographical references and index.
    ISBN 0-7425-0710-6 (cloth : alk. paper) — ISBN 0-7425-0711-4 (pbk. : alk. paper)
    1. Educational fund raising—United States. 2. Education, Highe—United States—
Finance. 3. Endowments—United States. I. Title.
    LB2336.E45 2006
    378.1'06—dc22

                                                                    2005017113

Printed in the United States of America

⊚ ™ The paper used in this publication meets the minimum requirements of American
National Standard for Information Sciences—Permanence of Paper for Printed Library
Materials, ANSI/NISO Z39.48–1992.

This volume is dedicated to John Stuart and Harriet Taylor Mill, for their continued inspiration, and to my husband, Paul Martin Lester, because, to paraphrase JSM, like all that I have written for many years, this book belongs as much to him as to me. The work as it stands has had the inestimable advantage of his revision.

Thanks to University of South Florida, St. Petersburg graduate students Rita Florez, Heath Hooper, and Jeff Neeley for creating a reasonable bibliography from existing fragments. Thanks to students and colleagues at the University of Montana (1992–2003) and the University of South Florida, St. Petersburg (2003–2005) for engaging in sometimes heated discussions about legitimate limitations on the kindness of strangers.

Contents

Part I

PHILANTHROPY IN HIGHER EDUCATION TODAY

Introduction

In the late 1980s my scholarly focus took a detour. Spurred on by grants from the Lilly Foundation and Kellogg, my primary research in journalism ethics turned to the ethics of university fund-raising. My newfound interest in philanthropy and higher education was unabashedly based on money. I was the founding director of the Ethics Institute at Dartmouth College. The sustainability of the institute was based directly on my ability to bring in funding for project support and institutional overhead.

However, my academic curiosity was soon engaged by the analogies I discovered between the tactics of investigative journalism and those of prospect research. The reasons offered for justification of ethically questionable journalistic methods, such as using information about a source to coerce disclosure or withholding information that might impede the source's cooperation, seemed eerily similar to those used by development officers to justify questionable methods of developing information about potential donors.

Attending my first conference on institutional advancement was not unlike attending an investigative reporters' and editors' conference. Hunting metaphors ruled the day at both. Development officers talked about "targets," as did investigative journalists. Both groups talked about "going in for the kill."

In the early 1990s, now committed to academic analysis of investigation, wherever it occurred, I conducted a seminar on ethics and prospect research with a group of development officers from elite institutions. In those pre–on-line research days, researchers worked with friendly credit reporting agencies to gather financial information relating to potential donors. They answered my seemingly naive question about why they thought that it was okay to access information about their prospects' recent purchases by saying, "They would have paid with cash if they wanted to keep their purchase secret." But when I suggested that research techniques be approved by potential subjects, their educative responses turned defensive. One officer from a school that was, even then, sitting on a multimillion-dollar endowment said in frustration, "You don't get it. This is war."

And from a certain perspective, that development officer was right. Soliciting and enticing gifts, what officers call "providing an opportunity to give," is a competitive practice. Representatives from nonprofits that have matched donor intent with a potential donor's capacity to give line up at the door of wealthy individuals. Donors make choices among deserving beneficiaries. Institutions of higher education want to make sure that they get their share. Yet, metaphors that emphasize the hunt for funds or perception of fund-raising as war cast the relationship between giver and institution in a way that contradicts the very nature of philanthropy.

Philanthropists are volunteers who provide funds that they are not ethically required to give. One might make a case that individuals who have been enriched from the high-quality education received at their alma maters have a responsibility to give back to the institution. But, they certainly have no stronger obligation to their college or university than they have to their primary or secondary school. Or, a particular individual might, on balance, feel that a religious organization provided the spiritual direction necessary. Another might be especially grateful to the hospital that provided treatment for a life-threatening illness. There certainly is no obligation for donors to give some particular amount to one's college or university.

Donors have a variety of motivations, from the most pure philanthropic action made on behalf of the public good to the most self-interested concern made to produce the best tax benefits. Regardless of their motivation, their acts of giving are acts of beneficence. The act provides resources to an institution that it had no call to have, and that provides benefits that would not be there otherwise. Donor intent is important, but only when it comes to the expectations that accompany the gift.

Hunting and war may not be the appropriate attitude for dealing with potential donors, but acquiescence to donor expectations raises ethical concerns as well. Ethically speaking, the strings that accompany a gift should be accepted or declined based on how well those expectations fit with the mission of the individual school and of higher education as a social institution. In keeping with the institutional mission, decisions regarding the solicitation and acceptance of gifts and under what terms should be determined in an open communication process with all relevant parties.

Philanthropy, the kindness of strangers, serves as a foundation of support for American higher education. It ought not be a foundation that ultimately destroys the integrity and credibility that give higher education its unique role.

Chapter One

The New Landscape of Higher Education Funding

Graduate student and staff assistants sat around a small conference table at the University of Montana's Ethics Center with a staff meeting agenda in hand. All eyes were focused on the small black speakerphone in the center of the table that linked the staff with the absent Ethics Center director.

The director was off to another conference and trying to keep up with the Ethic Center's activities between talking to potential donors. The staff and the disembodied director ran through the agenda that included project updates and future travel plans with the single most important topic of discussion saved for last—funding.

The single most pressing issue was how to get the money needed to run the programs and keep the doors open for another year. The group suggested and rejected potential revenue-generating projects and instead concentrated on the grant proposals in process. Much of the time was spent discussing how to get on the university's foundation solicitation list so that the school's development officers would also work to cultivate donors for the Ethics Center. In annual pleas, the alumni were already being urged to support the activities that they had enjoyed when they were students. The center's staff, faculty members, and members of the community who made up its board of directors had developed the expertise to turn friends into donors.

This scene is replayed around many campus conference tables in today's era of self-supporting higher education. Increasingly, academic programs, departments, centers, admissions offices, and student service programs are expected to find their own sources of financial support or to supplement institutional support.

For the small, lightly staffed center at the Practical Ethics Center at the University of Montana, this pressure was achingly obvious as the staff and its director worked to tailor their projects and programs to bring in revenue. Whether that meant provocative titles for summer course offerings or weighing the cost of investment against likely outcomes when marketing the courses, it was simply not possible to think about how to deliver academic programs without concurrently thinking about how quickly those programs could support themselves.

More than ever, fund-raising, entrepreneurship, and grant writing are indispensable in a higher education fiscal strategy. Private funding sources are increasingly the means by which schools deliver programs that were once supported through tuition or state or federal support. Successful fund development is the means by which schools that do it well become and remain the most powerful schools in the nation. Elite schools, best positioned to attract such support, get richer. Struggling schools close their doors. Public institutions cut programs, increase class size, and whittle down the faculty.

In the early years of the twenty-first century, the financial landscape of higher education reflects increased external support. It is a landscape that includes benefactors as program architects and auditors. It is a landscape in which sales and psychology propel "institutional advancement." And, perhaps most oddly, it is a landscape where hardly anybody pays taxes.

To understand the ethical issues raised by increased external funding on higher education, it is important to understand how those financial changes correlate with other changes in the institution and its place in society.

HIGHER EDUCATION BECAME MASS EDUCATION

In the twentieth century, a bachelor's degree evolved from being a stepping-stone to becoming an entry-level requirement for many careers. According to the former university president Clara M. Lovett, "advanced degrees have replaced the baccalaureate as gateways to leadership positions in most professions."[1]

Lovett claims that "The baccalaureate degree used to be the educational end point for a privileged elite." But, the credentials provided by higher education helped employers develop an objective hiring process that could stand up to charges of unfairness.[2]

With the GI bill providing lucrative inducements from the end of World War II through the Vietnam War era, higher education became mass education. The results were unquestionably positive. According to Lovett, "The 20th Century marked the ascendancy of American higher education to first place in the world. What made it so was a unique convergence of excellence in teaching and research, access for large numbers of students regardless of income or social class, and institutional pluralism."[3]

Indeed, some argue that, at this point, higher education is a right rather than a privilege. According to Adolph Reed, "Higher education is a basic social good. As such, it should be available to all, without cost, who meet admission standards. The federal government, as the guarantor of social rights, should bear primary responsibility for providing free college for all."[4]

If higher education is a basic social good, it can be argued that public funds should cover the costs. But, even extreme proposals such as Reed's argue to extend rather than create public support for education. State and federal governments do support higher education, despite declining direct subsidies. Federal subsidies come in the form of grant support for academic research and low-cost financial aid packages for students. Institutions, students, and their benefactors all benefit from higher education's tax-exempt status. Nevertheless, the rising cost of higher education threatens to cause a retreat from mass education to higher education as a privilege for the wealthy.

COSTS OF HIGHER EDUCATION KEEP GOING UP

A report to the U.S. Congress from the House Committee on Education and the Workforce in October 2003 detailed the rising costs of higher education:

- The cost of higher education has been rising significantly faster than the rate of inflation or the growth of family incomes for decades. . . . [D]uring the 1980s, the cost of attending college rose over three times as fast as median family income.
- . . . [O]ver the ten-year period ending in 2002–2003, *after adjusting for inflation,* average tuition and fees at both public and private four-year colleges and universities rose 38 percent.
- According to the Advisory Committee on Student Financial Assistance, cost factors prevent 48 percent of college-qualified high school graduates from attending a four-year institution, and 22 percent from attending any college at all.[5]

These increased costs translate directly into increased tuition burdens on families. According to one scholar, Robert Martin, "The relative real burden for students attending public universities has increased by approximately 80 percent during the period 1980–95, while for students attending private universities it has increased by 148 percent over the same period."[6]

Martin suggests that the reasons for steeply rising costs have not been adequately analyzed or understood. "The rate of increase in the average cost of educating students is excessive no matter what standard you use to evaluate it in relation to other costs in the U.S. economy."[7]

Martin points out that higher administrative costs have risen more dramatically than the costs of teaching or research: "Accelerating a four-decade pattern, expenditures for presidents, deans, and their assistants grew 26 percent faster than instructional budgets in the 1980s." More faculty are also teaching fewer students, with the number of faculty per one thousand students increased by 28 percent in public institutions and 26 percent in private institutions between 1976 and 1996.[8]

Families have traditionally paid less than the actual cost of educating students. The price charged is less than the total costs.[9] Whether the subsidy comes from state legislatures for public institutions or from actual wealth in private institutions, the average subsidy is about the same—$8,750 per student per year. But, what is actually charged in tuition varies considerably. In private education, "average expenditures are half again as large as in the public sector, but the average price of private institutions is six times higher."[10]

THE CASE FOR GOVERNMENTAL FUNDING

Higher education is a social good. It creates a more educated and, one hopes, a more enlightened citizenry. Research shows that higher education helps solve social and individual ills and builds on our cultural heritage to create future possibilities in science, technology, and the humanities.

As Robert Martin argues,

> Society chooses to subsidize education for a variety of sound reasons. The most important reason is that the sum of benefits received by society exceeds the private benefits individual students obtain from education. Current students are the direct beneficiaries of today's subsidies, and the subsidies are provided by the contributions and taxes paid by their elders. At each point in time, students are entrusted with a social contract, a contract that they are expected to pass forward to the next generation. If they fail to provide education subsidies to the next generation, at least in the same proportion as the subsidies they received, then they have not honored the social contract between generations.[11]

Theoretically, subsidized higher education implicitly rests on a multigenerational quid pro quo.

Martin also argues that public funding of higher education is in the self-interest of taxpayers. "By choosing to relieve ourselves of the current financial obligations, we have undermined society's ability to finance our own retirement."[12]

Reed notes that compared to other federal initiatives, higher education is cheap. "The total bill for all students currently enrolled in higher education is under $27 billion, less than one-third of what George W. Bush is spending on Iraq this year. Closing recently opened corporate tax loopholes would also more than meet the program's cost, even if enrollments doubled as a result of eliminating tuition as a constraint."[13]

GOVERNMENTAL FUNDING IS COMPETITIVE

If there is a social contract between generations for public funds to "pay forward" what has been offered to the current generation, higher education is not the only contender for a share of the subsidy. The pay forward argument can be applied equally well to other programs at the state and federal level used to advance the public good. All social goods are implicitly offered as quid pro quo—society provides a person with the implicit understanding that the individual will return the favor as a taxpayer and a contributing citizen. Whatever the argument for public support, higher education competes with defense (or homeland security) funding, welfare and medical programs, and business incentives as well as K–12 education and new pre-K initiatives. The increase in demands for public funding has coincided with politicians' promises for and citizens' expectations of lowered taxes.

Of the various publicly supported institutions, higher education is in a better place than most to absorb cuts in funding. Unlike other social institutions, higher education has potential for generating its own income and for coping with lost revenue. "Public colleges and universities respond to decreasing state support by increasing tuition. . . . Colleges and universities may also respond by cutting academic programs, staff and faculty and delaying major purchases."[14]

The result is that higher education is the easiest appropriation to cut:

First, higher education institutions have separate budgets with reserves of their own and perceived fiscal flexibility to absorb temporary fiscal adversity, unlike state agencies which do not have these features. Second, higher education is perceived as having more flexibility to translate budget changes into employee pay than state agencies, which are bound by statewide pay scales. Third, higher education is seen as having more flexibility to vary spending levels (e.g., through changes in courses offered and class sizes) than most programs, which have spending levels that are more fixed. Fourth, in most states, higher education has the ability to maintain and increase spending levels by shifting larger proportions of costs to users by tuition and fee increases.[15]

SUCCESS IN HIGHER EDUCATION IS HARD TO MEASURE

Increasingly, legislatures want to see outcomes to justify the public funding that higher education receives. "A 1997 survey by the State Higher Education Executive Officers (SHEEO) found that 37 of the 50 states reported some kind of accountability or performance reporting, with another five indicating plans to establish systems in the future. Most report only on public institutions, but a few include information about the private sector as well."[16]

According to Wellman, "state decision-makers are keenly interested in promoting efficiency and productivity in higher education. Skeptical of traditional methods of supporting institutions that equate quality with inputs rather than outcomes, they are looking for ways to maintain or increase instructional capacity while holding the line on new money."[17]

Traditionally, schools have snagged bragging rights and respect among peer institutions based on the competition of applicants, a low acceptance rate, and the quality of their incoming classes. However, state legislators and auditors are less concerned about the quality of students that schools attract. Instead, state funders look at measures such as retention, graduation, and the length of time between matriculation and graduation. They look at how institutions can achieve these outcomes with the least cost.

COMPETITION AMONG INSTITUTIONS
OF HIGHER EDUCATION

Competitive pressures between institutions, particularly for students who can foot their own bills, have resulted in marketing tactics that address students and their families as consumers who are looking for the best higher education that their money can buy and leave less wealthy students out of the picture.

Despite attempts by some well-endowed institutions to eliminate tuition costs for low-income students or to freeze tuition for a year or two, wealthy students are increasingly claiming the space at top colleges.[18] According to a *New York Times* article in the first part of 2004, "At prestigious universities around the country, from flagship state colleges to the Ivy League, more and more students from upper-income families are edging out those from the middle class, according to university data. . . . More members of this year's freshman class at the University of Michigan have parents making at least $200,000 a year than have parents making less than the national median of about $53,000, according to a survey of Michigan students."[19]

Students have become savvy in their quest for the best institution. "As the income of college graduates has risen much faster than that of less educated workers, getting into the right college has become an obsession in many upper-income high schools. . . . With the help of summer programs, preparation classes for college entrance examinations and sometimes their own private admission counselors, the students in these schools put together more impressive applications than they once did."[20] The combination of wealth and opportunity equals stronger college applications than less wealthy or connected high school graduates can provide. The ability to prepare a competitive application is increasingly dependent upon one's wealth, the quality of one's high school, and access to expert advice. Applicants with only intellect and desire to attend an elite school are at a disadvantage from the start.

Wealth also results in parents who contact advancement and admissions offices simultaneously in their quest for a place for their child. In 2003, the *Wall Street Journal* ran a story designed as a helpful guide for parents to decide how much to give to boost their child's chances at admission. Consider these passages:

> As competition for slots at selective colleges becomes ever more ferocious, affluent parents may be more inclined to pay to gain an edge, but just as uncertain about how to do it without seeming crass. A big donation—or the prospect of one—doesn't guarantee admission. It does, however, put applicants on the priority list of the college's fund-raising, or development, office.
>
> The question for many parents is how big is "big"? The price for special treatment rises with the college's endowment. Educational consultants say a five-figure donation—as low as $20,000—is enough to draw attention of a liberal-arts college with an endowment in the hundreds of millions. That's a relatively modest sum compared with the $140,000-plus parents pay for four years of tuition and housing.
>
> At an exclusive college, it can take at least $50,000 with some assurance that future donations will be even greater. At top-25 universities, a minimum of $100,000; for the top 10, at least $250,000 and often seven figures. Parents who aren't that flush can compensate by pledging stock or a portion of their estate through various deferred-giving arrangements.[21]

The *Wall Street Journal* also acknowledges the ethical concern:

> Some parents and educators consider it ethically questionable for people to take advantage of their wealth to push under-qualified children into selective colleges, perhaps edging out a more needy and academically superior applicant. In many cases, students may be happier and more successful at second-tier colleges that better suit their abilities. And dangling upfront donations invites a lifetime of solicitations from the university.
>
> College administrators are reluctant to discuss such preferences. But when pressed, Duke and others argue that tuition alone doesn't cover the cost of

education, while donations underwrite scholarships, faculty salaries and other expenses. They also say they admit only students who can flourish. Duke, for one, plans to limit these types of admissions to 65 students this year, and fewer next year.[22]

Federal funding, like parents willing to buy their offsprings' way into college, also favors the wealthiest colleges and universities. According to a 2003 report in the *New York Times,*

> The federal government typically gives the wealthiest private universities, which often serve the smallest percentage of low-income students, significantly more financial aid money than their struggling counterparts with much greater shares of poor students.
>
> Brown, for example, got $169.23 for every student who merely applied for financial aid in order to run its low-interest Perkins loan program in the 2000–1 academic year. Dartmouth got $174.88; Stanford, $211.80. . . . [T]he median for the nation's colleges was $14.38. . . .
>
> Nearly 200 colleges received less than $3 per applicant for financial aid. The University of Wisconsin at Madison got 21 cents.[23]

Institutions also compete against each other to best cater to today's student. It is thought that academics alone won't woo the young adult of the twenty-first century.

Resources have gone to nonacademic services that some have referred to as "mission creep." As part of a National Public Radio (NPR) report in early 2004, Representative Howard McKeon (R-CA) described some of the window dressing designed to attract students: "Ohio State University spent $140 million to build what many of their peers call a Taj Mahal featuring kayaks, canoes, indoor batting cages, rope course, massages and climbing wall big enough for 50 students to climb it simultaneously. The University of Cincinnati is spending $200 million on a Main Street of sorts . . . a mall-style student center."[24] Consumer-focused education in the twenty-first century takes into account the desires of young adults as much as their intellectual needs.

Another type of competition has appeared on the higher education scene at the turn of the twenty-first century—for-profit institutions that cater to nontraditional students through on-line and short, intensive residency programs.[25] Viewed as "glamour stocks" that rival Internet companies, for-profit institutions offer an approach to higher education decidedly different from the traditional campus. The University of "Phoenix teaches its 60,000 students with a total of 45 full-time faculty members and 4,500 adjuncts. Its libraries have no books— only journals and magazines available online. It operates in industrial locations and shopping malls rather than lovely parks."[26] But, nontraditional students who attend these marketing-focused institutions do not need to give up their jobs to complete basic or advanced degrees. Asynchronous on-line courses and weekend residency programs allow working students to complete degrees at a fraction of the price that it would cost if they returned to school and paid the overhead that traditional institutions charge above actual cost per credit.

Lovett argues that the for-profits offer a model that can lead higher education as a whole into the twenty-first century. This model, in her view, veers away from the mission creep of campus becoming the equivalent of a well-appointed camp and to better justification for state funding. "The transition from status quo to information-age organizations would benefit higher education by enhancing quality, expanding access, and protecting pluralism. It would not eliminate the need for public subsidies of institutions and students. . . . As elements of this country's 21st-century infrastructure, higher education's core functions—teaching and research—have a compelling claim to support from the public purse. This is not the case for services and amenities that students and communities might access off-campus or electronically, such as full-service campus health clinics, entertainment events for the general public, athletics, and financial and legal counseling."[27]

Some traditional schools have, intentionally or not, followed the lead of the for-profits by "using fewer full-time tenured faculty and more part-time adjuncts" or "capitalizing on an academic reputation to sell employee education to major business firms, directly or electronically."[28]

Lovett says, "Finally, colleges and universities could move decisively to dismantle industrial-age, Taylorite measures of time-on-task and productivity, such as semesters, credit hours, and graduation requirements that are only marginally related to mastery of subject matter and its applications. These late 19th Century constructs could be replaced by flexible entrance and exit procedures and by competency assessments available to students anytime their mentors judge them ready to be assessed."[29]

GREATER RELIANCE ON EXTERNAL FUNDING

Gone are the days when public academic institutions rested on their legislative appropriations. Public support became public assistance and is now, in many states, little more than public land upon which higher education takes place.

According to *Educational Marketer,* "State appropriations for higher education, which flattened in 2002–03," fell in 2004 "as a result of decreased tax revenue."[30] Lower state appropriations results in higher tuition and fees and the elimination of courses and faculty.[31]

The decline in state funding of higher education is seen as a combination of decreased tax base and shifting support to other services that compete for the state dollar. A summary from the National Center for Public Policy and Higher Education warns:

> Even if states experience normal economic growth over the next eight years, all but a handful of states will find it impossible, given their existing tax policies, to continue funding their current level of public services. . . . Further, due to demographic and economic factors in most states, the claims on the public purse will be greater for other programs than for higher education—continuing the trend that results in colleges and universities getting a consistently smaller slice of the state appropriations pie. If economic growth is slower than normal, if states continue to cut taxes, or if states increase spending in areas outside of higher education, then the outlook for support of public higher education will be even worse.[32]

The public university is no longer supported by, and in service to, the taxpaying public. Rather, private sources of funding, needed now to supplement public money and tuition, have created a "hybrid" university.

According to Eric Wentworth, then vice president of the Council for Advancement and Support of Education:

> The evolution to more corporate-like campus cultures has come to seem inevitable. Cost pressures have mounted inexorably. While colleges and universities relentlessly raise tuition year after year, they meet with growing resistance and resentment; occasionally there is even talk of government-mandated price controls. Federal financial aid for students has failed to keep pace with their needs. State governments, besieged with budget woes, have trimmed their own campus support.
>
>   In this environment, educational fund raising has gained greater strategic importance. At the same time, it has come under intense pressures. As institutional resource needs have soared, so has demand for more private support. Once icing on the cake, annual giving support now represents basic bread-and-butter revenue. Fund drives in recent years have become complex, high-stakes mega-campaigns.[33]

THE NEW PHILANTHROPIST

Into this mix of accountability, efficiency, higher tuition, and lower state appropriations, a new kind of philanthropist has appeared on campus. Called "new economy" do-gooders[34] or venture philanthropists,[35] these givers combine wealth with activism. They donate time, energy, and money as well as a watchful eye over the causes in which they invest. Donors take seats on the "boards of grantees, a strategy that most traditional foundations and many charities regard as intrusive because of the potential for undue influence over the grantees' missions and policies."[36]

Technology "made more people richer faster and at a younger age than any time in history. And these new millionaires, many of whom are under 40, aren't waiting to dole out their fortunes. True to their work-as-life code, they are, as a group, highly engaged with their causes, which they research meticulously, often with the help of professional charity consultants. And far from monuments and hospital wings, these new-economy donors are consumed with accountability and results."[37]

The new breed of givers—the approximately five million millionaires in the United States—helps fill the gap left by government funding. They bring to their philanthropy the skills that made them early successes in their own lives: "Many are marketers, innovators, and gifted managers. They have valuable connections and they're spry enough to initiate novel ways of giving."[38]

These givers are also motivated by failings in mainstream philanthropy. "They say an unwillingness by many foundations to support innovation among charities, to support their long-term infrastructure needs, and to demand tangible results from grantees has hindered the effectiveness of many groups."[39]

Letts and Grossman have identified six points "that distinguish venture capital practices from those in more traditional philanthropy." These include:

1. *Risk.* Venture capitalists are more likely to take and manage risk than traditional foundations.
2. *Performance measures.* Venture capitalists are more concerned with long-term outcomes.
3. *Closeness of a relationship.* Venture capitalists become involved with selection of personnel and strategic planning.
4. *Amount of funding.* Venture capitalists put a substantially higher percentage of project funding into chosen projects.
5. *Length of a relationship.* Venture capitalists plan on staying involved for far longer than most foundations.
6. *Exit strategy.* Venture capitalists' contributions come with exit strategy attached.[40]

An example of such a giver is Greg Carr, a graduate of the Master of Public Policy Program at the Kennedy School of Government, who made his millions in his thirties in voice mail and Internet companies. "In 1999 he gave $18 million to the Kennedy School of Government when, he says, 'I noticed that my alma mater didn't have a human-rights center.' It was the largest gift an alumnus had ever given the school, and funded the Carr Center for Human Rights."[41]

Carr said that he chose Harvard "because he realized that he'd get more for his money if he let academic and policymakers—experts in the human rights field—do the work that he could not."[42]

Carr had ended direct involvement with the day-to-day operations of the center by 2001, but "[d]uring a trial year in 1998–99, however, he was an 'active donor': working with faculty members to decide how the center should be structured and what issues it should pursue."[43]

Other donors create incentives to encourage better institutional involvement in the development of funds. One such example is Robert B. Pamplin Jr. At age fifty-two, Mr. Pamplin donated funds based on the ability of students, faculty and administrators to "Beat Bob." "For every student, staff member, and professor who showed up at the gym and 'Beat Bob' at his daunting fitness records—such as 625 sit-ups in 15 minutes or 116 continuous pushups—Mr. Pamplin gave $25,000 to the library fund. He donated smaller amounts for smaller feats, such as $250 for 50 sit-ups in one minute."[44]

Even foundations that have traditionally awarded grants to enable institutions of higher education to carry out goals identified at the schools are experimenting with more direct involvement. "The Alfred P. Sloan Foundation, which has pumped millions of dollars into distance-education projects over the past seven years, has shifted some of its focus from financing new programs to promoting existing distance-learning opportunities to students."[45]

The focus for the Sloan Foundation at the turn of the century was "on creating an online catalog—called the Sloan Consortium Catalog—where students can find information on various programs."[46]

The Posse Foundation provides another approach to creating change through donations. The foundation seeks high school seniors who demonstrate leadership potential and problem-solving skills in addition to having the potential for success in higher education. The foundation then puts the chosen students through thirty-four weeks of training to prepare them for campus life. The foundation also "seeks to work with colleges, large and small, that have strong academic reputations, that seek a more diverse set of students, that share the foundation's belief in minority students as 'agents of change' on the campus, and that will stick with the program for at least five years."[47] The foundation requires that institutions accept students in groups of ten and that the institutions overlook traditional factors such as grades and SAT scores. The foundation provides full scholarships for students, having given $17 million in scholarships to 234 students between 1990 when the first students matriculated through 2000.[48]

Even the more traditional foundations that support worthy projects and stay out of an institution's way are looking for benchmarks for success. "For example, a new core value of many foundations is impact analysis. Legislative action calling for more accountability on foundation-based support and increased return on charitable investments has forced foundations to reexamine their strategies and focus on efforts that can demonstrate high-impact results. . . . Universities, historically, have not been expected to develop and monitor quantifiable benchmarks and, more often, are experienced in implementing a worthy project whose impact is difficult to measure."[49]

Some administrators and faculty are uncomfortable with the new level of involvement by donors. For example, admissions officers at Rice University, which dropped out of the Posse Program after admitting eighteen students in 1994 and 1995, "bristled at admitting kids who, by traditional measures, were 'wildly under-qualified.' Lehigh quit the program largely because a rift had grown between the Posse Foundation and the minority engineering council, which "wanted to add more summer technology training and math training," explains Harvey G. Stenger, a former dean of Lehigh's College of Engineering. The foundation, for its part, "was more into creating the interpersonal bonds to survive," he says. "Lehigh agreed with the engineering council."[50]

Even though seventeen of the eighteen Posse students admitted to Rice graduated and all but two of the thirteen admitted to Lehigh completed their studies, the determining factor to separate from the program was not student success but institutional versus foundation control.

Others embrace the new style of donation. The Dr. Robert B. Pamplin Jr. School of Business Administration at the Roman Catholic University of Portland is a faith-based curriculum.

The school features ethics courses that, for example, scrutinize Nike's use of overseas labor. Students can also participate in an "adopt-a-business" program that puts their accounting and management skills to work for companies and retail stores in poor, inner-city areas.

Ronald P. Hill, then dean of the school, says the programs are of university design but were influenced by Mr. Pamplin's values. "He's a billionaire that doesn't just want to give money away but wants to change the way people think and do things, and he's thought very carefully about how he wants that to occur," Hill said.[51]

Philanthropy and higher education, long-time partners, have developed a new and essential level of intimacy. The short-term effects—money for the institutions, the satisfaction of being a change agent for donors, and the privatization of yet another social institution that may relieve the burdens of legislatures, some think permanently—may have costs of their own.

NOTES

Thanks to Michael Monahan for his assistance with this chapter.

1. Clara M. Lovett, "Cracks in the Bedrock: Can U.S. Higher Education Remain Number One?" *Change* (March 2002), http://www.findarticles.com/cf_dls/m1254/2_34/83667241/p1/article.jhtml (accessed 28 March 2004).

2. Ibid.

3. Ibid.

4. Adolph Reed, "Majoring in Debt," *The Progressive* (January 2004), http://www.findarticles.com/cf_0/m1295/1_68/112247537/print.jhtml (accessed 28 March 2004).

5. "The Skyrocketing Cost of Higher Education," http://edworkforce.house.gov/issues/108th/education/highereducation/factsheetcost101003.htm (accessed 21 November 2004); emphasis in original.

6. Robert Martin, "Why Tuition Costs Are Rising So Quickly," *Challenge* (July–August, 2002): 2.

7. Ibid.

8. Ibid.

9. Jane V. Wellman, "Assessing State Accountability Systems," *Change* (March 2001), http://www.findarticles.com/cf_o/m1254/2_33/71966507/print.jhtml (accessed 28 March 2004).

10. Ibid.

11. Martin, "Why Tuition Costs Are Rising So Quickly."

12. Ibid.

13. Reed, "Majoring in Debt."

14. National Education Association, "Financing Higher Education: A Crisis in State Funding," 2004, http://www.nea.org/he/fiscalcrisis/ (accessed 26 March 2004).

15. Highereducation.org, "Prospects for Funding Higher Education," 2004, http://www.highereducation.org/reports/hovey/hovey5.shtml (accessed 26 March 2004).

16. Wellman, "Assessing State Accountability Systems."

17. Ibid.

18. NPR, "Analysis: Rising College Tuition," 25 March 2004, http://nl.newsbank.com/nlsearch/we/Archives?p_action=doc&p_docid=1018CB (accessed 26 March 2004).

19. David Leonhardt, "As Wealthy Fill Top Colleges, Concerns Grow over Fairness," *New York Times,* 24 April 2004.

20. Ibid.

21. *Wall Street Journal,* "Buying Your Way into College: So Just How Much Do You Need to Donate to Get Your Kid In?" 12 March 2003.

22. Ibid.

23. Greg Winter, "Rich Colleges Receiving Richest Share of U.S. Aid," *New York Times,* 9 November 2003.

24. NPR, "Analysis: Rising College Tuition."

25. Julie Flaherty, "The Alternative Universe: A Guide," *Education Life,* April 25, 2004, 30.

26. Gordon C. Winston, "For-Profit Higher Education: Godzilla or Chicken Little?" *Change* (January–February 1999), http://www.findarticles.com/cf_0/m1254/1_31/54051223/print.jhtml (accessed 28 March 2004).

27. Lovett, "Cracks in the Bedrock."

28. Winston, "For-Profit Higher Education: Godzilla or Chicken Little?"

29. Ibid.

30. "Higher Education Takes a Hit in State Funding in 2003–2004," *Educational Marketer* (2004), http://www.findarticles.com/cf_dls/mODHM/1_35/112018933/print.jhtml (accessed 26 March 2004).

31. National Education Association, "Financing Higher Education: A Crisis in State Funding," http://www.nea.org/he/fiscalcrisis/ (accessed 26 March 2004).

32. Dennis Jones, "State Shortfalls Projected throughout the Decade," *The National Center for Public Policy and Higher Education Policy Alert* (2003): 1–2.

33. Eric B. Wentworth, "The Ethical Landscape," in *The Ethics of Asking,* ed. Deni Elliott, 1–15 (Baltimore: Johns Hopkins University Press, 1995).

34. Betsy Streisand, "The New Philanthropy: The Tech Economy May Have Collapsed, but Tech Millionaires Are Still Giving," *U.S. News and World Report,* 11 June 2001, http://www.usnews.com/usnews/issue/010611/biztech/philanthropy.htm (accessed 24 July 2001).

35. Thomas J. Billitteri, "Venturing a Bet on Giving," *Chronicle of Philanthropy* (1 June 2000): 1, 7, 10, 12, 23.

36. Ibid.

37. Streisand, "The New Philanthropy."

38. Katherine Dunn, "Philanthropy in a New Key," *Harvard Magazine* (May–June 2001): 39–44.

39. Bilitteri, "Venturing a Bet on Giving."

40. C. W. Letts, W. Ryan, and A. Grossman, "Virtuous Capital: What Foundations Can Learn from Venture Capitalists," *Harvard Business Review,* March–April 2000, cited in Morino Institute, "The New Economy and Venture Philanthropy: Excerpts from a Report," *Chronicle of Philanthropy,* 1 June 2000.

41. Dunn, "Philosophy in a New Key."

42. Ibid.

43. Ibid.

44. Scott Carlson, "An Oregon Philanthropist Spreads a Philosophy of Learning by Doing," *Chronicle of Higher Education* (21 January 2000): 33A.

45. Sarah Carr, "Sloan Foundation Turns Its Attention from Creating Programs to Promoting Them," *Chronicle of Higher Education* (2 June 2000): 49A.

46. Ibid.

47. John L. Pulley, "A Program That Believes in Going with the Posse," *Chronicle of Higher Education* (28 April 2000).

48. Ibid.

49. Alison R. Bernstein, "Is Philanthropy Abandoning Higher Education?" *The Presidency* (Fall 2003): 36–37.

50. Pulley, "A Program That Believes in Going with the Posse."

51. Carlson, "An Oregon Philanthropist Spreads a Philosophy of Learning by Doing," 34.

Chapter Two

Solicitation, Gifts, and Academic Mission

The economic picture of higher education has changed. Needs are greater, subsidies are fewer, and alternative funding is more alluring, whatever the quid pro quo. Nevertheless, institutional officials are ethically obligated to consider solicitation techniques, gifts, and donor requests against an appreciation of the unique role of higher education.

The mission of higher education serves as a legitimate basis for determining actions that support higher education. If the proposed action is contrary to the mission, the action is properly viewed as hindering the institution it seeks to promote. If the proposed action complements or furthers the mission, it is justifiable.

Higher education has a unique function in society—its administrators and faculty are among the best educated and most respected professionals, and its institutions and participants enjoy special benefits. The integrity of higher education is directly dependent on how well individual actions match an institution's mission.

The special role of higher education is best expressed in terms of its mission. The unique mission of higher education reflects the institution's societal role. Recognized social institutions such as government, medicine, journalism, and education have separate but complementary roles. In an ideal society, social institutions work harmoniously and comprehensively to mitigate some harms for citizens and to promote the aggregate good. Mission can also be thought of as the essence of the institution—the characteristics without which the institution would no longer be recognizable.

The "Statement of Ethics" by the Council for the Advancement and Support of Education (CASE) affirms the need to preserve institutional integrity in the process of development activities. The statement reads: "Institutional advancement professionals, by virtue of their responsibilities within the academic community, represent their colleges, universities, and schools to the larger society. They have, therefore, a special duty to exemplify the best qualities of their institutions, and to observe the highest standards of personal and professional conduct."[1]

The mission of higher education is complex and multifaceted. The expression of a mission by individual institutions should match geographical location, culture, and particular histories. The expression also reflects differences in the ranking of importance of individual aspects of the general mission. Some aspects give more focus to the teaching mission, others to research, and still others to the relationship between the institution and community or culture. The following points express what must be accepted by an institution that views itself as an example of higher education:

- Generally speaking, institutions of higher education promote academic values. According to Robinson and Moulton, "Academic values . . . promote the discovery and exchange of knowledge and ideas. In terms of academic values a better world is one where people are wiser, more knowledgeable, and more intellectually resourceful. The activities that go on in academic institutions are supposed to serve these goals."[2]
- Allan focuses on the practice of the institution rather than on direct goals. He says, "Students in attending a college should find themselves interacting with others in a milieu marked by human actions that are, or should be, conditioned by moral practices, by the resources that help people decide to do whatever they do in an appropriate manner." Open communication is essential. Allan says, "The essence of a college is that it is an agora for conversation. Whatever its mission, its methods, and the outcomes it might seek, it is first of all an environment where many voices can be heard conversing with each other."[3]
- In its "Statement on Professional Ethics," the American Association of University Professors (AAUP) would add that there is a responsibility to converse in a civil fashion. "Professors do not discriminate against or harass colleagues. They respect and defend the free inquiry of associates. In the exchange of criticism and ideas professors show due respect for the opinions of others."[4]
- The mission of the university is understood as not simply producing an educated student or new knowledge. There is a process that is essential to the setting. According to Peter Scott, "Universities not only express intellectual and scientific values directly through their teaching and research; they also embody powerful organisational values (notably in terms of collegial governance, institutional autonomy and academic freedom) and equally influ-

ential instrumental values (because of the increasingly potent role they play within the "knowledge society"); finally universities contribute crucially to the formation of wider social and cultural values."[5]

Indeed, as Amy Gutmann points out in *Democratic Education,* the setting of an academic institution in a democracy implies an adherence to the principal tenets of the democratic process. "Insofar as fostering free scholarly inquiry is the primary purpose of universities, neither their social value nor their autonomy from external political control varies directly with the degree to which they are internally democratized. But insofar as universities are also valued— and valuable—as communities, whose associational purposes are advanced by faculty and student participation, democratic societies have an interest in supporting a greater degree of self-governance within universities."[6]

Many scholars who write about the mission of higher education reflect the foundations that serve as the basis for evaluation for faculty and administrators within institutions. According to Edward Long, "Right practice in higher education involves concern about three dimensions of the campus experience, all of which must be addressed in appropriate ways by any college or university. These three functions, for which the term 'responsibilities' is more appropriate are: (1) the responsibility of the college or university for the identification, maturation, and enrichment of selfhood; (2) the responsibility of the college or university for the discovery/construction, extension, and dissemination of knowledge and culture; and, (3) the responsibility of the college or university for the well-being of society."[7]

Long's first area straddles the teaching and research aspects of the institutional mission. Teaching facilitates the development of students' intellectual powers; research defines the individual professor within the academic world. The AAUP addresses this part of the mission by stating that "Professors encourage the free pursuit of learning in their students. They hold before them the best scholarly and ethical standards of their discipline. Professors demonstrate respect for students as individuals and adhere to their proper roles as intellectual guides and counselors. Professors make every reasonable effort to foster honest academic conduct and to ensure that their evaluations of students reflect each student's true merit. They respect the confidential nature of the relationship between professor and student."[8]

Other scholars concentrate on the outcome for students. Robert Lipkin says that "a well-educated American university graduate should have the following characteristics: she should know enough about the dominant culture—including its science, social science, and humanities—to identify the dominant culture as a subject of criticism. Second, she should be trained in the analytic and critical skills necessary to thoroughly evaluate the dominant culture and be able to compare it with other cultures. Third, other cultures should be studied on their own in order to understand as many experiments in human flourishing as possible."[9]

The research aspect of the institutional mission as practiced by professors is described by AAUP. "Their primary responsibility to their subject is to seek and state the truth as they see it. To this end professors devote their energies to developing and improving their scholarly competence. They accept the obligation to exercise critical self-discipline and judgment in using, extending, and transmitting knowledge. They practice intellectual honesty."[10]

Gutmann adds that both scholar and institution have duties relating to research. "The duty of a scholar . . . is to avoid those influences that are likely to impede—or to give the appearance of impeding—scholarly judgment."[11]

And, "Just as the academic freedom of scholars carries with it an individual duty to resist improper influences, so the freedom of the academy carries with it an institutional duty not to exert improper influences on scholars. . . . By virtue of their democratic purpose, universities have not only a right to relative autonomy from external political control but also an obligation to create an environment that is conducive to the exercise of scholarly autonomy."[12]

The last foundation is the relationship between institution and community. According to Gutmann, "Universities are more likely to serve society well not by adopting the quantified values of the market, but by preserving a realm where the nonquantifiable values of intellectual excellence and integrity, and the supporting moral principles of nonrepression and nondiscrimination, flourish. In serving society well by preserving such a realm, a university acts as an educator of officeholders rather than simply a gatekeeper of office. Acting as an educator entails appreciating rather than abolishing the discrepancies between intellectual standards and marketing practices, since such discrepancies often signal a moral failing of the market rather than an intellectual failure of the university."[13]

The unique societal role of institutions of higher education requires focus on more than short-term societal needs. According to Paul Olscamp, writing on ethical obligations of college presidents, leaders in higher education have the responsibility of explaining how a curriculum advances an educational mission. "Doing so successfully presupposes that the university has an overarching vision of its comprehensive educational effort, into which every piece of the educational program fits like pieces of a picture puzzle. This also presupposes that the university leadership can relate this overall plan or concept to our societal needs, not just employment, but for purposes of good citizenry, the protection of legal and moral right, and social progress."[14]

It is also important to note that while the actions of administrators and professors are essential to the development and retention of the mission for higher education, appearance matters as well. Higher education enjoys a relatively high level of trust among the citizenry. For example, a national poll conducted by the *Chronicle of Higher Education* in 2003 found that "the public's confidence in private colleges was exceeded only by its trust in the U.S. military. Four-year and two-year public colleges ranked only slightly lower, just below local police forces."[15]

An institutional commitment to the mission sustains higher education. Community trust in higher education is based on the perceived commitment to the mission by the institution.

Aspects of the mission can be distilled to a set of guidelines to govern decisions regarding solicitation, gifts, and donor requests.

Generally speaking, institutional officers should choose actions that:

1. Promote scholarly inquiry or the unfettered exchange of knowledge and ideas.
2. Promote the ability of scholars and students to communicate freely.
3. Promote the ability of campus participants to sustain a self-governing institution.
4. Promote students or scholars in their quest to be critics, evaluators, and comparative analysts of all cultures, institutions and practices.
5. Promote antirepression or antidiscrimination within the campus community.
6. Promote the appearance of commitment to intellectual excellence and integrity.
7. Promote those areas in which higher education would serve as a critic of other social institutions.

These standards define the scope of ethically permitted actions for institutional decision makers. That is, it would be ethically prohibited and contradictory to a university's mission to act in violation of these standards. The standards also provide ethical ideals. Using the word "Promote" rather than a negative qualifier at the start of each statement illustrates how one can choose an action that enhances an institution's mission rather than simply refraining from those actions that hinder it. One hopes that most of the choices made by institutional officers would be those that are ethically ideal.[16]

If an institutional officer acts in ways that contradict a university's mission, there can be a conflict of interest. A conflict of interest occurs when an officer makes choices regarding a primary responsibility that promotes another interest. It should never be forgotten that the primary professional responsibility of administrators and faculty is to act in accordance with an institution's mission. An administrator or faculty member acting within their institutional role should never allow another interest to take precedent over a professional responsibility.

As the credibility of an institution is based on the public's trust that the institution is, indeed, acting in concert with its mission, the appearance of a conflict of interest can be as damaging as an actual conflict.

An institution can protect itself from negative publicity by

1. Committing itself to open communication,
2. Always using well-reasoned arguments, and
3. Having a transparent process of self-governance.

In the event of a dispute, the outcome can be ameliorated if all affected parties know of all the possible alternatives, if they have an adequate and thorough opportunity to provide input, and if the alternatives that are chosen are justified publicly as promoting the institution's mission. With such a procedure, decision makers are acting in an ethically permitted way regardless of the outcome. The fact that someone is unhappy with an outcome does not imply that there is something faulty with the process.

Traditionally, institutions of higher education have included activities not directly connected to its mission. Student and faculty services and athletics, for example, may not directly fulfill a university's mission, but that fact does not make those activities unethical. Showing the connection between those services and the unique role of higher education provides a basis for a justification. However, contradiction with an institution's mission provides a basis for regarding an action as ethically questionable and in need of deliberation.

NOTES

1. Council for the Advancement and Support of Education, "Statement of Ethics," reprinted in *The Ethics of Asking,* ed. Deni Elliott (Baltimore: Johns Hopkins University Press, 1995), 185.

2. George M. Robinson and Janice Moulton, *Ethical Problems in Higher Education* (Englewood Cliffs, NJ: Prentice-Hall, 1985), 13.

3. George Allan, *Rethinking College Education* (Lawrence: University of Kansas Press, 1997), 134, 175.

4. American Association of University Professors, "Statement on Professional Ethics," http://www.aaup.org/statements/Redbook/Rbethics.htm (accessed 16 November 2004).

5. Peter Scott, "Ethics 'in' and 'for' Higher Education," http://www.cepes.ro/September/scott_doc.htm (accessed 16 November 2004).

6. Amy Gutmann, *Democratic Education* (Princeton, NJ: Princeton University Press, 1987), 192.

7. Edward LeRoy Long Jr., *Higher Education as A Moral Enterprise* (Washington, DC: Georgetown University Press, 1992), 6.

8. American Association of University Professors, "Statement of Professional Ethics."

9. Robert Justin Lipkin, "The Idea of the Postmodern University," in *An Ethical Education,* ed. M. N. S. Sellers, 87–88 (Oxford, UK/Providence, RI: Berg, 1994).

10. American Association of University Professors, op. cit.

11. Gutmann, *Democratic Education,* 178.

12. Ibid., 179.

13. Ibid., 183.

14. Paul J. Olscamp, *Moral Leadership* (Lanham, MD: Rowman & Littlefield, 2003), 11.

15. Jeffrey Selingo, "What Americans Think about Higher Education," *The Chronicle of Higher Education* (2 May 2003), http://chronicle.com/free/v49/i34/34a01001.htm (accessed 7 December 2004).

16. See the writings of Bernard Gert, especially *Common Morality* (New York: Oxford University Press, 2004), for a particularly clear discussion on the distinctions between acts that are morally (or ethically) permitted and those that are morally ideal.

Chapter Three

The Business of Giving and Getting

Fund-raising and donating have become more business-oriented in the early twenty-first century, as differentiated from traditional notions that philanthropic action rises from the donor's "charitable impulse." As one development officer said, "Development is not a one-way relationship. It is an exchange. An exchange of values. And such an exchange, by definition, is always two-way."[1]

That today's philanthropists approach their giving from a contractual perspective does not necessarily raise ethical issues. However, the difference in donor approach and expectations combined with increased professionalism on the part of development officers creates an agreement among strangers that masks the philanthropic nature of the relationship. It can be more difficult for institutional officers to balance the need to treat gift giving as a supererogatory act while not allowing the donor to interfere with practices that support an institution's mission.

Fund-raising, which was once the collaborative effort of college presidents and alumni volunteers, is now staffed by professionals educated in marketing, finance, and tax law. In 2004, the Council for Advancement and Support of Education (CASE) counted more than thirty-two hundred institutional memberships in forty-seven countries. CASE describes itself as "the leading resource for professional development, information and standards in the fields of educational fund-raising, communications, and alumni relations."[2]

The Association of Professional Researchers for Advancement (APRA) boasted more than twenty-one hundred members.[3] The American Association of Fundraising Counsel (AAFRC) listed almost forty member firms in mid-2004 that provide clients, such as institutions of higher education, with advice regarding fund-raising and other aspects of advancement.[4]

Donating today is a calculated act that involves weighing potential outcomes and tax advantages, often requiring the advice of financial planners. Ethical issues related to new understandings regarding the contractual exchange of giving and getting are explored throughout this chapter.

THE DEVELOPMENT OF THE PHILANTHROPY PROFESSION

From the Greek root for "love of mankind," philanthropy, or the practice of giving to others, is as old as civilization itself. The Chinese philosopher Confucius "exalted universal benevolence as a personal virtue," while Hindu scriptures detailed that "giving to the needy . . . was an imperative duty, the fulfillment of which also rewarded the donor in a future state of existence." Buddhists established hospitals and giving as a way to spread their faith. In an Egyptian *Book of the Dead,* "a good man is identified as one who had given bread to the hungry, water to the thirsty, raiment to the naked, and a boat to one who had none."[5]

The Greeks "thought the word connoted good citizenship and democratic, humanitarian inclinations." However, they preferred gifts that would help the public at large—the Academy, the Lyceum, Alexander the Great's library in Egypt—than giving to poor individuals.[6]

The Romans thought that giving for "political and personal reasons was not truly philanthropic." Judaism "made charity a central and imperative duty for each believer," while the Talmudic rules in 1201 codified in the "Eight Degrees of Charity" agreed with the Romans in that an anonymous donation "was more meritorious."[7]

Christianity, as with Hinduism, emphasized giving as a way of assuring a path to a fulfilling afterlife. "Charity enhances life in this world by bringing the giver into closer spiritual relationship with God." After the end of the Greek and Roman Empires, the church assumed charitable duties "sponsoring gifts for hospitals, colleges, and monasteries." But with the Reformation and the end of monasteries in Tudor England, universities started to see a direct benefit of giving. "The merchant and gentry classes poured wealth into charitable and education institutions."[8]

Benjamin Franklin devoted himself to philanthropy by promoting funding for libraries and the College of Philadelphia (later the University of Pennsylvania). Franklin also formatted a practical guide for fund-raising that included (1) make a list of prospective donors, (2) personally visit each one, (3) make follow-up visits, and (4) use the media to gain publicity for your cause.[9]

In the late nineteenth and early twentieth centuries, Americans with great wealth desired to improve the quality of civilization generally by funding "existing colleges and universities, and or the establishment of new schools and universities associated with the benefactions of Cornell, Johns Hopkins, Vanderbilt, Vassar, Eastman, Stanford, and Rockefeller." Andrew Carnegie famously proclaimed that a wealthy person "should be ashamed to die rich." And with legislation regarding exempting gifts from taxation in 1936, a new era of giving resulted. However, because of abuses of the tax privilege, there were congressional investigations that led to more public control.[10]

The increasingly complicated practices of fund-raising and philanthropy resulted in the professionalism of advancement as a profession with its own degree programs. As early as 1985, "centers focusing on philanthropy" had "been established at Duke University and City University of New York." The American Association of Fundraising Counsel supported the development of courses for undergraduates at nine colleges.[11]

By the twenty-first century, universities offered graduate degree programs or nondegree certification programs in a variety of aspects relating to philanthropy, development, and management of nonprofit organizations. The Peabody College at Vanderbilt University, for example, offers a master's level degree in "Institutional Advancement in Higher Education," which includes studies in fund-raising.

Indiana University is a leader of higher education in philanthropy, with a Center on Philanthropy established in 1987. The Fund-Raising School, located in that center, has provided mid- and pre-career offerings since that time. The center offered the first master's degree in philanthropic studies. The university raised commitment to academic study in philanthropy to a new level in the fall of 2004 when it became home to the nation's first doctorate in philanthropic studies. The degree is interdisciplinary and includes academic work in ethics, religion, history, cultural perspectives, and the role of philanthropy and nonprofits.

The founder of the original programs in philanthropy at Indiana University, Robert L. Payton, was honored for his work by the Independent Sector in 2003. According to the Independent Sector, which describes itself as "the national leadership forum fostering private initiative for the public good," Payton can be credited for establishing philanthropy as a unique academic discipline. "As a result of his leadership, the study of 'philanthropics' is now taught at nearly 50 research centers while an estimated 500 colleges offer coursework on some aspect of the field. Additionally, 250 universities offer degree programs and as many as 50 graduate business schools and schools of public administration offer degree concentrations in nonprofit management."[12]

Payton argued in the 1980s for a return to recognition of philanthropy as "identifying the causes of human suffering and social misery and developing strategies to eliminate them."[13] However, the focus on the training of fund-raisers and other development professionals is away from the traditional view of philanthropy and toward a less personal, quid pro quo approach. Payton emphasizes the importance of the distinction between true philanthropy and exchange. "Philanthropy is voluntary rather than coerced. A philanthropic gift is different from taxes paid. Helping another person without receiving anything material in return is the difference between voluntary service and service in the marketplace."[14]

Distancing the processes associated with seeking gifts and making donations from the philanthropic motive makes it easier for both the fund-raiser and the benefactor to deny the essence of philanthropy—voluntary action for the public good—in the gift exchange.

A fund-raiser explains. "We attend classes and seminars and conferences about fund-raising. We refine sales and marketing techniques from the business world and apply them to fund-raising. We create imaginative fund-raising events and make deals with businesses in the cause of fund-raising. We give away book bags and other goodies to donors as part of our fund-raising program. The term, concept, and philosophy of philanthropy rarely comes up."[15]

The fact that philanthropy is voluntary, rather than required, is vital. Donors act in a supererogatory way. They deserve the respect associated with the recognition that someone has done more than what is ethically required.

Negotiating a gift is different, ethically speaking, from negotiating a contract that is mutually beneficial to both parties. In the latter case, for example, it is ethically permitted for either party to withhold information not required by law if disclosure is not in that party's self-interest. In negotiating a gift, the donor has a right to know everything that he or she might consider relevant in the giving of that gift. The fund-raiser or gift recipient has a proactive responsibility to seek information from the donor so that what is relevant for the donor to know becomes clear. The recipient has a proactive obligation to give that information to the donor, even if the specific knowledge may threaten the donation. Tricking a donor, or failing to disclose information that the donor would find relevant, constitutes cheating by the institution or its agent. The donor-recipient relationship is based on the donor's trust that the recipient will use the gift as the donor intended and that the donor understands the context in which the gift will be used. If a donor's assumptions of a gift's use are wrong, that is the fault of the potential recipient, not the donor. There should be no "donor beware" clause in a supererogatory act.

THE BUSINESS OF SEEKING FUNDS

Fund-raising is but one of a multitude of skills and concepts taught in course work for future and current nonprofit managers and staff. But, it is an important enough piece to rate certification of its own.

A professional association, the Certified Fund Raising Executive (CFRE), for example, provides a review of fund-raisers' experience and administers examinations to those seeking certification. The organization stresses that certification attests to a fund-raiser's recognition of knowledge, skills, achievement, and commitment to professional standards.

Certification, according to the organization, also leads to career advancement. "A major salary survey conducted by the Association of Fundraising Professionals (AFP), conducted in 2003, showed that fundraising professionals who are certified earned an average of 23% more than their non-certified counterparts."[16]

Colleges and universities are in competition for the philanthropic dollar. They are in competition with one another, with other charities, and with the potential donor's urge to keep wealth for oneself and one's heirs. Schools put tremendous resources toward the marketing of their cause. Stanford, for example, "has about 275 people involved in communicating and maintaining contact with alumni, researching and cultivating potential donors, acknowledging gifts, educating the public about the benefits of financial planning, planned giving and more."[17] Alumni relations have never been noticeably separate from fund-raising attempts, but a parody column from a 2000 *New Yorker* magazine lists a series of reunion "events" that hit close to home, developmentally speaking. In the schedule of events for a tongue-in-cheek twenty-fifth anniversary reunion, alumni have the following lectures to sample:

> Welcome talk by President Lootin, "The New Millennium and How Much More of Your Money We'll Need," . . . During the talk, development officers will pass Bloody Marys and pledge cards. . . .
>
> "Fund-Raising in Ancient Mesopotamia," which includes slides from "early cuneiform donor-pledge forms, which made Babylon U. the finest educational institution of the sixth century B.C. . . ."
>
> "Sexual Potency and Philanthropy." . . .
>
> "Leave It to Us!" . . . University lawyers explain the tax advantages of bequeathing your estate to the university, instead of to heirs who secretly despise you while pretending to love you.
>
> "Before alumni leave for the weekend, 'Attorneys and security personnel from Alumni Development meet with you to go over your irrevocable!—financial pledges.'"[18]

As the parody suggests, higher education fund-raising may stay shy of actual coercion or entrapment, but enticement is a big part of the pitch. An article in *CASE Currents* inadvertently echoes the parody's sentiment by saying, "The passionate philanthropist is one whose passions we have aroused, one to whom we offer what he or she most wants."[19]

The Charity Channel, an on-line site that describes itself as "a resource that connects you to your nonprofit colleagues across town, across the country, and around the world," counsels fund-raisers that "Major donors give in order to bring compelling dreams to life. They make gifts to those organizations that they believe have the capacity to deliver efficiently and effectively on those dreams. They are convinced not only by a powerful idea, but also because of their personal experience with the organization and the people who represent it." The challenge for the development officer is "to prepare donors so that they will be ready to make a major gift at the same time that your nonprofit is in need of that gift."[20]

Enticement is not ethically prohibited. Colleges and universities should market themselves to donors in an attempt to let donors know how their gifts could be used. As long as donors do not mistake an institutional officer's professional attempt to raise funds as an interpersonal attempt to make friends, the nature of the relationship is clear.

PROSPECT RESEARCH

The first hurdle for development officers is in determining where potential donations might be and how to connect the interests of the donor with those of the institution. Administrators of higher education have access to information regarding potential donors that other charities might not collect. "Internal researchers can check records that would be barred by law to outsiders. For example, school prospect researchers might check academic records to see if a professor who gave the prospect an 'A' grade was available to make a call, says one researcher."[21]

Prospect research "generally is defined as the ongoing investigative and synthesizing process by which an institution identifies prospective contributors, . . . assesses gift capacity and inclination, and explores a prospect's interests in order to motivate the prospect to contribute."[22]

Technology has changed the need for and the process of prospect research. "It used to be you'd sit a few alumni and friends around a table and review lists," says Steven Wilkerson, a Garrison, New York, fund-raising consultant. "Two local bankers could tell you the wealth of every rich graduate of a small college, but with the growing mobility of the population, that has become impossible."[23]

The Internet has extended the borders for research. In 1992, ten different companies offered search services with costs ranging from $2,000 to $20,000. Twelve years later, more than twenty-five different companies and consultants advertised specialized services at substantially higher costs.

According to the Association of Professional Researchers for Advancement (APRA),

> Although many fundraising organizations have utilized some form of research for years, today's advancement research comprises more than passing on word-of-mouth anecdotes, and locating and collecting data. Information is simply not enough anymore. Expert analysis is necessary to convert raw data and information into functional intelligence. Advancement researchers are the development professionals most able to meet the growing information needs of the fundraising community. Using the Internet and other current technologies, advancement researchers collect, evaluate, analyze, organize, package and disseminate publicly available information in a way that maximizes its usefulness and enables accurate and educated decision-making.[24]

For up to $40 per hour, in mid-2004, one consultant offered the following services:

1. Analysis of existing higher education databases.
2. Biographical, business/career, financial, and philanthropic information on potential givers.
3. Financial net worth and capacity estimate.
4. The most in-depth, comprehensive information available in the public domain.
5. Help identifying a wealth range to assist in determining the correct level of gift and also the right gifting vehicle.[25]

For $400 to $700 per prospect name, Grenzebach Research, which lists hundreds of clients on its website,[26] promised the following: "Relevant print and electronic databases are reviewed, including newspaper and periodical indexes, biographical sources, corporate affiliations and directorships, social registers, genealogical records, and business and financial sources. . . . In addition, all names are checked for affiliation with private foundations, corporate and personal. Listings are made of published gift data from directories. Electronic library research is conducted in relevant periodical and obituary indexes; cross-checking is done for key dates, family background, and social standing, and local histories and directories are researched at the state, county, city and township level. Where they exist, special resources are reviewed such as class books for some elite universities, published biographies, autobiographies and other business or personal documents, corporate proxy statements, real estate records, and all newspaper and periodical citations."[27]

What counts as relevant information, however, may be a matter of interpretation. According to a *Wall Street Journal* article:

The consulting firms are tight-lipped about their methods, but they combine demographic information with information on magazine subscriptions, car registrations and a host of other resources to pinpoint wealth.

Once researchers have a list of their rich but unknown prospects, they can do considerable additional work on-line. Using one database, they can check corporate credit records on closely held companies. Using another, they can get real estate records. In some states, they can get information on boat, yacht and airplane registrations. They still have to go to courthouses—useful for picking up rich heirs—and divorce settlements.[28]

From 2000 to 2004, charities and fund-raisers created privacy policies to reassure donors. Generally, the policies do not explain the limits of what information is gathered. Instead, the policies describe how information is used, under what conditions it can be shared, and how donors can decline from having information shared. According to the *Chronicle of Philanthropy,* "donors are becoming increasingly uncomfortable with the personal information that fund-raisers are gathering, and the ease with which it can now be obtained from the internet."[29]

Ethically speaking, institutions of higher education have a special obligation to protect privacy and confidentiality of their prospective donors. Higher education holds a respected place in society with its foundation in leadership development and the home of research that results in life-saving medical techniques and life-enhancing technology. As consistent with the mission of higher education, expectations for ethical behavior are greater for colleges and universities than other social institutions. They should be. Higher education sets the standard that others are expected to uphold; higher education serves as the critic of other social institutions and the judge of individuals. It is only reasonable that higher education be held to at least the same standard that it sets for others.

Prospective donors may feel that their privacy has been invaded if profiles are developed without their knowledge or consent. Privacy is both a property and a liberty right. It is a property right in that privacy is an individual's claim to be able to control information about oneself; it is a liberty right in that privacy is also an individual's claim to live life unobserved. Both of these claims are limited in that one cannot control public information or public observation.

The information gained from one's public self tends to be episodic and sporadic. However, when bits of information are compiled from public databases, the result is an extensive profile that may make the prospective donor more visible and vulnerable than the separate pieces of information alone. In addition, this piecemeal collection of data used to form a picture of the potential donor reminds one of a famous phrase associated with Gestalt psychology: "The whole is different than the sum of its parts." And, that whole picture may be so lacking in overall understanding and context that it provides a wholly inaccurate representation.

For example, consider these separate events in a person's life: A newspaper article appears announcing an appointment to an agency's board of directors; an alumnus is seen attending a local political function; records regarding the purchase of land are filed at the local county courthouse; a man and woman appear in open court to finalize their divorce settlement. Each of these actions is a public occurrence that is legitimately available for notice. However, the deliberate collection of all such materials creates a portrait that is suggestive, not necessarily of what the donor would want known by a development officer, and not necessarily of the picture that is going to expose donor intent. The fact that it is easier than ever to create broad portraits of potential donors does not imply that it is the individual's wish that such composites be created.

Imagine that one's employer developed surreptitious portraits of its employees based on material that could be legitimately collected—review of materials, including e-mail exchanges that occurred on the employees' computer plus random surveillance of employees' activities that occurred outside of their homes. It is reasonable that the employees would feel that their privacy had been violated, despite the ostensible legitimacy of what is being observed.

In unwarranted review of one's actions, there is both a liberty and a property claim at stake. Individuals have a reasonable expectation that they live life unobserved unless they are involved in activity that gives them special status as public figures, public officials, or criminals. Even then, the data that is collected and used without consent should be relevant to the reason for which it was gathered unless there is some overriding public need for that information. The claim to privacy holds whether information is being collected to help create a philanthropic match or whether it is being collected so that an employer has peace of mind regarding her top executives' after-work activities. If higher education is to be a model in areas in which it would serve as a critic for other social institutions, development officers must engage in only those acts of prospect research that are known and acceptable by those who are the subjects of such research. Transparency of process and open communication are hallmarks of how higher education sustains its high status within its community. A model for this is provided by the University of Vermont. The Prospect Research and Reference Tool page, which has been "cited as a virtual Swiss army-knife site by *CASE Currents*," lists all databases and reference sources that are used in prospect research.[30] This information is clearly available to prospective donors, as well as to the general public. Prospects know what information is being collected from them and from whom.

THE RATIONAL PHILANTHROPIST

Technology and the stock market in the 1990s created a new and younger philanthropist. The *New York Times,* in a special section called "Giving" in
December 1997, described various aspects of the fund-raising and donative
processes while profiling the new givers: "More hands-on and businesslike in
their approach, these boomer philanthropists—all in their 40s and early 50s—
have a different attitude than many of their elders. Harnessing that attitude to
their inherited or newly made millions, or billions in some cases, they have
already decided that they must be personally involved in creating more effective charities and communities that will lead to a better nation and world."[31]

Unlike previous generations of philanthropists, these younger donors, with
the skills that made them successful early in life, seek a return on their philanthropic investment. According to a *Chronicle of Higher Education* article
from 2001, "The traditional donor wants to leave a legacy. The new donor
often wants to change the world, and wants to do it now."[32]

But the author, a development professional, predicts that higher education
might have a more difficult time getting major gifts from this group. "If
donors want to make significant changes, they may look upon traditional institutions with suspicion. . . . When I was working as a lead campus development
officer and approached new philanthropists for support, it was a challenge to
secure their support for unrestricted funds for the campus. Many were equally
unwilling to support the endowment, which they often saw as perpetuating the
status quo."[33]

The new philanthropist wants outcomes and evidence of progress when
making gifts. They are interested in staying involved with the administration
of their gift and are more likely to support risky ventures than the traditional
donor. They are also not necessarily alumni of the school.

A donor's insistence on continuing a relationship based on the gift helps to
promote an institution's mission by keeping those involved with the project
focused on the task at hand. Meeting the short-term goal of the donor's assessment might have the long-term benefit of sustaining efficient use of the funds.
However, donor expectations must not interfere with the mission of higher
education.

UNRECOGNIZED CONSTITUENCIES

Traditionally, the core of the potential donor pool for most institutions was
thought to be middle-aged white male alumni. Institutions have been rethinking their target populations and discovering not only alumni of different gen-

der and color but philanthropists in the community with no connection to the institution aside from mutual interest in a project. On the other hand, donors are now looking more objectively at their alma maters and considering them as one of any number of deserving potential recipients.

Loyalty plays less of a role in motivating donors than in past years. According to Karen Putnam, director of Philanthropic Advisory Services, "Donors ask themselves such questions as 'Which organizations do I support at the current level, and which do I cut?' 'Do I take a chance with start-ups or stick with the tried and true?' 'Can I advance my philanthropic mission by giving larger grants to fewer grantees?'"[34]

As donors decide where to put their gifts based on observed need rather than on institutional loyalty, institutions are finding new constituencies that help replace alumni they have lost. Such is the case of University of Colorado and Bill and Claudia Coleman. The Colemans gave the University $250 million in 2001, at that time the largest single donation ever made to a public university, despite the fact that they had no connection to the school.

The donation, a gift to assist the school in developing advanced technology to help people with cognitive disabilities, came about through astute fund-raising. An article in *Matrix: The Magazine for Leaders in Education* detailed the gift's progression:

> Claudia Coleman has a niece with a cognitive disability. . . . Bill Caile, an alumnus and fund-raiser for the University's College of Engineering and Applied Sciences, knew the Coleman family and the issues that interested them. . . .
>
> Bill Coleman was invited to give a lecture to a freshman science class, followed by a tour of the university's Center for Lifelong Learning and Design. This research facility develops computer-assisted learning devices.
>
> The Colemans made small donations, watched how those were used and ultimately, gave $250 million.[35]

The story confirms, for the author, that "The right combination of networking, research, and personal attention can pay the biggest dividends in raising money for higher education."[36]

Traditionally, institutions of higher education have appealed to white male graduates. The assumption had been that "male graduates make money; female graduates marry into it. Development offices still schedule major solicitations of male graduates between the 25th and 50th class reunions, when earned income presumably crests. Fiscally speaking, college fund-raisers have traditionally found women most interesting after widowhood or inheritance gave them donatable goods—stocks and bonds, office buildings, oil wells, Van Goghs."[37]

But women with their own wealth and alumni of color are part of the new giving constituencies for higher education. Development officers are finding that they are different from their traditional counterparts. Martha Taylor, who was a vice president for the University of Wisconsin Foundation in 1997, said that women give differently than men. "Men often give to preserve. Women use their money for change, hoping to make things easier on those coming up, and often give to their children's colleges rather than their own for just that reason."[38]

An Independent Sector survey in 2000 showed that "a larger proportion of gifts made by women to women's colleges tend to be in the form of bequests." The explanation given is that women are more concerned than men about having enough money to support themselves until their death.[39]

Generally speaking, female givers were also distinguished from men in other ways. Women are less likely to be moved by how someone else gives. They don't want to know the giving levels of their peers and want their own gifts kept secret. Women are also more interested than their male counterparts in developing an ongoing relationship with the charity. A fund-raiser described a Vassar alumna who was "an active volunteer but never a big donor." After the woman died, the fund-raiser was "stunned" to find that Vassar would receive one-third of the women's estate—$9 million.[40]

Groups have formed to help women feel comfortable in their role as philanthropists. "There are nearly 100 women's funds like Priem's in the United States, according to the Women's Funding Network."[41] The groups pool resources, identify needs, and cooperatively make donations.

Because African Americans generally give within their own communities, "their giving does not register on the radar screen of traditional philanthropy," according to historian Marybeth Gasman, who has studied black philanthropy and education. Gasman suggests that African Americans will give in larger terms to their alma maters if they are asked and if they are approached by development officers of color. "Fund-raisers need to consider what motivates African Americans to give—ideas of racial uplift, being asked by a clergy member or friend, and specific causes, especially crises in the black community or individuals in need."[42]

Another new constituency for development is financial advisors. "I work at cultivating relationships with financial planners, lawyers, bank trust officers, estate professionals and accountants," says Arlene Kay, executive director of development at City College of New York (CCNY). "I want them attuned to CCNY's role in the community—even if only to ask the question, 'Do you want to include your alma mater or your parent's alma mater in your will?' After all, bequests serve as the backbone of any planned giving program."[43]

New constituencies do not create new ethical issues in higher education fund-raising unless those being approached have a fiduciary relationship with potential donors. It is good professional practice for a financial advisor or estate attorney to have potential giving opportunities available for discussion with their clients. However, it is not ethical for that advisor to promote a donation in which she has a personal interest. Whether the advisor is promised a kickback for helping to develop a potential giver or whether the advisor is simply seeking additional funds to promote her favorite charity, the advisor's chief interest must be to serve the best interest of a client. Anything else creates a conflict of interest.

THE BUSINESS OF DISBURSING FUNDS

Younger donors who see themselves with a world of giving options have created the need for professional donation advisors. "Just as fund-raising turned itself into a profession by bestowing degrees in fund-raising, the field of philanthropic advising will begin to develop professional, industry-wide parameters."[44]

According to Melissa Berman, director of a group that helps philanthropists decide where to give, "The impulse to charity is part of human nature, so there's a sense that it's supposed to be easy; in fact, it takes as much expertise as investing in stocks and bonds. Philanthropy is about making change, but first you have to figure out what it is you really want to change."[45]

And with current tax regulations, making change doesn't have to hurt. A recent report from the Independent Sector shows that the ability to take a tax deduction for charitable contributions plays a major role in donor decisions—at every income level—about how much to give.[46]

Philanthropy that is beneficial to one's taxes includes a variety of giving opportunities. For example, the gift of appreciated stock will almost always result in the donor realizing more return on a donation than if a capital gains penalty had to be paid after selling the stock. Charitable gift annuities allow a continued income as well as a tax deduction; a charitable lead trust allows a charity to make use of income for a specific time and then returns the principle to one's heirs.[47]

According to a survey conducted by The Philanthropy Institute (TPI) in Boston,

> donors want their financial advisors to talk about charitable planning because it helps to bring their goals into focus. Reps can help evaluate charities and suggest alternative ways to give, including tactics that are most tax-friendly. Advisors who develop these skills can develop greater client loyalty. In addition, the discussion

of philanthropic goals often leads to connections to the next generation of a client's family. . . . Once the advisor is involved in the client's philanthropic planning, he can make sure that gifts are made in the most effective and tax-advantaged ways. For example, a rep can help a client decide whether to give appreciated stock (thus avoiding a capital gains hit) and choose which securities to sell.[48]

Donor-advised funds (DAFs) are a way donors can get immediate tax benefits without committing to a charity first. Institutions of higher education have begun cashing in by forming these funds for their alumni and friends. "Campus-based DAF's often require that donors commit a portion of their account—usually 50 percent—to the campus. Cornell ensures this by separating each account into two pools, one for grants to Cornell and the other for outside charitable recipients."[49]

CREATIVE ACCOUNTING

With the announcement of campaigns designed to raise millions and even billions of dollars, how those funds are used or counted has become an issue. CASE published standards of accounting and reporting as early as 1982 but has continued to update those guidelines, with the latest issues in July 2003 (see Selected Readings).

The tendency to present a distorted picture of an institution occurs most often in fund-raising and student recruitment, according to CASE. "The distortions are probably most diverse and subtle in fund-raising. They include, for example, altering statistics, exaggerating needs, hiding information that could dissuade donors, and using money for purposes other than the one for which it was raised."[50]

Shifts in the stock market during campaign periods have resulted in lower than expected outcomes. For example, in July 2003, "Two weeks before the deadline, Georgetown's Third Century Campaign has turned into a squeaker, charitably speaking. Although school officials remain optimistic about several major donations in the works, the total stands at $923 million after two years of declining contributions." The slowing down of the economy affected other large, multiyear fund-raising campaigns including those at Rice, Mills College, and Worcester Polytechnic Institute.[51]

A sluggish economy, along with fiscal conservatism, can also lead institutions of higher education to spend endowment interest at a particularly low rate. Despite a generous real return of 10 percent, "universities on average withdrew a mere 5.4 percent of endowment value in fiscal year, 1999."[52]

How to report gifts and how to decide how much to put toward short-term needs and long-term investment will always be subjects of scholarly debate. But principles that protect the integrity and credibility of higher education help guide institutional officers to justifiable choices. The principle that one should not do anything that would diminish the appearance of an institution's commitment to intellectual excellence and integrity implies that whatever actions taken in acquiring, reporting, and using a gift should be public and offered for discussion among relevant constituencies.

NOTES

1. Jim Toscano, "To Give . . . and to Receive: Examining the Exchange Process," *Charity Channel,* 4 May 2003, http://charitychannel.com/publish/templates/?a=137 &z=0 (accessed 21 May 2004).

2. See various CASE press releases at http://classic.case.org/.

3. "About APRA," http://www.aprahome.org/aboutapra/index.html (accessed 18 May 2004).

4. "About the AAFRC," http://www.aafrc.org/about_aafrc/ (accessed 22 May 2004).

5. Merle Curti, "Philanthropy," *Dictionary of the History of Ideas,* http://etext.lib.virginia.edu/cgi-local/DHI/dhi.cgi?id=dv3-60 (accessed 14 December 2004).

6. Ibid.

7. Ibid.

8. Ibid.

9. Ibid.

10. Ibid.

11. Kathleen Teltsch, "Studying Philanthropy," *New York Times,* 18 November 1986.

12. Independent Sector, "Independent Sector Announces Robert L. Payton as 2003 John W. Gardner Leadership Award Recipient," News release, 2003 May 29.

13. Robert L. Payton, "Philanthropy as Moral Discourse," PaytonPapers.org, http://www.paytonpapers.org/output/ESS0020_1.shtm (accessed 3 August 2005).

14. Robert L. Payton, "Open Letter on Philanthropic Values," PaytonPapers.org, http://www.paytonpapers.org/output/ESS0003_1.htm (accessed 3 August 2005).

15. Irving Warner, "In Their Eagerness to Perfect Tehchiques, Fund Raisers Lose Sight of Philanthropy," *Chronicle of Philanthropy* (5 October 1993): 43–44, 43.

16. Certified Fund Raising Executive, "Why Certify?" http://www.cfre.org/index.php?action=website-view&WebSiteID=34&WebPageID=492 (accessed 31 July 2005).

17. Judith Harkham Semas, "Planning for Planned Giving," *Matrix: The Magazine*

for Leaders in Education, June 2001, http://www.findarticles.com/p/articles/mi_m0HJE/is_3_2/ai_79961312 (accessed 23 March 2004).

18. Christopher Buckley, "Reunion Schedule," *New Yorker,* 5 June 2000, 41.

19. Jan Krukowski, "The Passionate Philanthropist," *CASE Currents,* April 1979, p. 38.

20. Gayle Gifford, "Cultivating Major Donors: Part 2," Charity Channel, 7 May 2002, http://charitychannel.com/publish/templates/?a=592&z=0 (accessed 16 May 2004).

21. "Nonprofits Dig into Databases for Big Donors," *Wall Street Journal,* 8 September 1992.

22. Mary Lou Siebert, Deni Elliott, and Marilyn Batt Dunn, "Handling Prospect Research," in *The Ethics of Asking,* ed. Deni Elliott, 73–85 (Baltimore: Johns Hopkins University Press, 1995), 74.

23. "Nonprofits Dig into Databases for Big Donors," *Wall Street Journal,* 8 September 1992.

24. Association of Professional Researchers Advancement, "Advancement Research for Professionals," http://www.aprahome.org/aboutapra/advancementpros .htm (accessed 31 July 2005).

25. Summarized from ResearchProspects.com, http://www.researchprospects.com/ (accessed 3 August 2005).

26. Grenzebach Glier & Associates, Inc., "Our Clients A–Z," http://www .grenzebachglier.com/clients/clients.htm (accessed 3 August 2005).

27. "Grenzebach Research," undated printed description of the company's process of "confidential prospect research."

28. "Nonprofits Dig into Databases for Big Donors," *Wall Street Journal,* 8 September 1992.

29. Holly Hall. "Donors Raise a Red Flag Over Privacy," *Chronicle of Philanthropy,* 23 March 2000, 41–42.

30. "Prospect Research and Reference Tools," http://www.uvm.edu/~prospect (accessed 14 December 2004).

31. Judith Miller, "A Hands-On Generation Transforms the Landscape of Philanthropy," *New York Times,* 9 December 1997.

32. Mary Marcy, "How to Reach the New Donors," *Chronicle of Higher Education* (6 July 2001): B13–14.

33. Ibid.

34. Karen Putnam, "We're Talking Triage," *Trusts & Estates,* January 2004, 38.

35. Ibid.

36. Stephanie Brenowitz. "All Gifts Great and Small." *Matrix: The Magazine for Leaders in Education* (April 2001), http://www.findarticles.com/p/articles/mi_m0HJE/is_2_2/ai_79961284 (accessed 28 March 2004).

37. Anne Matthews, "Alma Maters Court Their Daughters," *New York Times Magazine,* 7 April 1991, 73.

38. Ibid., 74.

39. Meg Sommerfeld, "A Close Look at Ways to Increase Giving by Women—and to Instill the Habit in Girls," *Chronicle of Philanthropy,* 5 October 2000.

40. Ibid.

41. Katherine Dunn, "Philanthropy in a New Key," *Harvard Magazine* (May–June 2001): 43.

42. Marla Misek, "Creating a New Comfort Zone," *CASE Currents* (January 2004): 23–24.

43. Semas, "Planning for Planned Giving."

44. Putnam, "We're Talking Triage," 39.

45. Claudia Deutsch, "Learning to Cast Bread upon the Waters, Wisely," *New York Times,* 14 March 2004.

46. Independent Sector, "Giving and Volunteering in the United States 2001," http://www.independentsector.org/programs/research/gv01main.html (accessed 3 August 2005).

47. Floyd Norris, "Doing Well by Doing Good: Uncle Sam Can Help," *New York Times,* 9 December 1997.

48. Registered Rep, "Help Your Clients and Your Practice with Charitable Giving," http://registeredrep.com/mag/finance_help_clients_practice (accessed 3 August 2005).

49. Christopher Toward, "Are You Ready for Donor-Advised Funds?" *CASE Currents Online,* January 1999, http://www.case.org/Currents/ViewIssue.cfm?content ItemID=370 (accessed 17 June 2000).

50. Ronald Kind, "Painting the Wrong Picture," *CASE Currents,* 27–30 January 1987, 28.

51. Amy Argetsinger, "Fundraising Gets Tougher for Colleges," *Washington Post,* 17 June 2003, http://www.uh.edu/admin/media/topstories/2003/wpost/200306/20030617fund.html (accessed 14 May 2004).

52. Donald Frey, "University Endowment Returns Are Underspent," *Challenge,* July–August 2002, http://www.findarticles.com/cf_0/m1093/4_45/89871071 (accessed 28 March 2004).

Chapter Four

What Donors Want

As institutions of higher education are increasingly dependent on external donors, those responsible for financial operations have become more willing to allow donors to assert more control.

THE RALPH ENGELSTAD ARENA AT THE UNIVERSITY OF NORTH DAKOTA

Should a donation be accepted from a man who has thrown Adolph Hitler birthday parties amid a large collection of Nazi memorabilia and insists that a controversial university mascot be retained despite public protests?[1]

The University of North Dakota's (UND) Grand Forks campus has one of the most luxurious and well-appointed hockey stadiums in American collegiate sports. From a state-of-the-art scoreboard, leather seats, and a climate-controlled room to provide storage for hockey sticks and Italian marble floors, the $100 million Ralph Engelstad Arena is an elaborate monument to its namesake, a former UND "Fighting Sioux" hockey player. Locals refer to the arena as "Ralph's Palace."[2] The donor's story is a classic "local boy makes good and gives back" tale, if not for the controversy surrounding both the donor and the Fighting Sioux team name. One may assume that any financial officer would be thrilled to receive a $100 million gift. But Engelstad's donation, like the man himself, was not without controversy.

Engelstad collected Nazi memorabilia. And, with University efforts to change the school's team name, this case led to a controversy that seemed to be a classic fund-raising struggle. Should the school accept donations from an alumnus with a neo-Nazi collection? Should the donor's demand that the team continue to be called "The Fighting Sioux" legitimate quid pro quo for the donation?

Engelstad was a casino owner. His holdings included the Imperial Palace hotels in Las Vegas, Nevada, and Biloxi, Mississippi.[3] He was also a UND alumnus with a history of generous giving to his alma mater. In 1989, he donated $5 million to refurbish the university's old hockey arena. Engelstad, who played as a Sioux goaltender on scholarship during 1948–1950,[4] also received publicity at the time of his donation for his reputation as a collector of German Nationalist memorabilia. In 1988 he was fined $1.5 million by the Nevada Gaming Commission for holding Nazi theme parties in his establishments in 1986 and 1988 (coinciding with the anniversary of Hitler's birthday, 20 April) as well as for displaying Nazi memorabilia.[5]

Before accepting the $5 million to renovate the old hockey arena, UND sent a delegation to Las Vegas to investigate the Gaming Commission fine; included on the delegation were UND fund-raising officers, who were facilitating the possible gift. Though many on the delegation found Engelstad's collection distasteful, they found him guilty only of having "bad taste."[6] UND accepted the donation, and the newly refurbished arena was named for Engelstad.

The decision to accept the $5 million is still a sore spot for some members of the 1989 UND delegation. UND English professor Elizabeth Hampsten was a member of the delegation. She insists that Engelstad did not show the delegation the most objectionable memorabilia. Regardless, what they were allowed to see provided for her a reasonable basis for not accepting the gift. For example, one display included a bust of Hitler, wearing Engelstad's hat.[7]

In December of 1998, Engelstad announced his intention to fund a new hockey arena. He said that his decision to fund the $100 million, 400,000 square foot arena was based on his desire to share a portion of his "good fortune with the UND Hockey Team."[8]

However, while the stadium was under construction, UND was moving toward what turned out to be a deal breaker for Engelstad: the school was contemplating changing the Fighting Sioux team name.[9]

In the late 1990s, the national movement to reverse the long tradition of naming sports teams after Indian tribes had gained attention at UND, which is known as one of the major centers of Native American education in the nation. Among other sources of UND Indian pride, the Indians Into Medicine program claims to train a fifth of the Native American doctors in the country.[10]

Native American students are the largest minority on campus, with more than four hundred enrolled.[11] The UND Indian Association was founded in 1968. As both Indian student enrollment and Indian on-campus organizations increased in number, so did protests against the use of Indian names and symbols.[12] The Indian name and logo became an openly divisive issue by the early

1970s, when an ice sculpture of a suggestively posed Native American woman ignited a fight between a Native American man and a group of Anglo fraternity brothers.[13]

In May of 2000, UND president Charles Kupchella put together a campus commission to consider changing the Fighting Sioux name and logo. The two previous UND presidents, Thomas Clifford and Kendall Baker, had dealt with various facets of Indian stereotyping on the UND campus, and both presidents worked with Indian groups to eliminate clearly demeaning and offensive uses of Native American imagery.[14]

In e-mail messages to members of the North Dakota Board of Education—the body that would need to approve the change—Kupchella said that he was "prepared to outline steps whereby we would cease using the nickname after a period of several years. . . . I see no choice but to respect the request by the Sioux tribes that we quit using their nickname."[15]

Kupchella's commission was still in the course of its work when the president received a letter from Engelstad in December 2000 saying that he would end his support of the hockey arena (a "pay as you build" arrangement had been made, with Engelstad being directly billed by contractors during construction) if the mascot name and logo were changed. Thirty-five million dollars into the construction, Engelstad said in his letter to Kupchella that he would consider his investment up to that point a business loss. In his letter, he also stated: "Commitments were made to me by others and yourself regarding the Sioux logo. . . . These promises have not been kept, and I, as a businessman, cannot proceed while this cloud is still hanging above me."[16] The North Dakota Board of Education, which also received copies of the letter, voted 8–0 to keep the name, thus ending the work of the UND commission.[17]

The board denied that Engelstad's letter to Kupchella was the deciding factor in voting to keep the team name. The board's decision was reportedly made on the basis of a survey, commissioned by the Bureau of Governmental Affairs, that showed that 83.4 percent of the student body was either "opposed" or "strongly opposed" to changing the Fighting Sioux name.[18]

The Ralph Englestad Arena celebrated its inaugural year to sell-out crowds in 2001–2002.[19] There are more than two thousand Fighting Sioux logos (featuring a Sioux chief in headdress) located in the arena.[20] Many of them are on the floors and ice and are walked or skated on daily.

The North Dakota Board of Education gave approval in June 2003 for a fifty thousand square foot basketball/volleyball facility to be added to the arena. The building will be named the Ralph Englestad Arena Sports Center. Most of the cost of the $7 million addition will be funded through "current revenue sources and planned expansions of advertising, ticketing and suite revenues."[21]

Native students at the University of North Dakota continue to protest the use of the Fighting Sioux mascot and logo. One writer points out, "Since 1969, more than 600 schools across the country have dropped nicknames deemed offensive by Native American groups. . . . All of the North Dakota tribes have passed resolutions denouncing the name. . . . Money may have bought an arena here, but it didn't buy racial harmony."[22]

A NEW LOOK AT DONOR EXPECTATIONS

Since the last twenty years, donor expectations and higher education's willingness to accommodate donors have drastically changed. In the past, universities could easily ignore a donor's intention for how monies would be used.

One of the earliest examples of disregarding donor intent occurred in the founding of Dartmouth College.[23] Dartmouth's founding president, Eleazar Wheelock, educated a Mohegan Indian, Samson Occom, in 1743. Occom was a prize student, taking "just four years to advance from rudimentary literacy to fluency in English, and relative proficiency in Latin, Greek, and Hebrew."[24] Wheelock was so pleased with his success that he decided to start a school to educate Indian missionaries. "The Plan is such that all the Benefit done or proposed to be done to the English is Subservient in the Best Manner to the Indian Cause."[25] Along with a white missionary, Reverend Nathaniel Whitaker, Occom was sent to raise funds for the school. Based on positive reception to Occom's three hundred sermons delivered in England and Scotland, Occom and Whitaker were extremely successful, raising £12,000, or the equivalent of approximately $250,000 today. But when Occom returned from England, Wheelock had other ideas about the money. He changed his mind about training Indians to be missionaries. Instead, he decided to use the money to educate young men of European parentage. In fact, "by 1775, Wheelock had used up the entire English fund for the construction of buildings at Dartmouth."[26]

Such disregard for the wishes of donors is less likely thanks to the media. Institutions, even those that use private funds, cannot operate outside of the public eye. And because of increased media interest, administrators and donors can no longer assume that negotiations will remain confidential. Confounding that scrutiny is an institution's willingness to let donors and vocal activists play a direct role in gift-related decisions.

Unfortunately, the media have plenty to report about the new level of donor expectations. The academic world was horrified in 1988 when it looked as though Harvard officials were willing to give a husband and wife donor team honorary titles with positions on two advisory committees in exchange for $500,000. Around the same time, Duke turned down a $20 million gift that was offered if the donor could help select the faculty for the institute he pledged to fund. Finally, Smith College turned down an offer to fund a chair in economics from a donor after he demanded that his daughter be appointed to the selection committee.[27]

But with budget cutbacks and favorable tax incentives available to wealthy individuals, times have changed. The willingness of the University of North Dakota to keep a donor happy despite public protests is echoed by the University of Oregon's (UO) work in 2001 to patch things up with its major donor. Philip Knight, a UO alumnus and founder of the Nike sports shoe company had contributed more than $50 million to his alma mater by spring 2000. But when he found that the university had joined the Workers' Rights Consortium (WRC), an activist group engaged in protecting workers' rights in overseas factories, Knight withdrew a $30 million gift. "With this move the University inserted itself into the new global economy where I make my living, and inserted itself on the wrong side, fumbling a teachable moment," Knight said.[28]

Some faculty supported the university's decision, saying, "UO's associating with the WRC is only strengthened by Knight's retaliation; it speaks volumes to the necessity of the WRC." This e-mail, from a UO law professor, posted on UO's senate site, observes, "Phil Knight has got a lot of nerve expecting to be consulted first, before the public University of the State of Oregon makes a policy decision concerning human rights. Perhaps he thinks this is really a private university—i.e., his."[29] Alumni, on the other hand, were critical of President Dave Frohnmayar's decision to join the Workers' Rights Consortium.

By September 2001, the spat had ended and Knight said that he would renew donations to the University of Oregon. Frohnmayar had responded to Knight's protest and his withdrawal of funds by agreeing to join the Fair Labor Association, a trade-based watchdog group supported by Nike. "But, in February, the state Board of Education adopted a policy that banned the university from joining any watchdog group."[30]

While traditionally donors may have seen themselves as donating to their alma maters as a way of helping the school continue its good work, schools are showing increased willingness to play to the self-interest of potential donors. "Naming," traditionally the reward for a substantial gift, such as a building or an endowed chair, is now used to attract those interested in giving smaller amounts. Chapman University in Orange County, California, offers naming opportunities for gardens, elevators, and a sound-editing room. Colgate University in Hamilton, New York, named a connector road for a donor, along with the school's recreational climbing wall, first-aid room, and a pole-vault area. At the University of Arkansas, a donor can have his or her name on rock benches and a lighthouse. The Ohio State University offers a soil and plant laboratory, a mud room, and the heating and cooling system for naming. Cottey College in Nevada, Missouri, entices philanthropists with naming opportunities for library books, flowerpots, piano benches, and an automatic door opener.[31]

Donors, too, are making their wishes for recognition known. In exchange for $100,000 to Duke, Evelyn Y. Davis requested a plaque that was mounted outside the student center to be "polished and visible."[32]

Unfortunately, enticing naming with a variety of recognition possibilities without adequate vetting of a donor sometimes encourages hoaxes. The University of Washington, University of New Hampshire, University of Florida, and Warren Wilson College found themselves the recipients of bad pledges from Ravi Desai, who represented himself as a dot-com entrepreneur with a yen for poetry. Of the more than $5 million in pledges made to the four universities, only $8,770 was realized. Meanwhile, Desai was recognized in press releases and during public ceremonies including football games. He was also given free meals and a substantial amount of time from administrators at all four schools. Finally, in March 2003, news reports connected Desai with the hoaxes.[33]

THE TIMES THEY ARE A-CHANGIN': THE CURIOUS PRACTICE OF HONORARY DEGREES

Despite the fact that he was born in Duluth, Minnesota, and dropped out of the University of Minnesota to become a professional musician, Robert Allen Zimmerman, or Bob Dylan to his fans, nevertheless received an honorary degree from the University of St. Andrews in Scotland. Conveniently, he was in town playing two sold-out concerts. The doctorate was Dylan's second honorary—in 1970 he received one from Princeton University.[34]

Giving honorary degrees to anyone from civic leaders to celebrities is not new for academic institutions, but the practice comes with a dubious history. In fact, the first time the award was given was around 1478 by administrators of Oxford University to Lionel Woodville, brother-in-law of King Edward IV. The degree was a blatant attempt to win the good favor of the king. Over the years, the practice has been praised as a way of "recognizing achievement" of gifted and important individuals and panned as a crude attempt for a university to draw publicity to itself by the choice.[35]

Cambridge University has bestowed the high honor on Albert Einstein, Nelson Mandela, and Mother Teresa with little criticism. As with Great Britain, throughout America universities invite well-known celebrities in the hope of enticing them to give an inspirational speech during the graduation ceremony with an honorary doctorate. Sometimes, however, only a "B-list" star is available. There have been instances when degrees were given to reality television show and soap opera "stars" and singers needing an ego boost.[36]

The not so implicit hope as well is that the wealthy speaker will also feel obligated to make a contribution. Rick Skinner, president of Royal Roads University in Victoria, British Columbia, is matter-of-fact about the connection between a degree and a contribution, "There's more than an implied expectation that a person might want to give back to the university conveying the degree."[37]

University administrators would be wise to have a clear motivation for honoring a person for a lifetime of work for humanity by giving a degree that others have worked many years through academia to achieve. Truly honoring someone for their contribution and not pandering to publicity or donation is the only justification for giving a celebrity such an unusual and rare honor.

WHAT MOTIVATES DONORS

Different people donate for different reasons and at different times. While no one can truly know the motivations behind a gift—sometimes even the donor is not clear or suffers from self-deception—the primary role of the fund-raiser is to understand the donor's motivations, acquire the funds, and work with the donor to see that the funds are put to the best use for all concerned. If at all possible, the gift should match the donor's reasons for giving.

Donors give money for some combination of seven basic reasons:

1. *Religious, spiritual, or philosophical beliefs.* Beliefs can be externally motivated, such as donors who respond because they think that their religious beliefs require them to give, internally motivated because they believe that philanthropic activity is part of what it means to be a good person, or motivated by the belief that being wealthy requires them to give back to the community so that a kind of justice in the world is achieved.
2. *Guilt.* Philanthropy can be a way of making up for recognized past sins. Community funds can be arranged to allow for those who had taken money inappropriately to anonymously make restitution.
3. *Recognition.* Giving with one's name attached achieves immortality. According to one study, "the number of donors who give anonymously—and thus clearly signal that they do not want recognition—is probably fewer than 10 in 100."
4. *Self-preservation and fear.* Some give as a way of buying protection or in response to ad campaigns that capitalize on fear.

5. *Tax rewards.* Philanthropic giving has increasingly become a way of sheltering funds.
6. *Obligation.* Obligation differs from guilt in that obligation notices a benefit received rather than a past wrongdoing. Obligation can recognize the need to pay-back or to provide support at least at the amount that had been provided to the donor.
7. *Pride and self-respect.* Some people give because they want to be seen by themselves and by others as the kind of person who would give to the cause.[38]

Some of these motivations are more closely aligned than others with giving to higher education. Givers motivated by religious or philosophical beliefs are more likely to find the neediest cause in town or their religion's favorite charity than give to a comparatively wealthy school. Those motivated by fear will respond to nonprofits likely to relieve their concern. Those motivated by guilt will look for ways to pay their recognized debt to society. But, those motivated by recognition, tax rewards, obligation, and pride are likely to look to their alma maters for philanthropic outlet. Of these, only "obligation" comes close to the traditional notion of philanthropy as altruistic action.

DONOR RELATIONSHIPS GONE BAD

Relationships between donors and institutions seem to go bad when there is misunderstanding regarding donor intent or when institutions accept gifts with conditions that are difficult to execute. Donor relationships also go bad because of political disagreements among those who accept or execute the gifts. Here are some typical examples:

- Charles and Marie Robertson gave Princeton $35 million in 1961 to establish an endowment to help graduate students prepare themselves for careers in government service, particularly in international relations and affairs. The heirs of the estate attempted to have the endowment, now worth $600 million, returned. "In 2002, according to Princeton's own data, the program funded by the Robertson Foundation produced 63 graduates. Of these, only 9 took positions with the federal government. What's more, only 3 of these 9 students had an international focus to their studies."[39] The heirs claimed that the intent of the donation had been ignored. As of this writing, the case has not been resolved.
- In 1991, Lee M. Bass gave $20 million to Yale to fund a program in Western civilization, but his donation came with a catch. Bass required that he be

able to approve the professors who would be hired to teach in the program. When the gift still hadn't been executed four years later, Yale returned the gift. Some expressed outrage that Bass would seek such involvement, but others suggested that the problem was that few on the faculty thought that Yale really needed another Western civilization program.[40]

- In 2000, Texas Tech University rejected a $12.5 million gift on the grounds that it fell short by half what was needed to fully fund a new law school. However, the donor claimed that the rejection of his gift was because he was the lawyer who led the state's $17 billion lawsuit against the tobacco industry.[41]
- More than one thousand contributors anted up $250,000 in 1991 to support the Anita Faye Hill Professorship of Law at the University of Oklahoma after Hill accused then Supreme Court nominee Clarence Thomas of sexual harassment. In 1999, the university abandoned the professorship and returned the donations and the state's matching funds because an activist "had threatened to lead a petition drive to cut off funding for the law school if the endowment was not dropped."[42] The chair had been intended to honor a scholar with a national reputation in sexual harassment and women's rights. One opponent compared Hill's chair to "a Jeffrey Dahmer Chair in the school of cooking."[43]

NEGOTIATING INDIVIDUAL GIFTS

Giving is often a self-serving activity for the donor and the recipient. Donors naturally wonder what a donation will get them, while institutions want to use funding sources that best serve their academic mission. Confounding the relationship between the two is the fact that donors and institutions of higher education are more likely to sue one another than ever before. Extreme care, therefore, should be made when negotiating a contract. Below are a few tips to keep in mind:

1. Communication is key. Development officers should, as much as possible, clarify and articulate a donor's intent and then ensure that the faculty and administrators who will execute the funded project are equally aware and supportive of the donor's intent.
2. Contract specifications. Acknowledging the contractual nature of the exchange is increasingly important. But, the contract should exist not just between donor and institution but within the institution as well. Promises made by administrators who move on before a gift is fully executed may leave a legacy not appreciated and not likely to be honored by their suc-

cessors. Agendas may change. But, as the understanding exists between the donor and the institution, contracts should bind institutions as well as donors to live up to their promises and do so in a timely fashion.
3. Matching expectations. Gifts should be accepted and terms agreed upon so that there is a clear fit with the school's mission and strategic planning. Millions of dollars provide strong motivation to try to do what a potential donor would like. However, projects that don't fit with an institution's mission or the political climate of the community should be rejected.

Despite all of the trappings of business and complicated motivations, philanthropy is still a voluntary act for the public good. Colleges and universities owe their donors more than the donors owe the institution.

NOTES

1. This case study involving the Ralph Engelstad Arena is from John Squillante, M.A. in Philosophy, "Teaching Ethics Emphasis," unpublished master's thesis, University of Montana, 2005. Ralph Engelstad died in November 2002.
2. Dan Gunderson, "'Ice Palace' Opens at UND," *Minnesota Public Radio,* 5 October 2001, http://news.minnesota.publicradio.org/features/200110/05_gundersond_arena-m/ (accessed 2 January 2002).
3. Dale Wetzel, "Engelstad Vowed to Pull Arena Funding If Controversial Indian Name Dropped," *Associated Press,* 15 January 2001.
4. Message written by employees of the Imperial Palace Hotel and Casino in Las Vegas, Nevada, on 27 November 2002, http://theralph.com/new2/Arena_Info_Section/RalphEngelstad.htm.
5. Winona LaDuke, "Not the Fighting Sioux: The University of North Dakota's Mascot," *The Circle* 23(3) (March 2002).
6. Andrew Brownstein, "A Battle over a Name in the Land of the Sioux," *Chronicle of Higher Education* (23 February 2001).
7. Ibid.
8. Message written by employees of the Imperial Palace Hotel and Casino in Las Vegas, Nevada, on 27 November 2002, http://theralph.com/new2/Arena_Info_Section/RalphEngelstad.htm.
9. Wetzel, "Engelstad Vowed to Pull Arena Funding If Controversial Indian Name Dropped."
10. Brownstein, "A Battle over a Name in the Land of the Sioux."
11. "Opportunities for American Indians," http://www.und.edu/newviewbook/ (accessed 29 June 2004).
12. "NCAA 'American Indian Mascot Survey,'" http://www.und.edu/news/messages/904.html (accessed 15 December 2004).
13. Kaufman King, "Puck Politics," Salon.com, 8 June 2002, http://dir.salon.com/

news/sports/bounds/2001/03/08/north_dakota/index.html?sid=1017665 (accessed 9 September 2002).

14. "NCAA 'American Indian Mascot Survey.'"

15. Ibid.

16. Wetzel, "Engelstad Vowed to Pull Arena Funding If Controversial Indian Name Dropped."

17. Ibid.

18. "NCAA 'American Indian Mascot Survey.'"

19. "Ralph Engelstad Arena—Home of the Fighting Sioux," http://www .theralph.com/new2/Arena_Info_Section/Arena_Info_Main.htm (accessed 3 August 2005).

20. LaDuke, "Not the Fighting Sioux."

21. UND Media Relations, "REA Sports Center Gets Approval from State Board," http://www.geocities.com/grovers50/menbball/0203news/0626arena.htm (accessed 29 June 2004).

22. Daryl Sager, "Paying the Price for Offensive Mascots, Logos," *Native Voice,* http://www.naja.com/nativevoice2003/1darylcol.html (accessed 29 June 2004).

23. Coincidentally, it was while I worked at Dartmouth that I was principal investigator on a comprehensive ethical analysis of higher education fund-raising.

24. Bernd Peyer, "The Betrayal of Samson Occom," *Dartmouth Alumni Magazine,* November 1998, 32–37.

25. Ibid., 34.

26. Ibid., 36.

27. "The Hard Sell behind the Ivy," *U.S. News & World Report,* 11 April 1988, 54.

28. "Nike CEO Retracts University Donation over Human Rights," SocialFunds.com, http://www.socialfunds.com/news/print.cgi?sfArticleId=237 (accessed 16 May 2004).

29. E-mail written by Howard Grooters, http://darkwing.uoregon.edu/ ~uosenate/dirsen990/dirextra/grooters20apr00.html (accessed 29 June 2004).

30. Boaz Herzog, "Bearing Gift, CEO Returns to UO Fold," *The Oregonian,* 26 September 2001, A01.

31. "Picture This: Your Name on a . . . Flowerpot," *New York Times,* 9 November 2003.

32. "Give & Take," *Chronicle of Higher Education* (26 April 1998): 6.

33. Martin Van Der Werf, "Donor Leaves Colleges Waiting for Major Gifts Promises for Poetry Programs," *Chronicle of Higher Education* (6 April 2001): A38.

34. "Honorary Degree for Dylan," *The Sentinel* (Stoke), 23 June 2004, 4.

35. Judith O'Reilly, "I'm a Celebrity, Get Me an Honorary Degree," *Sunday Times* (London), 12 September 2004, University Guide 10.

36. Ibid.

37. Jim Gibson, "Degree of Unease," *Times Colonist* (Victoria, British Columbia), 28 June 2004, D4.

38. Paul H. Schneiter, *The Art of Asking: How to Solicit Philanthropic Gifts* (Fund Raising Institute, 1985).

Chapter Four

39. John J. Miller, "Giving and Taking Away: A Controversy at Princeton Offers Broad Lessons—Robertson Foundation Lawsuit," *National Review,* 29 September 2003, http://www.findarticles.com/p/articles/mi_m1282/is_18_55/ai_109411351 (accessed 8 August 2005).

40. Joye Mercer, "Yale U. Returns a $20-Million Gift to Donor after Impasse over How It Would Be Used," *Chronicle of Higher Education* (24 March 1995): A36.

41. Scott Street, "Texas Tech Rejects a $12.5-Million Gift Leaving the Donor and Others Wondering Why," *Chronicle of Higher Education* (8 December 2000): A32.

42. "Anita Hill Professorship Abandoned," http://www.adversity.net/education_3.htm (accessed 29 June 2004).

43. Maria Russo, "Cold Shoulder?" *Lingua Franca,* 13–15 February 1998.

Chapter Five

What Corporations Buy

Academic institutions have never existed in isolation from communities. Direct relationships exist between business and academic institutions to the benefit of both. Faculty, students, and staff support local business as part of their normal lives. Local business supplies products and services necessary to keep the academic institution functioning.

This is a relationship of mutual benefit, mutual dependency, and mutual power. This relationship allows both parties to maintain separate identities in the community and to have their separate, but often complementary, missions.

The mission of higher education, broadly speaking, has two goals: (1) to transmit knowledge through its teaching function, and (2) to create new knowledge through its research function. Higher education prepares future teachers and researchers through an established apprenticeship program that includes graduate school, postdoc fellowships, and the tenure track system for academic appointments. While it is imperative for colleges and universities to cobble together sufficient funding to support current and future activities that relate to the mission, money is but one of the many resources necessary to promote the fulfillment of the academic mission.

Business, defined here to include industry and corporations, has the mission of creating and selling products and services with the goal of making a profit for owners or stockholders. R. E. Spier says that the mission of a corporation "is to achieve its own survival through the generation of surplus monies which it uses to buy the favor of its shareholders . . . and the loyalty of its employees."[1]

Making money and providing service are necessarily linked. Profit is the ultimate measure of success for business. But making money is not linked in any necessary way to the mission of higher education.

Generally speaking, higher education and business pursue their missions separate from one another. Overlap, when it occurs, is for the mutual benefit of both parties.

Consequently, business-university partnerships that occur when business pays for academic research can cross or blur the borders needed for the parties to maintain their separate identities and missions. As one scholar explains, "The core values of the academy and the core values of business are in conflict. . . . To the industrialist, paying for research implies ownership of the results, which are used to establish proprietary competitive advantage if at all possible."[2]

According to one investigator, business-university research partnerships raise three areas of concern that include "the selection of research questions, biasing of research outcomes, and the public's perception of science."[3] Despite these concerns, the pull toward industry and corporate-supported research is strong, especially since governmental support can no longer be guaranteed. Given such a situation, a 1993 *New York Times* article reported that administrators at the University of Miami pondered "where to turn for money?"[4] The answer, of course, is the private sector.

In 1999, it was reported that 20 percent of the Massachusetts Institute of Technology's (MIT) funding came "from industry and this proportion is growing." In the 1998–1999 annual report, Florida State University Vice President for Research Raymond E. Bye Jr. reported that funding from the private sector accounts for 9 percent, with expectations that the amount will "greatly increase."[5]

In a 2001 statement, the American Association of University Professors (AAUP) expressed concern about the trend toward corporate funding. "Although corporate funding of academic research accounts for a relatively small percentage of all university research funds—approximately seven percent of the total—that percentage has grown more rapidly than support from all other sources over the past two decades."[6]

Research universities, struggling with continuing or expanding current levels of work in the face of federal cutbacks, naturally seek other funding and are relieved that business is becoming more interested.

It is because of federal sponsorship that there is increased dependence of higher education on external support. This condition can be traced back to World War II, "when professors were enlisted in the drive to win the war. After the war, university research never returned to the casual, almost sleepy affair it had been. Enticed by Federal money and willing to undergo the peer review required to prove a project worthwhile, thousands of professors turned their attention from the classroom to the laboratory."[7] Due to this shift, the mission of higher education changed. Most institutions switched their primary focus on teaching to research. The result is that today research is the primary consideration for those interested in tenure and promotion. In the latter half of the twentieth century, declining governmental support for research could have led to a reemphasis on the teaching mission for higher education over the research mission. Instead, it led faculty, administrators, and legislators to think creatively about how to continue funding an expanding and, some would say, changing research mission.

Indeed, some state legislatures are envisioning business-university partnerships as a way out of the fiscal drain that public higher education puts on state budgets and as providing a method for economic development for the state as well. State legislatures are encouraging, and in many cases providing, the seed money for research universities to transform "scientific discoveries into new businesses and, eventually, centers of emerging industry near their campuses."[8]

The University of Maryland, for example, encourages "faculty members to conduct research for commercial interests. The state offers to match what companies pay them for such work, up to $70,000 annually per faculty member."[9]

Yet when the profitability of research becomes a goal for academic institutions or when they enter into business partnerships that capitalize on that, a conflict of interests is created.

While these conflicts are a struggle for individual faculty and administrations, it is the entire social institution of higher education that is likely to suffer. If the public perceives that the mission of higher education has changed from the pursuit of pure knowledge to making money for itself or for its business partners, the credibility of the social institution is at risk.

A Harris Poll from February 2004 found that "major educational institutions, such as colleges and universities," came in second only to the military in the level of confidence of those surveyed. In the survey, respondents ranked, in order, the following social institutions below higher education: the medical profession, the White House, the U.S. Supreme Court, organized religion, the executive branch of the federal government, Wall Street, television news, the press, organized labor, the U.S. Congress, major corporations, and law firms.[10]

Considering that major companies are near the bottom of the list and that education is near the top, too close an association between the two is likely to diminish trust in education rather than elevate trust in business. Americans have learned that who controls the purse strings generally wins over principle. Business support of higher education is not intrinsically problematic, but it must be achieved in a way that promotes the more vulnerable party in the relationship—higher education within its traditional mission.

THE PHILANTHROPIC NATURE OF CORPORATIONS

Corporations have a long and distinguished tradition of advancing the needs of higher education. As philanthropy guru Robert L. Payton observed in the late 1980s, corporate philanthropy has been around since the late nineteenth century. Philanthropic contributions from Andrew Carnegie, John D. Rockefeller, and the founders of Sears and Roebuck provided models for using the financial clout of business to improve education, health care, and the general culture. As Payton points out, "The United Way has done more to educate the public about the principles of giving than any other institution except the church—and the United Way is preeminently an achievement of American business."[11]

According to a Council of Foundation's report from the mid-1980s, "Corporate philanthropy is based on the premise that a corporation has many of the duties and responsibilities of citizenship and, as such, shares with citizens the obligation to contribute to the well-being of the community. Corporations should engage in philanthropic activities, advocates say, because these activities benefit the community in which the corporation operates, help to ensure a stable and enlightened society, and generate a positive image of the corporation in the eyes of its employees, its customers, and the public."[12]

American industries historically have recognized their responsibility to invest in the "long-term well-being of the system that makes corporations possible," said Robert L. Payton, then president of the Exxon Education Foundation.[13]

According to Nelson Aldrich, contributing editor to *Worth*, "Most corporate giving . . . is actually a long-term investment in community building—in increasing the competence and self-respect of the workforce, in sustaining its culture and health—which in turn is a long-term investment in the general well-being and good name of the corporation."[14]

One way of viewing corporate philanthropy is that community support is best woven into the overall mission, vision, and goals of the business. Marc Benioff, author of *Compassionate Capitalism*—how corporations can make doing good an integral part of doing well—proposes a model of philanthropy that reflects this view of business:

> The model of philanthropy . . . sees business and community needs as closely aligned, and encourages companies to make serving the community a central focus. . . . The new model says that philanthropy must be woven into every thread of corporate existence so that it becomes a part of the cultural fabric and cannot be pulled out without pulling apart the corporation itself. Organizations that have service as a core value of their culture will see both intrinsic and external returns. . . . It is simply part of being human to be able to give, and companies that provide the opportunity will find that it energizes employees and executives.[15]

While this altruistic notion of business engaged with community spurs philanthropic giving, the basic self-interest of the company provides a basis for giving as well. Business may trickle support to any number of campus initiatives without a quid pro quo, but research partnerships carry expectations. Payton wonders, "When does something stop being called 'philanthropy' and start being called 'business'? The source of funds may be one answer; the expenditure may come from the corporation's marketing, promotion, personnel, public affairs, or corporate contributions department. The result for the community or the nonprofit recipient may be the same, but technically the first four expenditures are 'business' and the last is 'philanthropy.'"[16]

An article in the December 2002 issue of the *Harvard Business Review* said "that corporate philanthropy should be designed to give corporations a leg up on competitors. 'Philanthropy can often be the most cost-effective way—and sometimes the only way—to improve competitive context. It enables companies to leverage not only their own resources, but also the existing efforts and infrastructure of nonprofits and other institutions.'"[17]

THE RISE OF CAUSE-DIRECTED GIVING AND ACADEMIC RECEPTIVENESS

The 1980s is considered a benchmark for the growth of business support of academic research. Federal funding was holding constant or declining, research was getting increasingly expensive, and Congress looked for a way to encourage higher education to keep up the good work. According to one observer, "The change in the way universities view working with businesses and making money from research is generally traced back to Congress' passage of the Bayh-Dole Act of 1980, which gave universities the right to retain patents to intellectual property that they developed with federal support."[18]

The Supreme Court also focused attention on the financial outcomes of research in 1980 in determining that "genes, bugs, and cell lines could be patented, that life forms in and of themselves could be patented. That stimulated an enormous amount of investment opportunity."[19]

Universities had incentives to give priority to research that was likely to result in marketable or patentable products, and business was more interested in funding research that could contribute to the bottom line. According to Norman Bowie, "One of the more significant developments in the 1980's is the growth of partnerships between education and industry."[20]

In addition, businesses became more strategic in their giving as universities competed against one another to be the most attractive partner. Payton contends that "cause-related" giving is "marketing, not philanthropy."[21] He adds, "Many avenues are open to corporations that want to give in a cause-related way, or to make charitable contributions that still have a direct bearing on the company's interests. Examples are donations of money or equipment for university research and development in the company's field; the donation advances knowledge, may lead to market opportunities, and—not incidentally—may attract bright graduates to work for the company. Major high-technology corporations regularly give cash and computers to leading universities for these reasons."[22]

Examples of this kind of giving abound:

- "AT&T has picked a number of causes, such as lifting minority enrollment in engineering schools, that relates to its own interests."[23]
- B. Dalton Booksellers, a company that sells books for profit, is spending "$3 million over four years to fight functional illiteracy."[24]
- United Technologies Corporation (UTC) focused on arts and cultures because, according to its manager of corporate contributions, "Quite simply, we have found support of the arts to be the single most effective way of positioning UTC as a distinctive, imaginative, and quality-minded corporation in the minds of both customers and opinion leaders around the world." UTC learned that it could demand exclusivity of sponsorship for enough funding.[25]

Attaching strings, particularly strings that lead to the company's bottom line, is a given of business-university partnerships. Consider the contract between the Scripps Research Institute in La Jolla, California, and the Swiss company Sandoz Pharmaceuticals Corporation. Scripps is one of the largest nonprofit research centers in the United States and includes "more than 270 professors, 800 postdoctoral fellows, 1500 laboratory technicians, administrative and support personnel, and 126 Ph.D. students."[26]

Scripps entered an agreement with Sandoz that would provide $300 million in unrestricted support to last, at least, until 2007. "But the support was not entirely unrestricted: Under the contract, Sandoz, based in Switzerland, has the first rights to any and all discoveries made at Scripps."[27]

According to an AAUP report, Novartis Corporation and the Department of Plant and Microbial Biology at the University of California, Berkeley, developed a similar agreement in 1998: "Under a five-year, $25 million arrangement, Novartis is funding research in the department and will receive licensing rights to a proportion of the number of discoveries by the department's researchers equal to the company's share of the department's total research budget, whether or not the discoveries result directly from company-sponsored research."[28]

Giving for a specific cause, strategic giving, and the discovery of natural connections between academic research and business interests have clear advantages to corporations, universities, and the general public.

ADVANTAGES OF BUSINESS-UNIVERSITY PARTNERSHIPS

Some advantages are obvious, others are more subtle.

According to Norman Bowie, "the corporation receives three distinct advantages from business-university partnerships: access to information, access to potential commercial products, and access to creative, intelligent faculty and students. . . . The most obvious advantage [for a university] is money and lots of it. . . . Substituting these partnerships for open-ended giving provides a way for chief executive officers to tell stockholders that there is a return on the money provided to universities."[29]

The symbiotic nature of these advantageous relationships is evident in a description of Northwestern University's Kellogg School of Management corporate affiliates program. Corporations that give $5,000 or more each year to the school have important access. "As corporate affiliates, these corporate partners have the opportunity to interact with Kellogg's world-class faculty and outstanding students as speakers in class, panelists and keynote speakers for student conferences, participants in case studies and research initiatives and many other ways. . . . Additionally, corporate support remains integral to the activities of our academic research centers including the Center for Research in Technology and Innovation, which is receiving significant support from Motorola this year."[30]

The less obvious advantages involve the positive side of bringing business values to academic research. Researchers working on their own timeline may not work as quickly as those funded with business-controlled deadlines. The result, according to some, is research efficiency. "[B]usiness/university research partnerships will put time pressures on some who might otherwise be more relaxed in their research."[31]

In addition, business is more likely to fund applied research, or the research that will produce products with marketable worth. Faster, more efficiently applied research results in "products of interest to the general public more quickly." According to Bowie, "Taxpayers may well argue that their support of public universities justifies and perhaps even obligates universities to engage in applied research."[32]

CRITICISMS OF BUSINESS-UNIVERSITY PARTNERSHIPS

The advantages to the business partner may become disadvantages to the university partner when business expectations get in the way of a university's mission.

The problem begins, according to Bowie, when the business partner "tries to impose the same rules at the university level that apply in the corporate context, that is, that the researcher needs the permission of the business sponsor before the research can be published. . . . Most major business/university contracts presently in force provide exclusive rights to the industry sponsor of the research."[33]

The bias can begin as early as the choice of a research question or may not be evident until the publication of the research findings. For example, "In the field of weed science the choice of research questions is heavily influenced by the interests of chemical-industry benefactors. . . . The few studies that have been published suggest that researchers studying a drug and funded by manufacturers are more likely to reach a favorable interpretation of its safety, efficacy, or cost-effectiveness than those studying the same drug but funded by not-for-profit institutions.[34]

While evidence of problems created by business-university partnerships is more than anecdotal, it is undoubtedly limited. An American Association for the Advancement of Science (AAAS) report points out, "Little is known about the number of academic scientists who may be experiencing professional dilemmas because of restrictive controls on communication and sharing of research results."[35]

According to a study conducted in the late 1990s, "20 percent of 2,052 life science faculty that they surveyed indicated that publication of their research results had been delayed by more than six months at least once mostly for protection of proprietary value. Those with industrial support were more likely (11 percent) than those without such support (six percent) to refuse requests from other academic scientists to share research results or materials."[36]

Limitations on publication or inability to access data can have a profound effect on scientists who are serving a business master while attempting to jump through academic hoops. "[L]ife scientists working with industry who delay more than 6 months to publish their research may have salary issues, tenure decisions, or other institutional career incentives tied to their decision."[37]

Yet, academic institutions may be constrained from supporting researchers who are being pressured by the business partner if it is supporting more than one research project. "The failure of administrators to recognize threats to academic freedom, as well as to the public interest, is a common criticism within cases where researchers find themselves up against large companies that may be funding other projects at the same university."[38] For example:

Nancy Olivieri, [a researcher] at Toronto's Hospital for Sick Children, became convinced that use of the drug deferiprone [known commercially as Apotex] on children with thalassemia [a genetic blood disorder] had dangerous side effects. The manufacturer of the drug . . . that funded Olivieri's study cancelled her research and threatened her with a breach of contract suit should she inform her patients or publish her negative findings. When Betty J. Dong, a researcher at University of California, San Francisco, and her colleagues found the effectiveness of a new synthetic thyroid drug, Sythroid, to be equivalent to three other thyroid drugs, the drug's manufacturer Boots/Knoll Pharmaceutical refused to allow publication based on a contractual agreement that Dong had signed prohibiting disclosure of proprietary information. . . . Having signed non-disclosure agreements with the companies, both Olivieri and Dong found that their universities, daunted by monetary and legal stakes, would not support them. . . .

In another much watched case, research by David Kern, an occupational health physician at Memorial Hospital of Rhode Island and an associate professor at Brown University's School of Medicine, revealed an outbreak of lung disease at the Microfibres, Inc. textile plant in Pawtucket, Rhode Island. Kern's initial attempts to publicize findings of this new occupational disease were viewed by the company, hospital, and university administrators as breaching a confidentiality agreement with Microfibres over nondisclosure of its trade secrets.[39]

When administrators side with their researchers, they are likely to find themselves face-to-face with company lawyers with arbitration agreements that administrators signed as terms of the agreement.

For example, Immune Response Corporation, which has funded AIDS research at the University of California at San Francisco, accused "James O. Kahn, the lead researcher on a study the company funded in 2000, of omitting favorable data in his report, that was published in the *Journal of the American Medical Association.* . . . The company . . . also charged that the university had violated an agreement to keep certain findings confidential."[40]

Ronald Collins, director for the new Integrity in Science project at the Washington-based Center for Science in the Public Interest, said that Dr. Kahn's actions and the university's backing of him were especially "gutsy" because both parties knew they might have to resolve any ensuing dispute in an arbitration rather than an open-court proceeding. Since arbitrations are private and are conducted without a jury, they cannot be appealed and are "generally more sympathetic to industry," said Mr. Collins.[41]

Congressional oversight committees are also concerned about the influence of business on academic research as well as about how business might benefit from federal grant funding. The mix of federal funding and private contracts with research universities can result in indirect federal funding of private enterprise, some of it foreign.

For example, when Scripps entered into its contract with Sandoz, it also received approximately $70 million in grants from the National Institutes of Health (NIH), which led one congressional representative to observe that the Scripps-Sandoz alliance put the federal government in the position of subsidizing a foreign corporation. The director of the NIH "strongly criticized the Scripps-Sandoz contract," saying it "forbids free enterprise and forbids the free exchange of ideas."[42]

Models exist to show what happens when academic values are co-opted by commercial values. "The dangers of academic research that focuses too narrowly on commercial values should be evident from the unintended consequences of agricultural research and extension at land-grant universities," according to Paul B. Thompson of the technology policy center at Texas A&M. "People have bought into the idea," said Thompson, "that anything that can be marketed is in the public interest."[43]

Thompson also stated that "Strong federal support led to an agricultural revolution that produced a cornucopia of cheap food. But the aftermath also included technologies that may poison farmland, he says. And the technologies have promoted large businesses over family farms and contributed to the social and economic decline of many rural communities."[44] Consequently, science and engineering departments generally will have a distinct financial advantage over humanity and art departments.

CONFLICTS OF INTEREST AT THE MICRO AND MACRO LEVEL

A conflict of interests exists when "professional judgment concerning a primary interest . . . tends to be unduly influenced by a secondary interest (such as financial gain)."[45]

Universities, funding agencies, and the editors of refereed journals that publish academic research have been concerned for some time about conflicts of interest among individual researchers. Since the mid-1980s schools have required disclosure or placed limitations on how commercial funding could be used or placed limitations on consulting hours for researchers funded by commercial interests. Administrators are concerned that faculty continue to have primary loyalty to their academic positions and that commercial interests not be allowed to hijack a faculty's research agenda.

According to Bowie, "Allowing faculty members to be affiliated with biotech firms presents the same kind of difficulty as allowing members of the business school faculty to sit on corporate boards. Some institutions may not trust their professors to give sufficient time to their university responsibilities; these institutions will forbid or constrain such affiliation."[46]

For the AAUP, "The increasingly complex and controversial relationships among universities, researchers, and corporations led the federal government in 1995 to require researchers who receive grants from the National Science

Foundation or the Public Health Service . . . to disclose to their institutions any 'significant financial interests . . . that would reasonably appear to be affected by [their] research.' Specifically, researchers must report any income . . . greater than $10,000 that they receive from a corporation that could benefit from their research, or any equity interest greater than $10,000 that exceeds five percent ownership interest in such a corporation."[47]

Universities have followed this model, or developed more limitations, such as having no monetary limit for the disclosure requirement or requiring approval from the school before researchers can accept "a fiduciary role with a company, if such a position is related to their academic duties."[48]

Similarly, journals that published the results of research have been under increasing pressure to require authors to disclose any personal financial interests that they might have in research being reviewed for publication. An analysis of fourteen publications reported in 1996 showed that one-third of all research examined had at least one lead author with a financial interest in the research described in the article.[49] Virtually none of the authors had disclosed those interests.

A further study conducted by the same lead investigator in 1997 found that of 1,396 high-impact journals, 15.8 percent of them had disclosure policies, but only 6 percent had "templates" asking each author to identify the kind and quantity of a potential conflict. In contrast to the pilot study, investigators found that only 0.5 percent (327 of the 61,134 articles examined) of the original research items had at least one author's disclosure of personal financial research. In this later study, investigators concluded that "based on the previously mentioned pilot study, higher disclosure rates in the template journals, and the growth of commercialization in the biomedical sciences, we believe that poor compliance is the more likely explanation for low disclosure rates in most journals with COI [conflict of interest] policies."[50]

But influences on researchers may include restrictions "such as the non-disclosure of research findings, delay of publication, or licensing of research tools or processes are becoming more common."[51]

Just as it is important for administrators to pay attention to potential conflicts of interest for individual researchers, they must be aware of potential conflicts for the college or university as a whole. The "professional judgment" of administrators about a primary interest (the academic mission) can be compromised by the undue influence of a secondary interest (financial support for the institution).

For example, administrators might be willing to let the institution sacrifice basic research for the more lucrative applied research, or they might be willing to enter into contractual obligations regarding confidentiality, nondisclosure, and proprietary agreements that provide short-term financial support at the cost of the long-term academic mission.

DEALING WITH CONFLICTS

Business-university partnerships can be fruitful endeavors for both, but strict controls are necessary to protect the academic mission.

The AAUP offers a set of guidelines that favor faculty involvement, include university and faculty conflicts of interest, and allow flexibility. Interestingly, however, what is missing from the AAUP guidelines is the need for faculty and administrators to be first committed to the academic mission. With that in mind, the following prelude is necessary.

The basic commitment of higher education is in serving as a trustee for the body of knowledge. That position must always take priority over the right of a corporation to its intellectual property.[52]

The AAUP guidelines include:

1. Consistent with principles of sound academic governance, the faculty should have a major role not only in formulating the institution's policy with respect to research undertaken in collaboration with industry, but also in developing the institution's plan for assessing the effectiveness of policy.
2. The faculty should work to ensure that the university's plan for monitoring the institution's conflict of interest policy is consistent with the principles of academic freedom. There should be emphasis on ensuring that the source and purpose of all corporate-funded contracts can be publicly disclosed. Such contracts should explicitly provide for the open communication of research results, not subject to the sponsor's permission for publication.
3. The faculty should call for, and participate in, the periodic review of the impact of industrially sponsored research on the education of students, and on the recruitment and evaluation of researchers and postdoctoral fellows.
4. The faculty should insist that regular procedures be in place to deal with alleged violations by an individual of the university's conflict of interest policy.
5. Because research relationships with industry are not static, the faculty, in order to ensure that the assessment of conflict of interest policies is responsive to changing needs, should regularly review the policies themselves as well as the instruments for conducting the assessment.[53]

Except for the need for academic freedom stressed in guideline two, the AAUP list is process- rather than content-oriented. The guidelines put the governing of higher education research in the hands of the faculty, where it should be. Administration exists to support faculty teaching and research. While administration serves as a handy liaison between researchers and funders and as a source of accountability for the quality and completeness of research provided, neither business nor universities should forget that it is the faculty researcher upon whom research depends. Faculty, as a consensual group, is less likely to lose sight of the research and educational mission than either the business partner, administrators, or individual researchers.

Individual faculties at any institution may come to slightly different decisions regarding how to best protect their overall research agenda. Some may be purists, agreeing with scholars who argue the following: "If a university collaborated with a business sponsor in withholding an invention from the market, the university would be in violation of its central mission to add to the body of knowledge. Similarly, a university cannot refuse to conduct research on the grounds that the research may yield an invention that would compete with the product of another university sponsor."[54]

However, others might be more probusiness. "Since one of the central missions of the university is to add to the store of knowledge and to bring new knowledge to the community of scholars as quickly as possible, the university should maintain both publication rights and the ownership of all patents. Since the protection of trade secrets and the patenting of inventions can be justified on the grounds that such devices enhance basic research, rather than hinder it, prohibitions against the release of proprietary information received by the university partner in pursuing the research are justified."[55]

On the other hand, faculties might agree with Norman Bowie, who says that "trade secrets are necessary if basic research is to be undertaken. In the absence of trade secrets, other firms would be able to ride free on the basic research of others. Hence firms would be unwilling to undertake basic research. Since increasing research is a core task of the university and since these business/university partnerships are designed to enhance the ability of the university to engage in research, the anti-free-rider argument would apply in the university context as well. Corporations do have a legitimate right to insist that their proprietary information be protected."[56]

Using an anti-free-rider argument to protect basic research leads to interesting ironies in that, theoretically at least, the basis for academic research is free and open exchange of ideas. While a published research article is not a recipe, replication of the study is the criterion by which researchers judge the adequacy of the work. In this way of thinking, all researchers are "free riders" on the shoulders of scholars who have come before. The ability to think beyond what has been done is what separates an exemplary scholar from one who is simply adequate, just as the ability to rake in the profits separates an exemplary business from one that is simply surviving. Faculty are in the best position to determine how to best protect the institution of higher education.

A faculty member is not likely to forget that a business-university research partnership is borne from mutual self-interest, not philanthropy that springs from corporate awareness of the importance of supporting the communities in which they function.

The Council for Advancement and Support of Education has proposed guidelines that would make the division between corporate contracts and corporate philanthropy more clear than it has been. "Colleges and universities would no longer be allowed to count as gifts the money that pharmaceutical companies pay them to operate clinical-research trials, according to new guidelines developed by the Council for Advancement and Support of Education. Because clinical trials are contractual agreements, their proceeds do not qualify as gifts, the council has decided. . . . The standards also deal with specific gift types, like the so-called 'megagifts' of software that have become frequent. In order to pass the scrutiny of the Internal Revenue Service, institutions must be certain that such donations have no strings attached. Often software companies make such donations with the stipulation that an institution train its students to use the software. Such an arrangement is a contract and cannot be counted as a gift."[57]

Universities, corporations, and the IRS may struggle with making these divisions, but a faculty member should know the difference between sponsored research and having an uninvited partner in the lab.

NOTES

1. R. E. Spier, "Ethics and the Funding of Research and Development at Universities," *Science and Engineering Ethics* 4 (1998): 375–384.

2. Norman E. Bowie, "Business-University Partnerships," in *Morality, Responsibility and the University,* ed. Steven M. Cahn (Philadelphia: Temple University Press, 1990), 209.

3. Sheldon Krimsky, "Journal Policies on Conflict of Interest: If This Is the Therapy, What's the Disease?" *Psychotherapy and Psychosomatics* 70 (2001): 115–117.

4. Anthony DePalma, "Universities' Reliance on Companies Raises Vexing Questions for Research," *New York Times,* 17 March 1993.

5. "Report from Dr. Raymond E. Bye Jr., Vice President for Research," Office of Research Annual Report, Florida State University, 1999, http://www.research.fsu.edu/activity/1999/vprpt.html (accessed 28 June 2004).

6. AAUP, "Statement on Corporate Funding of Academic Research," 2001, http://www.aaup.org/statements/Redbook/repcorf.htm (accessed 27 May 2004).

7. DePalma, "Universities' Reliance on Companies Raises Vexing Questions for Research."

8. Peter Schmidt, "Public Universities Get Money to Attract High-Tech Industry," *Chronicle of Higher Education* (25 February 2000): A42.

9. Ibid.

10. "Major Institutions," PollingReport.com, http://www.pollingreport.com/institut .htm (accessed 19 June 2004).

11. Robert L. Payton, "Giving Gets Unfashionable," *New York Times,* 21 February 1988.

12. Council on Foundations, "Moral Obligation or Marketing Tool?" *Examining the Roles of Corporate Philanthropy,* Washington, DC, 4.

13. Ibid., 5.

14. Kristen Philipkoski, "Who's Giving Up the Most?" http://www.wired.com/ news/technology/0,1282,32716,00.html (accessed 15 December 2004).

15. Mark Benioff and Karen Southwick, *Compassionate Capitalism* (Franklin Lakes, NJ: Career Press, 2004), 17.

16. Council on Foundations, "Moral Obligation or Marketing Tool?" 22.

17. Michael E. Porter and Mark R. Kramer, "The Competitive Advantage of Corporate Philanthropy," *Harvard Business Review,* December 2002, reported in Benioff and Southwick, *Compassionate Capitalism,* 128–129.

18. Schmidt, "Public Universities Get Money to Attract High-Tech Industry."

19. Karen Young Kreeger, "Studies Call Attention to Ethics of Industry Support," *The Scientist* 11 (1997), http://www.the-scientist.com/1997/03/31/1/3 (accessed 3 August 2005).

20. Bowie, "Business-University Partnerships."

21. Council on Foundations, "Moral Obligation or Marketing Tool?" 6.

22. Ibid., 25.

23. Payton, "Giving Gets Unfashionable."

24. Council on Foundations, "Moral Obligation or Marketing Tool?" 9.

25. Ibid., 13.

26. "About TSRI: Introduction," http://www.scripps.edu/intro/intro.html (accessed 26 June 2004).

27. DePalma, "Universities' Reliance on Companies Raises Vexing Questions for Research."

28. AAUP, "Statement on Corporate Funding of Academic Research."

29. Bowie, "Business-University Partnerships," 198.

30. Kellogg School of Management, "Development Update: Kellogg Corporate Partners Lend Support," *Kellogg World Alumni Magazine* (Spring 2002), http://www .kellogg.northwestern.edu/kwo/spr02/facultynews/development.htm (accessed 28 June 2004).

31. Bowie, "Business-University Partnerships," 199.

32. Ibid.

33. Ibid., 202.

34. Sheldon Krimsky and L. S. Rothenberg, "Conflict of Interest Policies in Science and Medical Journals: Editorial Practices and Author Disclosures," *Science and Engineering Ethics Journal* 7 (2001): 115.

35. Amy Crumpton, "Secrecy in Science: Professional Ethics Report," Washington, DC: American Association for the Advancement of Science, 1999, 7.

36. Ibid.

37. Ibid.

38. Ibid., 1.

39. Ibid.

40. Katherine S. Mangan, "Company Seeks $10-Million from Scientist and University," *Chronicle of Higher Education* (17 November 2000): A50.

41. Ibid.

42. DePalma, "Universities' Reliance on Companies Raises Vexing Questions for Research."

43. Collen Cordes, "Debate Flares over Growing Pressures on Academe for Ties with Industry," *Chronicle of Higher Education* (16 September 1992).

44. Ibid.

45. Krimsky, "Journal Policies on Conflict of Interest: If This Is the Therapy, What's the Disease?" 206.

46. Bowie, "Business-University Partnerships," 204.

47. Ibid., 207.

48. AAUP, "Statement on Corporate Funding of Academic Research."

49. Sheldon Krimsky et al., "Financial Interests of Authors in Scientific Journals: A Pilot Study of 14 Publications," *Science and Engineering Ethics Journal* 2 (1996): 396–410.

50. Krimsky, "Journal Policies on Conflict of Interest: If This Is the Therapy, What's the Disease?" 205–218.

51. Crumpton, "Secrecy in Science: Professional Ethics Report," 1, 7.

52. Bowie, "Business-University Partnerships," 201.

53. AAUP, "Statement on Corporate Funding of Academic Research."

54. Bowie, "Business-University Partnerships," 203.

55. Ibid.

56. Ibid., 201.

57. John L. Pulley, "Guidelines Proposed to Tighten Reporting on Colleges' Gifts," *Chronicle of Higher Education* (19 July 2002): A27.

Chapter Six

Recipients as Givers

- A student-run foundation has awarded over its fifty-year history $800,000 to thirty-eight hundred students.[1]
- An alumni donor gave to an annual fund drive after being approached by a freshman woman who was in the same freshman-year dorm and sorority when the donor had attended the school.[2]
- One university reported that almost half of the $348,025 raised in the fall 2001 Excellence Fund Drive—an annual giving campaign earmarked for immediate needs—came from faculty and staff donors.[3]
- Elizabeth Hoffman, president of the University of Colorado, explained that every employee's gift is important. "Just recently," President Hoffman said, "we had an administrative assistant give $101 to the chancellor's campaign, her entire bonus check. We gave her a standing ovation."[4]

These examples can be read as fund-raising success stories, but they carry particular ethical baggage. In each case, persons who would typically benefit from a school's fund-raising campaign—students, faculty, and staff—are, in addition, donors or fund-raisers. Their role as solicitors or gift-givers puts them in a different, and potentially conflicting, role from the one that they fulfill as an employee of an institution.

Ethical issues arise from the multiple roles created when a recipient is also a fund-raiser or a donor. Sharing prospect information can lead to privacy and confidentiality concerns for the donor. The additional role can interfere with peer and power relationships that are found in a person's primary affiliation. Conflicts of interest and commitment are a dilemma for the institution when beneficiaries become fund-raisers or donors.

STUDENTS AS FUND-RAISERS

Traditionally, students have been expected to be boosters for their college or university. From the expectation that students will sit on the "right" side of the field at the football game to the expectation that students will call up their collective and competitive spirit to make an annual class gift, involving students in institutional advancement is not new. However, a new sense of urgency has intensified and formalized the expectations of students as fund-raisers in a way that makes ethical issues in the practice more obvious. In addition, the fact that something has been a traditional expectation does not imply that the expectation is necessarily ethical.

For example, it is not unusual for students to call alumni to encourage them to give in annual campaigns. Specific students are chosen to make particular calls because of some point of connection with the alumni in question. The current and former students share departmental or professional interests, race, gender, or extracurricular interests. The former student is thus, implicitly, encouraged to support someone like him- or herself. The implicit assumptions behind these connections are rarely considered or questioned, yet there are many, including:

1. A desire among former and current students to connect with one another.
2. The unstated belief that graduates should donate to their alma mater and, given the opportunity, will.
3. The assumed responsibility of graduates to donate despite the lack of any internal motivation on the part of alumni.
4. The realization by the student that, upon graduation, the institution will expect that same effort from him or her.
5. That it is reasonable to expect students to participate in fund-raising activities for the school.
6. That there is no privacy concern in collecting information regarding a graduate's activities as a student and using that information for development purposes or with sharing it with a current student.

Research backs up the belief that students who become involved in philanthropic activities on behalf of their school will give more later in life. A survey in 2000 that examined the giving activity of alumni who had been involved in fund-raising as students compared with those who had not confirmed that student fund-raisers were more likely to later give. "Overall, IUSF [Indiana University Student Foundation] member alumni have donated significantly higher average amounts to Indiana University than non-member alumni. In some cases, member alumni gave six times the amount non-members gave." According to this author, "The model suggests that serious philanthropy results from a process through which a donor identifies with an organization and its cause. Individuals identify with the cause by becoming involved in an organization whose benefits can be learned and internalized and where they can interact with others who share similar values."[5]

For some elite undergraduate institutions, the process of helping students internalizing the values that turn into later gifts begins with freshman orientation. According to one highly successful development officer, freshmen learn that they have philanthropic responsibilities and are provided examples and campus lore relating to gift development and giving by past students and classes. If that message is successful, the development officer expects 100 percent participation from current students in annual fund drives. Recent alumni are persuaded, shamed, and cajoled to give throughout the first ten years following graduation. The continuing relationship is not meant to result in major gifts when students are in school or in the years that they are establishing careers and families. However, the long-standing relationship and the developed habit of giving yields substantial gifts when income peaks.[6]

By the time undergraduates arrive on campus, almost all of them will have had experience raising funds. From selling Girl Scout cookies to holding bake sales and car washes to pay for band uniforms or extracurricular trips, students learned during K–12 how to ask parents, neighbors, friends, and even strangers in the community to help fund their efforts. But there are ethically relevant differences between what happened at the precollege level from what transpires once the students become undergraduates.

There is a difference of degree in both the expected impact of fund-raising and the motivation behind student involvement. At the precollege level, students have the experience of giving of themselves to help advance some obvious community good or the experience of making themselves instruments for bringing about some personally desired end.

As undergraduate fund-raisers, students are commonly provided a minimal goal that they are expected to achieve, with prodding to be competitive with classes of the past or other current groups. Just what the donations are expected to fund is usually far more vague than the trip to the state capitol that high school car washes made possible. In a similar way, undergraduates may have some vague belief that they will benefit from the donated funds, but the benefit is less clear than a seat on the bus for the class trip. Undergraduates learn to solicit on behalf of the institution upon which they depend for their degrees. This is a far more complicated kind of agency than soliciting Christmas gifts for disadvantaged children.

Lacking such clear self-interest or beneficiaries outside of the social group, fund-raising undergraduates operate as general agents and benefactors of the institution. A power differential is created between the wealthier and less wealthy students. The role of agent or of peer-benefactor has the potential of creating conflicts with the primary role of a student.

Undergraduate fund-raisers are often matched with potential donors based on shared characteristics for specifically targeted prospects. Students are expected to capitalize on their connections with prospects as a basis for motivating donations. This is conceptually different from the asking they did as precollege students from those with whom they had previously established relationships (parents, teachers, neighbors, family, and friends) or those with whom they had no relationship, such as strangers buying cookies or paying for a car wash at a fund-raiser. They could legitimately expect those within their network of care to support their activities; they could legitimately expect strangers to support the cause or want the product or service offered. At the undergraduate level, their basis for expectation of donation are shared characteristics.

The undergraduate student's primary role includes a multitude of facets: inherent characteristics such as ethnicity and gender, departmental affiliation, personal interests, and extracurricular involvements. When fund-raising, students may be expected to treat any of those markers as enticements to motivate others to give. The ethically relevant assumption is that it is appropriate for students and their institutions to exploit their own and others' characteristics to motivate giving behavior.

An associated ethical concern is the gleaning, using, and sharing of alumni information for purposes of solicitation. Alumni may consider the use of information related to their college experience for fund-raising to be an invasion of privacy, just as patients might reasonably object to information about their diagnosis, treatment, and financial situation used by a hospital to target them for donations. Just as patients might consider their medical records an inappropriate mine for hospital foundation fund-raisers, alumni might consider it a violation of confidentiality to share information about them with current students if they have not been given the opportunity to withhold consent.

Ethical prospect research precludes the access and use of information without prospective donor knowledge, and graduating students should have the ability to prohibit the use of information to be used for development purposes. Current students should not feel obligated to exploit their personal characteristics to solicit funds from alumni. Creating an assumed obligation potentially disables students in their quest to be critics of the institution and its practices by creating peer pressure to do the institution's work.

Although financially deprived children may be those who most directly benefit from fund-raising activities during K–12, they are rarely identified or targeted because of concerns of labeling or ridicule. At the college level, students receiving financial assistance are aware of the special help, are expected to be grateful for it, and, later, are expected to give back, at least at the level that was given to them.

When undergraduate fund-raising creates scholarship funds or creates a pool of money to be used to donate on behalf of less wealthy peers to fulfill the challenge of 100 percent participation in class drives, the distinction between benefactor-peers and recipient-peers creates a difference in the student-student relationship.

For example, when students give to students, as through an endowment fund at North Carolina State University to provide "a partial scholarship each year to a child of migrant farm workers,"[7] student-donors may have expectations of what is appropriate use of those scholarship dollars by student-recipients. That changes the peer relationship in that it can lead students to judge one another's actions based on appropriate use of donating dollars. By way of analogy, the identity of a recipient of a cadaver donation is often concealed from donor families, in part to protect the ability of the recipient to live his or her life away from the donor family's scrutiny. In a similar way, student recipients may feel observed and obligated to choose their actions based on real or perceived donor desires.

The assumption of a student as a donor can also directly complicate the student-scholar role. In 2002, a University of Utah economics professor, Anne L. Yeagle, was criticized for offering extra credit for students who raised money for a charity. Students could raise their final grade a full letter by bringing in the maximum $100 for a charity that provides funds for medicine and education in Kenya. "The offer didn't sit well with some students, who claimed Ms. Yeagle was selling grades."[8] The instructor was criticized for exchanging grades for donated dollars, but coerced voluntary action is acceptable in higher education.

Service learning is increasingly considered a legitimate part of undergraduate education. The difference between giving service and giving donations is not a difference in kind. Both qualify as examples of philanthropy—voluntary action for the public good. Schools that give credit for service learning experiences explicitly reinforce the notion that giving to one's community is an expectation of the educated person.

Some schools have made service learning a requirement for graduation. California State University, Monterey Bay (CSUMB), explains its connection between the community and the classroom: "By explicitly making these issues [diversity, compassion, justice, social responsibility] part of the curriculum, students actively clarify their own conception of service as they participate in the community. Service learning enables moral and civic learning to become a component of the curriculum. Learning becomes a tool for both individual and social betterment. Through service learning, CSUMB students acquire the knowledge, skills and awareness to become more culturally aware, self-reflective and responsive community participants."[9]

Service learning, like an expected donation, also communicates that it is the action, not inner motivation, that makes one a good citizen. Students are not likely to feel free to criticize, evaluate, or analyze institutions and their practices if the school has already blessed the institution as appropriate for students' philanthropic activity.

WEALTH AS A CATEGORY FOR ADMISSION

Wealthy families donate to institutions in the hopes of influencing admissions or retention. In doing so, they create conflicts of interest for the institution. A conflict of interest is any financial interest or obligation that is not compatible with the proper discharge of one's primary duty.

The primary duty of admissions officers is to admit qualified students with an eye toward creating a diverse and broadly talented student body. The wealth of the student's family is not connected to that essential mission.

However, the likelihood of significant donation has influenced admissions for some time. In 1989, John Hennessy, then provost of the University of Vermont, defended that school's practice of admitting seven to ten students each year because of the wealth of their families and the families' likelihood of giving to the school. "Mr. Hennessy said the policy of considering potential donors in a few out-of-state admissions was just as legitimate as considering academic qualifications, ethnic backgrounds and special talents like athletic and musical abilities. . . . Spokesmen for several associations representing higher education said that colleges and universities have made it a practice for a number of years to reserve some places in their freshmen classes for students from families who could be counted on to make significant contributions to the institutions. But, the spokesman said they had never heard of such a policy being explicitly stated." One Vermont state representative objected to the practice. "I think admissions to our educational institutions should be based on a student's ability, not the family's wealth."[10]

Times have changed, both in terms of institutions' willingness to admit to the practice of development admissions and to the acceptance, if not the acceptability, of the practice. According to a *Wall Street Journal* article from May 2003, "Maude Bunn's SAT scores weren't high enough for a typical student to earn admission to Duke University. But Ms. Bunn had something else going for her—coffeemakers. Her ancestors built a fortune on them. And with Duke hoping to woo her wealthy parents as donors, she got in."[11]

While Duke is not the only elite institution practicing development admissions, it has been the most willing to speak to journalists about the practice:

> While children of the wealthy have long had advantages getting into colleges, a look at how "development admissions" work at Duke shows how institutionalized the process has become at some major universities. The school accepts just 23% of applicants, rejecting more than 600 high-school valedictorians a year. Three-fourths of its students have SATs above 1320.
>
> Yet in recent years, Duke says it has relaxed these standards to admit 100 to 125 students annually as a result of family wealth or connections, up from about 20 a decade ago. These students aren't alumni children and were tentatively rejected, or wait-listed, in the regular admissions review. More than half of them enroll, constituting an estimated 3% to 5% of Duke's student body of 6,200.
>
> The strategy appears to be paying off. For the last six years, Duke says it has led all universities nationwide in unrestricted gifts to its annual fund from nonalumni parents: about $3.1 million in 2001–2002.[12]

College advisors acknowledge the practice, also creating an analogy with athletic and celebrity admits. According to one admissions assistance company,

> Once in a while, Harvard will admit a student with a composite 1000 SAT score. He might be a hockey player. Another student with a 950 score will sometimes get into Brown. She might be the daughter of a movie star. The same score will sometimes get an earnest applicant into Duke. His grandfather may have put up the money for a library.
>
> Nearly all admissions committees at private colleges and universities pay close attention to the applications submitted by legacies and the children of big donors. Why? Because without big-time taxpayer support, private schools depend heavily on gifts from grateful alumni and thoughtful big donors. These preferences are controversial, of course, but they won't go away anytime soon. Somebody has to pay the bills. Is a new library worth a kid on campus with subpar SAT scores? Yes.[13]

Katherine Cohen, a founder of another educational consulting service,

> says that development offices routinely speak to donors on the verge of giving when their children are juniors and seniors in high school. She argues that development cases are particularly important for the name recognition of a school.
>
> "Usually there's a conversation that takes place between the development office and the family," Cohen said. "The development office may reach out to different families. They know, for example, if a legacy is applying and the parents really have not done anything for the school. They have a list of high net

worth individuals, famous people, things like that, whose kids are applying to college."[14]

The process, according to *Wall Street Journal* writer Daniel Golden, is well coordinated between development and admissions offices. The development office, at least at Duke, starts the process by identifying "500 likely applicants with rich or powerful parents who are not alumni. . . . It cultivates them with campus tours and basic admissions advice; for instance, applying early increases their chances. It also relays the names to the admissions office, which returns word if any of the students forgot to apply—so development can remind them."[15]

This yields "at least 160 high-priority applicants." Usually 30 to 40 are admitted on merit alone. The admissions officer and senior vice president for development "debate these 120 cases, weighing their family's likely contribution against their academic shortcomings." Despite admission officer concerns, "most of the 120 students are admitted."[16]

Ethically speaking, development admissions are different from admissions that give extra consideration to those with athletic or musical talents. Theoretically, at least, the student-athlete or student-performer who receives a scholarship based on talent is first and foremost a student-scholar. They meet academic standards and bring extra talent. That is the justification of the talent-based scholarships that they receive. The guiding justification, whether widely practiced or not, is that scholarships are awarded based on the extra measure that the student brings to campus.

Admitting a class that will contribute to a well-rounded student body provides justification for accepting students with slightly varying numbers in terms of test scores and cumulative high school averages. The justification here is that each admission contributes equally, but differently, to the class makeup and therefore merits the same consideration for matriculation. Thus, the high school newspaper editor who writes well but who struggles with math, the exceedingly bright but non-social intellectual, and the community activist all have a place in creating a well-rounded class.

Admission based on wealth, however, contributes nothing, conceptually speaking, to improving the school's talent base or in rounding out the set of abilities, interests, and accomplishments traditionally considered in college applications. Parental influence or wealth, while potentially good for the institution's coffers, does not relate to a student's ability to contribute to the school's educational function or environment.

That concern is probably not relevant to the parent of the subpar student. One such parent mused, "Did my normal child take the place of somebody who could really make a difference in the world? Sure, yes, to an extent. But there are so many things you can lose sleep over. I'm happy for me and my child."[17]

However, such concerns should be relevant to an institution of higher education. While it may not be surprising that people who are used to their wealth buying what they wish would find such ethical concerns irrelevant, it doesn't follow that the institution must choose the economic over the ethical. Duke, like other prestigious institutions that make admission decisions based on gifts and pledges, has a solid and substantial endowment. It costs the institution little to take the high road and costs substantially in credibility for it to choose otherwise.

Development and admissions offices work together to develop parent givers in more surreptitious ways as well. Fund-raising offices are cooperating with admissions offices in the following ways, according to a report in an ethics journal:

1. Asking parents to complete information cards that seem directed to the registrar's office, but that actually end up in the development office.
2. Seeking parents' social security numbers, which are then used to determine income and property holdings.
3. Allowing the development office access to student applications.
4. Scanning student applications to determine parents with the most lucrative occupations.[18]

The development of these prospective parent-donor lists creates the same privacy and confidentiality concerns that arise in the development of alumni prospects. The parents may well object to information that they provided in support of their child's application being diverted for development purposes; they may object to information being shared between admissions and development offices without their knowledge or consent.

FACULTY AS FUND-RAISERS

It was about three years after I completed my M.A. degree that I got a call from one of my professors. I was well into my doctoral work and was touched that the professor would call to see how things were going. We chatted for a few minutes, and I got caught up on the news of other professors and some of my classmates who had since finished the program.

"I'm hoping that you will contribute to our department's fund drive," he said. At first, I was confused. "A department fund drive? That's new," I responded.

The professor agreed that it was a new concept, but now departments were encouraged to fund-raise on their own to defray the costs of faculty travel and to build a scholarship fund. My next reaction was one of uncomfortable surprise that the department would be asking me for money. I was a starving graduate student, living some weeks on oranges, crackers, and cottage cheese. Nevertheless, I sent a check for $25, which represented a substantial portion of my monthly teaching assistant income. At the time, I reasoned that it was better to pinch a few more pennies but feel that I could go back to the professor for a letter of recommendation if I needed it. The next year, I was less surprised by the call, but I still gave. The following year, I said, "No, thank you," and that was the last call I received. It was also the year that I removed my M.A. professors' names from my reference list. I also learned that anonymous donations provide the best protection against further solicitation and also provided the best test of whether I really *wanted* to give to a cause.

Professors who call alumni asking them to give may be naive as to the negative implications of the request. Such calls are illegitimate. The alumni perception can reasonably be that having a continuing good relationship with the department depends on the gift. For recent graduates from a program who may still be in school or paying back student loans and in need of the good will of the asking department, the "opportunity to give" may feel more like blackmail than philanthropy.

When faculty are asked by development officers to meet with prospective donors who are particularly interested in the faculty's research, faculty play an appropriate role in the fund-raising process. The faculty member is doing what she is paid to do by the institution: produce notable research. That the prospective donor is interested in the good work that the faculty member would be doing anyway is what might be termed good luck or a happy coincidence. Institutions may capitalize on their faculty's good work to bring in donations, but not on the connections that faculty members have built with students in fulfilling their primary teaching role.

FACULTY AS DONORS

It was only a matter of time before faculty members were asked to donate to the colleges and universities that employ them. Providing faculty an "opportunity to give" goes back at least to the 1970s, when United Way convinced institutions of higher education, as well as corporations and news organizations, to distribute pledge cards to their employees at the office. Controversy arose over whether employees were being coerced to give or not—United

Way claimed that was not their intention. It was natural for the schools themselves to decide to cash in on the process.

Most schools have separate solicitations of employees at different times of the year—one for United Way supported agencies and the other for the school's own annual campaign. Donations may be made through payroll deduction in both cases. Many schools have fund-raising campaigns coordinated through departments. Departmental secretaries or administrative assistants often serve as the collection point. Department members are asked to return sealed envelopes with their pledge or designation that they will not contribute. The departmental point person is expected to remind all faculty members to return their envelopes. Often that person is rewarded for "100 percent return." Theoretically, administrators may gain access to information regarding an employee's level of giving. Departments often receive back a list of the names of donors who have directed gifts toward the department. While this disclosure allows departments to thank their donors, it also allows the departments to identify faculty and staff who did not give.

According to the Council for Advancement and Support of Education (CASE), "Faculty giving is a touchy subject in advancement. Some faculty members feel that receiving a solicitation from their institution is a bit like encountering a hungry crocodile—a beast they believe has already consumed a limb or two and is coming back for more. Faculty members are well aware of their institution's imperfections. In addition, they often feel underpaid and under-appreciated. Whipping a bit of Times New Roman into billowy paragraphs about academic excellence isn't likely to move this often cynical audience—unless it's toward a paper shredder."[19]

CASE recommends that faculty be enlisted to ask other faculty to give and that the campaign focus on faculty productivity. "Promoting the institution's needs at the same time you acknowledge the faculty's primary contribution—their work—can cultivate a general feeling of good will even among those who are unreceptive to the campaign."[20]

The dual role of faculty-donors creates ethical issues similar to those created by the dual role of student-donors. Faculty peer relationships are changed by the knowledge that some are donating and others are not. Faculty-student relationships are changed by the awareness that faculty have personally provided the funds for a scholarship. Faculty may feel empowered to implicitly or explicitly demand more of scholarship students when their personal dollars are making it possible for the student to be in school.

There also is the issue that faculty are deducting from their salaries what had once been provided to them in addition to their salaries. The amount that faculty are "giving back" to the institution is therefore twice the amount of the gift. Along with the portion of their salaries that they are refunding to the school, they have lost the travel funds or other benefits that used to be institutionally provided.

In addition, there is a clear danger of faculty donations replacing institutional support. Once an administration sees that departmental members will pitch in to support faculty travel, scholarships, or library funds, the administration can divert its support to operating costs that are not so easy to replace.

However, the biggest ethical issue in creating multiple roles for faculty and students is that the additional, developmental-based roles can conflict with their primary institutional obligations.

Fund-raising and donating on behalf of the institution creates a sacred cow. Unfettered inquiry or exchange of ideas regarding institutional fund-raising is not likely to happen as long as fund-raising and donations are expected from scholars and students. Communication can be blocked and primary relationships can be difficult to maintain when developmental expectations get in the way. Creating a difference in peers between who gave and who did not can lead to discrimination.

NOTES

1. "Breaking Away in the Race for Donors," *Philanthropy Matters* 10(2) (2000): 3.
2. Stephanie Carr, "Stanford's 1990 Graduates Didn't Wait Long to Give Back in a Big Way," *Chronicle of Higher Education* (20 October 2000): 35.
3. "Excellence Fund Reaches Goals," News Forum, University of Montana, http://www.umt.edu/urelations/nf/archive/121800/excell.htm (accessed 23 May 2004).
4. Stephanie Brenowitz, "All Gifts Great & Small," *Matrix: The Magazine for Leaders in Education,* April 2001, http://www.findarticles.com/cf_0/mOHJE/2_2/ 79961284 (accessed 28 March 2004).
5. "Breaking Away in the Race for Donors," 3.
6. Personal communication, 17 September 2000.
7. "Give and Take," *Chronicle of Higher Education* (7 December 2001): A23.
8. "Gifts Make the Grade," *Chronicle of Higher Education* (2 August 2002).
9. "Transforming Learning through Community Service: CSU Monterey Bay's Service Learning Prism," http://service.csumb.edu/overview/prism2.html (accessed 18 May 2004).
10. Lee A. Daniels, "Potential Donors Figure in Entry to Vermont U," *New York Times,* 8 November 1989.
11. Daniel Golden, "Money Talks: Many Colleges Admit Sub-Par Students Because They're Rich," *Wall Street Journal: Classroom Edition,* May 2003, http://www.wsj classroomedition.com/archive/03may/EDUC_moneytalks.htm (accessed 27 May 2004).
12. Ibid.

13. "Hooked and Unhooked," ThickEnvelope.com, https://www.thickenvelope .com/college-admission-3.aspx (accessed 26 May 2004).

14. Jon Cohen, "Scrutinizing Special Admissions Policies: Pending Reforms May Not Target Privileged Application Process," *Yale Herald* 34(9) (1 November 2002), http://www.yaleherald.com/article.php?Article=1318 (accessed 27 May 2004).

15. Daniel Golden, "Colleges Bend Rules to Admit Rich Applicants," *College Journal from the Wall Street Journal,* 24 February 2003, http://www.collegejournal.com/ aidadmissions/newstrends/20030224-golden.html (accessed 27 May 2004).

16. Ibid.

17. Ibid.

18. "You May Already Be . . . a Donor," *Ethics: Easier Said Than Done* (1995): 25.

19. Susan Sarver, "Proceed with Caution," *CASE Currents,* July/August 2001, http://www.case.org/currents/2001/viewarticle.cfm?CONTENTitemid=2870 (accessed 3 August 2005).

20. Ibid.

Chapter Seven

Conclusion

The best defense against unethical practices relating to philanthropy in higher education is the process that protects higher education in so many other ways—decisions regarding the solicitation and acceptance of gifts should be subject to open discussion and input from the faculty.

Faculty governance models have proved successful in the development and administration of curriculum, in addressing faculty and student misconduct in research and classroom activities, and in creating and maintaining standards in many other realms of campus life.

At least since the articulation of the Statement on Governance by the American Association of University Professors (AAUP) in 1966, the importance of a faculty's voice has been an established principle of American higher education. That statement, in part, reads:

> Effective planning demands that the broadest possible exchange of information and opinion should be the rule for communication among the components of a college or university. The channels of communication should be established and maintained by joint endeavor. Distinction should be observed between the institutional system of communication and the system of responsibility for the making of decisions.
>
> A second area calling for joint effort in internal operation is that of decisions regarding existing or prospective physical resources. The board, president, and faculty should all seek agreement on basic decisions regarding buildings and other facilities to be used in the educational work of the institution.[1]

The management of private and corporate gifts fits into both planning and prospective physical resources. The potential for damage to academic integrity and credibility by decisions that make donors' interests a priority over an institution's mission obligate advancement officers and administrators to bring these decisions to the campus community.

The researcher who is promised years of support for his work and his students is not in the best position to determine if a potential giver's stipulations are consistent with or contrary to the overall mission. The vice president for research may be swayed by the substantial overhead that such a gift brings. But, the broader voice of campuswide faculty governance, whether in the form of a faculty senate or a standing committee, adds the probability of dispassionate review of the benefits of accepting the gift with its strings attached against the benefits of declining the gift.

An open process with open communication will not avoid all ethical problems. The willingness of admissions officers to admit subpar but wealthy students doesn't mitigate the harm done to the perception of the university and its students. The willingness of university administrators to abdicate the mission by allowing a corporate interest to own research data and determine its use does not mitigate the harm caused to the academic field that is dependent on the sharing of research results. But an open process with a broad set of faculty voices is certain to create vigorous discussion on questionable proposals. Decisions made by one campus become fodder for discussion in higher education as a whole.

Institutions may be more dependent on the kindness of strangers in the twenty-first century than at any time in history, but it doesn't follow that individual and corporate givers must be provided a seat at the academic or governance table. Schools have been dependent on tuition and state funding without allowing students or legislatures to dictate the academic agenda. However, protecting higher education from forces more inclined to favor economic factors over a mission will require increased vigilance by the faculty.

NOTE

1. "Statement on Government of Colleges and Universities," American Association of University Professors, http://www.aaup.org/statements/Redbook/Govern.htm (accessed 14 December 2004).

Part II

SELECTED READINGS

The following five selected readings are intended to illuminate different aspects that form the foundation of a justifiable theory of philanthropy in higher education. "Conceptions of Ethics in Educational Administration," by Lynn G. Beck and Joseph Murphy describes the ethical requirements for educational leadership. In "The Ethics and Values of Fund Raising," Robert L. Payton provides a rationale for the philanthropic support of higher education and the important role of the President in providing leadership for philanthropy. W. Bruce Cook and William F. Lasher provide a careful analysis of the perspectives of college and university presidents who have raised $100 million or more and identify markers of effectiveness from that study in "Toward a Theory of Fund Raising in Higher Education." Philosopher Allen Buchanan examines an important distinction in "Justice and Charity," concluding that the traditional methods of distinguishing the two fail. Neil Levy ends the section by taking a provocative stand in "Against Philanthropy, Individual and Corporate." Levy argues that essential services should be provided by government rather than through the kindness of strangers. The remaining question is whether higher education qualifies as essential to the public good.

Conceptions of Ethics in Educational Administration

Lynn G. Beck and Joseph Murphy

We cannot expect to find in our society a single set of moral concepts. . . .
Conceptual conflict is endemic in our situation because of the depth of our
moral conflicts. Each of us therefore has to choose both with whom we
wish to be morally bound and by what ends, rules, and virtues we wish to
be guided.

Alasdair MacIntyre, from *A Short History of Ethics* (1966), p. 268

In the recent rebirth of interest in educational ethics, two themes stand out in the area of school administration. The Gist is a belief that education is "invested from the outset with a moral character" (Hodgkinson, 1991, p. 26). The second, a natural extension of the first, is the belief that educators must become aware of the ethical implications of their work and that they must continually strive to make and be guided by morally sound decisions and to encourage others to do the same. Interestingly, despite agreements on these ideas, scholars seem to differ—at times slightly and at times rather dramatically—in their interpretations and understandings of ethics and its relationship to practice and decision making.

As we sought to understand the current status of ethics in educational administration programs, we realized that we needed some way of thinking about the various conceptions of ethics, values, and morals as they relate to educational leadership. After pondering the various recommendations for the development of "moral imagination and interpersonal competence" (Greenfield,

"Conceptions of Ethics in Educational Administration," by Lynn G. Beck and Joseph Murphy, in *Ethics in Educational Leadership Programs,* Corwin Press Inc., 1994, pp. 1–17.

1987, p. 70), we discovered that authors writing on this topic seem to think about ethics in one of two general ways. Many concentrate upon identifying, explicating, analyzing, and justifying certain principles or "concepts used by administrators in ethical reasoning and [in] the process of ethical reflection itself" (Strike, Haller, & Soltis, 1988, p. 6). Others, taking a slightly different approach, assume that reasoning and decision making are only a part of what morality encompasses. It is concerned with the way in which we typically regard ourselves and others (and the social and physical world in which we live) as well as how we act; with the range of stable dispositions, attitudes, and emotions that incline us to see and act as we do (Crittenden, 1984, p. 18).

Those holding this view tend to stress the need for experiences within preparation programs that shape not only the thought of administrators but also their perceptions, beliefs, assumptions, emotions, and commitments. In the sections that follow, we discuss these two broad ways of thinking about ethics, noting several more specific interpretations and applications of these concepts as manifested in the work of several authors who have influenced the preparation programs we examined.[1]

This chapter opens with a general discussion of the notion that ethics provide principles to guide administrators toward morally sound decisions and continues with an examination of three ways this assumption has influenced efforts to prepare ethical leaders. We first discuss scholarship predicated upon the idea that knowledge of various philosophical principles can assist administrators in "the process of ethical reasoning" (Strike, Haller, & Soltis, 1988, p. xi). Next, we look at efforts to equip administrators to understand and interpret "relevant laws and regulations" (Crittenden, 1984, p. 28). Finally, we explore work that concentrates upon the importance of professional codes of conduct in the development of ethical practice.

In the second section the focus shifts to an examination of the idea that ethics provide a perspective on educational purposes, roles, and practices and that the development of ethical leaders requires cultivating certain fundamental ways of thinking and understanding. As in the previous section, we begin with a general discussion of the idea that ethical persons perceive the world, their roles, and others in certain distinctive ways. We then look at three manifestations of this view in administrative literature. First, we discuss scholarship that suggests that moral leaders will seek to identify education's deepest and finest purposes and allow these purposes to influence their thinking and acting. Next, we look at the work of authors who stress the importance of understanding education as a social enterprise and who argue that ethical administrators will seek to uphold certain political values and ideas. Finally, we turn our attention to those who stress that moral leadership requires seeing schools as inhabited by persons and making decisions and engaging in actions that honor, respect, and support individuals.

ETHICS AS PRINCIPLES, PROVIDING GUIDELINES FOR DECISION MAKING AND PROBLEM SOLVING

Much of the recent attention to ethics has arisen in response to a growing awareness of the complex dilemmas facing educational leaders. Today, administrators must discover ways to work with teachers, students, and parents representing a wide range of circumstances. Within their schools, they must cultivate a shared vision, meaningful and coherent professional and personal experiences, and a sense of membership in a community of learning with persons who may have some profound differences in living conditions, values, and beliefs. Complicating this challenge is the fact that many of the norms, ideals, and assumptions that once provided a fairly stable framework to guide leaders are under attack (e.g., Mitchell, 1990a).

In an effort to identify ways educators might respond to multifaceted challenges and value-linked conflicts, some scholars have emphasized the importance of identifying principles that can guide leaders in untangling quandaries and resolving dilemmas. For some, these take the form of "moral principles" that can be applied to specific cases to provide guidance in "ethical reasoning" (Strike, Haller, & Soltis, 1988, p. 4). Others look to policies and laws emanating from some superordinate governing body for help in solving complicated problems (see, for example, Cohen, 1976; Mitchell, 1990a; 1990b). Still others emphasize the importance of professionals developing their own codes of conduct to guide them in the decision-making process (Kultgen, 1988).

Ethics as Philosophical Principles

In his essay, "The Moral Context of Decision Making in Education," Brian Crittenden (1984) argues for the existence of "at least some moral values that are generally recognized and that can be upheld objectively" (p. 16). For him these values center around "respect for human life" and include "such notions as love, loyalty, justice, honesty, courage, . . . generosity, . . . truth telling and promise keeping, and [respect for] political authority, property, and family" (p. 16). Because these values are linked to "common needs and capacities of human beings, to the characteristic condition on which the flourishing of life depends, and to human experience" (p. 22), Crittenden asserts that universal principles supportive of basic human values can be developed and that these can provide guidance to educational leaders seeking to make moral decisions and "to rationally justify their decisions as thoroughly as possible" (p. 35).

In his discussion, Crittenden concentrates on the possibility that principles *do* exist that can provide criteria for administrators seeking to determine "the appropriate educational means for achieving a predetermined end" (p. 33). He does not offer a comprehensive discussion of specific principles, however. Strike et al. (1988), following Crittenden's line of thinking, do offer such a discussion. In *The Ethics of School Administration* these authors draw a distinction between "*facts, moral principles,* and *preferences*" (p. 36, emphasis in the original) and demonstrate the interplay of these three phenomena in the decision-making process. Presenting cases containing an array of facts about a problematic condition, Strike and his coauthors invite readers to consider their own preferences and those of others in the situation, and they define and discuss concepts related to the cases in question and suggest ways that certain ethical principles can guide leaders in evaluating preferences, interpreting concepts, and making decisions. Two of the central ethical principles discussed are the principle of benefit maximization and the principle of equal respect. The first of these "holds that, whenever we are faced with a choice, the best and most just decision is the one that results in *the* most good or the greatest benefit for the most people" (p. 16). The latter, in turn, "requires that we act in ways that respect the equal worth of moral agents. It requires that we regard human beings as having intrinsic worth and treat them accordingly" (p. 17). Using these and other moral guidelines—such as the principle of equal treatment and the principle of noninterference—Strike et al. (1988) demonstrate the ways moral principles might inform and guide educational leaders who must make "hard choices . . . under complex and ambiguous circumstances" (p. 3). Throughout their book, they are not pretending to claim that there is "one right answer to every moral dilemma"[1] (p. 3). Rather, they are attempting to assist administrators in making good decisions and wise choices that are based upon broadly accepted moral principles and not merely upon the personal preferences of the decision maker.

Similarly, building upon the work of Gastil (1977), Sergiovanni (1980) offers a set of "pluralistic criteria" to guide decision makers in "problem analysis and the selection from among alternatives" (p. 3) in the quest for "solutions for concrete, practical problems" (Hills, 1978, p. 2; quoted in Sergiovanni, 1980, p. 16).[2] He suggests that four principles form a sound and helpful framework within which leaders can consider various options. The first, concerning the value of utility, asserts that administrators must be "concerned with the practical, with social maximization, with costs and benefits, and with other standards of production and achievement" (p. 4). Sergiovanni's second principle emphasizes the notion of "transcendence" (p. 4). In his discussion of this concept, he writes that decision makers must assess "the capacity of an alternative to increase the potential of society for achieving humanness in the pursuit of happiness" (p. 4) and calls on educational leaders to "give attention to the potential of each (possible decision) to help individual organizations, the community, and society to move beyond the ordinary, to grow to new levels of understanding, to higher standards of operation" (p. 4). Sergiovanni next concentrates upon justice: "As educational administrators and policy makers evaluate decision alternatives, they [should] give attention to the extent each provides for a just distribution of benefits" (p. 4). Finally, he asserts that, "As decision makers and policy makers evaluate decision alternatives on the basis of utility, transcendence, and justice, they should consider as well the ethical questions which surface" (p. 5). Acknowledging that these questions are often difficult to answer, he nevertheless argues that morally sound consideration of solutions to dilemmas must take into account the boundaries or limits imposed by personal and professional ethical commitments and beliefs. Like Strike et al. (1988), Sergiovanni does not present these principles as a formula. Rather, he suggests that they can serve as useful guidelines for educators confronting complex problems which compel decisions and solutions.

Ethics as Embodied in Laws and Public Policies

Crittenden (1984) suggests that persons seeking to understand the ethical challenges facing school leaders would do well "to distinguish between the basic social morality—the values and practices without which society could hardly survive and would certainly not be tolerable—and the comprehensible bodies of moral belief about what is good or desirable for social and individual human life" (p. 18). In his view, the task of an educational leader is that of a trustee of a public, social good, and persons who undertake this task must allow themselves to be guided by certain tenets of public morality:

> At a minimum, the basic social morality includes the practices of justice, truth telling and honesty, concern for others at least to the extent of avoiding the infliction of injury, mutual help in satisfying essential physical and cultural needs, and the willingness to recognize the claims that others make on us on the basis of these practices. (pp. 18–19)

Crittenden asserts that, within pluralistic societies,

> it is obvious that decisions in the domain of public morality should be based on the principles of the essential core of social morality together with those values on which the policy of moral pluralism itself directly depends (personal freedom, the equal worth of all individuals as moral agents, tolerance of diverse ways of

thinking and acting, the use of non-violent persuasions). In the political and legal systems of the society *these values are translated into more specific principles and procedures (for example, consent of the governed, majority rule, due process of laws [and] various specific rights of freedom.* (p. 21, emphasis added)

In his view, public administrators are thus under obligation to seek guidance from principles and procedures embodied in laws and public policies as they make decisions. Indeed, he asserts:

> In many of the decisions, general as well as particular, made by educational administrators, the application or interpretation of legally binding directives is the main issue. In moral terms, educational administrators have a duty to ensure that the decisions they make accord with the relevant laws and regulations. The scope of their authority even at the highest levels, is itself at least broadly determined by law. (p. 28)

Crittenden suggests that, in a society that has accepted certain fundamental values (i.e., respect for individuals), laws established by representatives of its citizens can and should serve as moral directives. To be sure, he does not claim that educational leaders must blindly and unthinkingly enforce laws as "clear-cut rules" (p. 31). Rather, he sees the task of administrators as one of interpreting laws and public policies in ways that meet the needs of particular situations and remain true to the principles undergirding the legal directives.

Beauchamp and Childress (1984), although they do not use the words "laws" and "public policies," frame their discussion of moral decision making in ways that support Crittenden's assertions. In essence, they argue for "the place of rules" (p. 57) in administrative thinking and reject the notion that situational ethics can provide adequate guidance for persons facing difficult and complex dilemmas. Their advocacy of "some rules and derivative principles" is based upon belief in the existence of some "virtually exceptionless or absolute principles" (p. 59). These authors suggest that some of these absolutes—those that "refer to traits of character whose development and expression are always good"—are likely to be covered by philosophical principles. However, they also suggest that many of the absolutes find their expression in public laws with clearly defined terminology (i.e., murder as unjustified killing) that have "exceptions built into them" (p. 59). Further, Beauchamp and Childress assert that rights—"justified claims that individual and groups can make upon others or upon society" (p. 61)—and duties and obligations established by these rights are, within democratic societies such as ours, defined in laws and policies and guarded by constitutionally established processes for interpreting and changing legal directives. Thus, like Crittenden, Beauchamp and Childress argue that educational administrators in societies whose governments are committed to certain fundamental principles, such as justice, tolerance, and respect for and fair treatment of all persons, can and should look to laws and public policies for ethical guidance.

Codes of Ethics as Guides to Decisions

The beliefs that ethics are embodied in legal directives and that ethical leaders have a mandate to look to policies for assistance as they seek pathways through troublesome situations presuppose several things. First, they assume that people—functioning collectively through some form of democratic government—are equipped to determine the ways individuals should act and interact. Second, they assume that laws and policies as crafted by representatives of individuals will embody the intentions of society and, further, that they will create mechanisms for protest and change if those are desirable. Finally, they presume that educational leaders are responsible to enact and support the will of society as expressed in laws and public policies. A related view of ethics shifts the onus for establishing ethical rules and guidelines from society to the educational profession. Those holding this view emphasize the importance of professional codes of ethics in decision making.

In *Ethics and Professionalism* (1988) John Kultgen examines, in some detail, the belief that professions, because they "represent the highest level of competence in our civilization," and because they are dedicated to "truth and service [in ways that] cut across political and cultural boundaries" (p. x), are the institutions best able to provide ethical guidance to their members. Surveying the history of this belief, he discusses the influence of Durkheim (1950/1957) and Whitehead (1933), "the two men who inaugurated modern thinking about professions" (Kultgen, 1988, p. 43). Kultgen suggests that these scholars held "Utopian conceptions of professionalism" (p. 43), in that they assumed both that membership in a profession means that one possesses a degree of "competence to attain those ends whose immediate dominance is evident to enlightened wisdom" (Whitehead, 1933, pp. 71–79) and that such membership accords "moral authority" (Whitehead, 1933, pp. 71–79) to such a person. A logical extension of this idea is that the collective insights of individual authorities carry moral weight and can provide guidelines for the "happy coordination of individual emotions, purposes, affections, and actions" (Whitehead, 1933, pp. 71–79) in the pursuit of "freedom, truth, and beauty" (Kultgen, 1988, p. 46). Thus Durkheim and Whitehead helped to establish a belief that professions can serve in at least a limited way as moral *milieux*. With the right ideals they can improve the way people do their work, encourage them to consider the social consequences, and cultivate a heightened and more enlightened commitment to the common good (Kultgen, 1988, p. 45).

Recent decades have witnessed much cynicism regarding the beliefs that "human beings are so constituted that under favorable conditions they will take the moral point of view" (Kultgen, 1988, pp. 47–48) and that professions provide such conditions. However, Kultgen argues that these ideas do contain a "valid kernel" (p. 45) that must not be overlooked. He then examines various ways that professions and then codes of ethics can provide "guidance for those practitioners who have not thought through moral issues . . . [and who face] difficult dilemmas" (p. 216). Indeed, he asserts that "debates over confidentiality, conflict of interest, bribery, paternalism, whistle-blowing, credit for the work of others, social responsibilities, etc." (p. 216) require "hard thinking and searching dialogue" (p. 216) and that a code can summarize the results of such activities for persons who do not have the time and inclination to engage in them:

> A rational code would contain the results individuals would have reached for themselves if they had reasoned objectively long enough on an adequate base of experience. If such a code is available, it relieves professionals of most of the burden of ethical inquiry. After all, their primary responsibility is to heal, counsel, minister, design, etc., not to puzzle over ethical questions. Most in matter of fact do not reflect on ethics until faced with difficult questions, when the pressure of action prevents careful thought. It would simplify their moral universe to have solutions at hand which had been worked on the collective experience and wisdom of the moral community. (p. 216)

To be sure, Kultgen does not suggest that codes can be treated as formulas or prescriptions and he emphasizes "the need for personal judgment" (p. 216) on the part of those looking to them. He does, however, propose that codes can provide important and useful guidelines regarding ideals, behaviors, and decisions.

ETHICS AS PERSPECTIVES INFORMING PERCEPTIONS, CHARACTER, AND BELIEFS

Certain assumptions undergird and unite the views of ethics discussed in the preceding sections. For example, each presupposes that the primary function of ethics is to guide individuals as they approach dilemmas that require hard choices between competing values (Pincoffs, 1971). Each view also tends to emphasize the importance of a systematic and rational approach to ethical behavior, for each presents a set of tenets that can guide the thinking of decision makers. The preceding views also presume that a function of ethics is to help individuals avoid being swayed by their emotions and personal interests, concerns, and beliefs as they seek to choose morally sound strategies and activities from a range of alternatives (Hauerwas & Burrell, 1977).

The belief that ethics are and should be concerned with "action-guiding rules and principles, choice and decision, universality and impartiality, and obligation and right action" (Blum, 1991, p. 701) has been explicitly or implicitly accepted by many who write about the ethics of educational leaders. However, a small but growing number of individuals have begun to examine the moral challenges facing administrators in ways that suggest an expanded notion of ethics. In the sections that follow, we discuss three themes that permeate the scholarship that assumes that ethics inform not only decision making but the perceptions, character, and beliefs of educators operating individually and corporately. The first theme emphasizes that moral leadership requires a consideration of the fundamental purposes of education, of the nature of schools as institutions, and of the roles and responsibilities of educational leaders. Those advocating this perspective (e.g., Greenfield, 1988; Hodgkinson, 1991; Sergiovanni, 1992; Starratt, 1991) see ethics as informing administrators' understandings of themselves as moral agents and of their schools as moral agencies. The second theme concentrates more specifically upon the responsibility of schools to contribute to the public good. A number of scholars (e.g., Giroux, 1988; Purpel, 1989) stress that ethics must assist educators in gaining a robust understanding of the common or public good and in determining morally sound ways to pursue this good. The third theme is anchored in the belief that persons, not principles, provide the fundamental *raison d'etre* of applied moral philosophy. Those articulating this idea (e.g., Beck, 1992, 1994a; Gilligan, 1982; Noddings, 1984, 1992) insist that ethics should encourage and assist persons in developing lasting commitments to understand and care for others.

Ethics as a Way of Understanding Purposes, Roles, and Institutions

Drawing upon the work of Iris Murdoch (1970), Lawrence Blum (1991) asserts that traditional notions of ethics, which "focus on action-guiding rules and principles, on choice and decision, on universality and impartiality, and on obligation and right action" (p. 701), fail to take into account the facts that "in any given situation moral perception comes on the scene prior to moral judgment; moral perception can lead to moral action outside the operation of judgment entirely; and, more generally, perception, involves moral capacities not encompassed by moral judgments" (p. 702). For Blum, developing these capacities requires cultivating the ability to recognize in situations those details that are morally significant. However, it also requires understanding the panoply of purpose (including moral purpose) undergirding human interactions. Thus Blum argues that ethics must be concerned with how people perceive themselves, others, and their shared experiences. Hauerwas and Burrell

(1977) arrive at a similar conclusion when they assert that contemporary ethicists' concentration "on problems—situations in which it is hard to know what to do—as paradigmatic concerns for moral analysis" (p. 18) is inadequate. Such emphasis fails to realize the ethical significance of the capacity to identify certain situations as problematic, to assume that one has a right and responsibility to seek some kind of solution, to perceive a repertoire of alternatives from which to choose; to make right choices informed by one's "virtue and character" (p. 20). Like Blum, they suggest that ethics must be concerned with developing right ways of thinking about people and their relationships.

In recent years several scholars have written about the ethics of educational leadership in ways that are consonant with the conceptions of Blum (1991) and Hauerwas and Burrell (1977). Two scholars whose discussions of ethics demonstrate expanded ways of thinking are T. B. Greenfield (1979) and Christopher Hodgkinson (1991). Greenfield's insistence that organizations are born out of the beliefs, emotions, thoughts, volitions, and experiences of individuals emphasizes certain ways of understanding leadership. In his view, the tasks of all members of organizations—especially of leaders—have moral dimensions, because they require, at every point, working with, protecting, and honoring people. Greenfield (1979) writes that leaders who function in ethically sound or right ways must "engage in a continuing process of discovery aimed at gaining an understanding of ourselves and of others" (p. 109). Thus, both in his approach to organizational study and in his claim that scholars and leaders must pursue *understanding* as a foundation to ethical behavior, Greenfield exemplifies the idea that ethics are rightly concerned with the ways individuals think about themselves, others, and the organizations and experiences they share.

In *Educational Leadership: The Moral Art* (1991), Hodgkinson, like Greenfield, suggests that administrators must be aware that because education has "relevance to all aspects of the human condition, [it] is also invested from the outset with a moral character" (p. 27). He argues that leaders must be guided by more than "mere pragmatism, positivism, philistinism, and careerism" (p. 165)—that they must develop "extraordinary value sensitivity" (p. 164). For Hodgkinson, this requires continuous reflection upon the values undergirding educational efforts and upon the role of leaders in honoring those values. In order to encourage this, he presents new ways of thinking about the fundamental purposes of schooling.

In recent works (1992, 1993a, 1993b), Sergiovanni, too, argues that the ethical practice of leadership requires wrestling with foundational questions. In *Moral Leadership: Getting to the Heart of School Improvement* (1992), he challenges scholars and practitioners to think about the meanings they attach to words such as "education," "schools," and "leadership," In his view, ethical practice, i.e., "doing the right things" (p. 4), requires educators to commit themselves to developing a "virtuous school," that is both "moral and effective" (p. 107). As they cultivate such a school, Sergiovanni challenges leaders to concentrate not merely upon what they do and think, but also upon who they *are* and upon what they believe and feel. He further asks both scholars and practitioners to think seriously about "the basic theories and root metaphors that shape the way we understand schools and shape the way we understand leadership and management within them" (1993b, p. 2). Sergiovanni suggests that, historically, education has borrowed "its fundamental frames for thinking about how schools should be structured and coordinated, how compliance within them should be achieved, what leadership is, and how it works" (p. 2) and that educators have thus passively allowed others to define their work (see also Mikios, 1990). He sees in this passivity a moral failure that can be rectified as scholars and practitioners begin "to decide which theory should dominate which spheres of our lives" (p. 20). In making these claims, he insists that ethics must do more than assist administrators in making decisions and that, as a field, ethics must help scholars and practitioners understand the purposes, values, and commitments behind their work. Yet another scholar who concurs with this expanded notion of ethics is Robert J. Starratt (1991). In "Building an Ethical School: A Theory for Practice in Educational Leadership," he argues that the primary ethical task facing school leaders "is to establish an ethical school environment in which education can take place ethically" (p. 187). Starratt suggests that administrators seeking to fulfill this task allow themselves to be guided by a "multi-dimensional ethic" (p. 199) that emphasizes, simultaneously, caring, critique, and justice. In his view, these three ethical perspectives are needed by leaders seeking to react morally to specific dilemmas and challenges as well as to engage proactively in the comprehensive task of the "building of an ethical school as an integral part of a national effort to restructure schools" (p. 199). For Starratt, a commitment to multiple ethical perspectives will promote the development of "an ethical consciousness" (p. 201). Such a consciousness will enable leaders to avoid being "captured by sentimentality, by rationalistic simplification, or by social naivete" (p. 200) and to approach each and every activity in ways that honor individuals and their varied communities.

Ethics as Politics

A number of scholars, although not disagreeing with the perspectives of Sergiovanni, Starratt, and others cited in the previous section, emphasize the importance of educators' adopting a more specific ethical perspective. Henry Giroux (1988) and David Purpel (1989) are among those most vocal in calling on administrators, teachers, and those who work with them in colleges and universities to recognize that schools must play a key role in the development of a just and caring society. For these scholars, ethics, politics, and schooling go hand in hand, because all, ideally, should provide mechanisms for improving the human condition. In his call for a "politics of ethics" (p. 37), Giroux asks educators to consider the ways their pedagogies, curricula, and organizational structures further social and political ends. Additionally, he challenges them to allow a "radical theory of ethics" (p. 59) to guide them as they develop "nouns of solidarity, sympathy, caring, friendship, and love" and as they "promote the material conditions and forms of solidarity that point to a better life . . . [and] contribute to actualizing what Agnes Heller (1985) has called the universal values of life and freedom" (p. 59).

David Purpel's (1989) perspective on ethics is similar to Giroux's in that he sees "intimate relationships among society, culture, and education" (p. x). He contends that most people operating within these three spheres have, in the past, ignored the moral and spiritual implications of their activities. This, in his view, has led to "an impoverished civic discourse that celebrates freedom as a form of possessive individualism and treats the concept of democracy as if it were at odds with the notion of community" (p. xv). Purpel asserts that ethics of social justice and compassion must be conjoined as educators reshape both the structures and the cultures of schools so they can become "just, loving, and joyous communities" (p. 123) in which all persons can grow and learn. He further asserts that, as educators and others give voice to "our mythic goals, our sacred aspirations, and our moral commitments" (p. 122) within schools, we will help to move the larger world toward the realization of "a society based on a serious and continuing commitment to peace, joy, love, social justice, equality, and community" (p. 152).

Ethics Grounded in a Commitment to Persons

Carol Gilligan's watershed book, *In a Different Voice* (1982), expressed a notion of ethics that, in the past decade, has received a fair amount of attention in educational circles. Gilligan's research challenged the Kohlbergian concept that the highest level of moral development is reached when a person looks to universal ethical principles for guidance in solving moral dilemmas. Troubled by the fact that Kohlberg's research had been exclusively with males, Gilligan replicated the studies that led to the formulation of his theories, but this time with young women. She found that many of her subjects were aware of impersonal principles but rejected them as the pivotal guides in solving ethical dilemmas, preferring instead to ground their responses in a commitment to solve problems in ways that were most beneficial to individual persons. Gilligan posits an alternative way of thinking about ethics, suggesting that a commitment to care for persons and to promote their growth and development to the greatest extent possible can provide a viable ethical perspective which is as mature as an objective, principle-driven orientation.

Nel Noddings (1984, 1988a, 1988b, 1992) has been a key figure in developing a model of the ways in which an ethical perspective centered on caring and on the promotion of personal development might influence education. She suggests that such an orientation would shape conceptions of educational purposes and pedagogical and organizational strategies for achieving those purposes. For Noddings, schools must focus, first and foremost, on promoting the development, health, and happiness of individual human beings and, because persons are fundamentally relational, they must also focus on developing capacities for "interpersonal caring" (1992, p. 18).

Noddings suggests that this focus, influenced throughout by an ethic of care, would in all likelihood lead to many changes in our schools. For example, she argues that teaching and learning, influenced by caring, would be much more individualized than they are currently. Asserting that "caring teachers listen and respond differentially to their students" (p. 19), she writes:

> We need to give up the notion of an ideal of the educated person and replace it with a multiplicity of models designed to accommodate the multiple capacities and interests of students. We need to recognize multiple identities. For example, an 11th grader may be a black, a woman, a teenager, a Smith, an American, a New Yorker, a Methodist, a person who loves math, and so on. As she exercises these identities, she may use different languages, adopt different postures, relate differently to those around her. But whoever she is at a given moment, what she is engaged in, she needs—as we all do—to be cared for. Her need for care may require formal respect, informal interaction, expert advice, just a flicker of recognition, or sustained affection. (Noddings, 1992, p. 173)

In addition to introducing more personal pedagogies, Noddings notes that an ethic of care would influence thinking about curricular issues: "I have argued that education should be organized around themes of care rather than the traditional disciplines. All students should be engaged in a general education that guides them in caring for self, intimate others, global others, plants, animals, and the environment, the human-made world and ideas" (1992, p. 173). She also asserts that such an ethic would shape our understandings of assessment: "We should move away from the question, Has Johnny learned X? to the far more pertinent question, What has Johnny learned?" (1992, p. 179). Noddings suggests that teachers, principals, and parents should join with students to evaluate the answer to this question and then "roll up [their] sleeves and work together to accomplish what [they] deem important" (p. 180).

Drawing upon many of the ideas offered by Nodding, Beck (1992, 1994a) concentrates upon the ways an ethic of care, with its focus upon people and their development, can and should inform the practice and preparation of educational administrators. She asserts that this ethic's concepts of the nature and purpose of humans and their communities are philosophically and practically appropriate for schools and for their leaders. After defining this ethic in some detail, Beck explores its relevance for principals, superintendents, and other school executives. For example, she presents research that suggests relationships among a caring ethos, student achievement, and teachers' sense of efficacy, and she offers evidence that the orientation, commitments, and behaviors of administrators can do much to cultivate or destroy a nurturing, supportive culture. She then discusses roles that a caring administrator might embrace and suggests that such a person would seek to be "a values-driven organizer," "a creative and capable pedagogue," and "cultivator of a nurturing culture" (1994a, p. 78). In Beck's view, schools exist for people—to promote their growth and health and that of the various social networks. Thus she contends that ethical perspectives that focus upon personal and community well-being are consistent with the fundamental purposes of education and appropriate to guide educational leaders.

CONCLUDING THOUGHTS

As MacIntyre (1966) notes in the quotation that opens this chapter, we do not possess "a single set of moral concepts" (p. 268) to use in discussions of ethics. We assert that this plurality extends beyond multiple understandings of concepts and encompasses the varied ways we think about ethics and their relationships to personal and professional interactions. We contend that a robust understanding of the ways educational administration programs are addressing issues of ethics requires that we examine not only course content and pedagogical strategies, but also the assumptions about ethics that guide programmatic decisions. In subsequent chapters, we will seek to ground the analysis of our research findings in the framework presented in this chapter.

NOTES

1. In dividing an understanding of ethics into categories, we do not mean to imply that these are neatly circumscribed, philosophical camps. They are not, and most authors we cite make no claim to have discovered the "real" or "true" meaning of ethics. They do, however, emphasize different ways of thinking. These emphases provided the basis for our division of this section into two major categories with three subfoci in each.

2. In later work (e.g., 1992, 1993a, 1993b), Sergiovanni, although not denying the importance of rational decision making, tends to emphasize the ways ethical commitments provide perspectives on education's deepest purposes and underlying metaphors and to argue that these commitments must shape the being as well as the thinking of school leaders.

REFERENCES

Beauchamp, T.L & Childress, J.F. (1984). Morality, ethics and ethical theories. In P.A. Sola (Ed.), *Ethics, education and administrative decisions: A book of readings* (pp. 39–67). New York: Peter Lang.

Beck, L. G. (1992). Meeting future challenges: The place of a caring ethics in educational administration. *American Journal of Education.* 100 (3), 254–296.

Beck, L.G. (1994). *Reclaiming educational administration as a caring profession.* New York: Teachers College Press.

Blum, L. (1991). Moral perception and particularity. *Ethics*, 101, 701–725.

Cohen, D.K. (1976). Loss as a theme in social policy. *Harvard Educational Review*, 46, 553–571.

Crittenden, B. (1984The moral context of decision making in education. In P.A. Sola (Ed.), *Ethics, values, and administrative decisions: A book of readings* (pp. 15–38). New York: Peter Lang.

Durkheim, E. (1957). *Professional ethics and civic morals.* (C. Brookfield Trans.). London: Routledge & Kegan Paul (Original Work published in 1950).

Gastil, R.D. (1977). *Social humanities.* San Francisco: Jossey-Bass.

Gilligan, C. (1982). *In a different voice: Psychological theory and women's development.* Cambridge, MA: Harvard University Press.

Giroux, H. A. (1988). *Schooling and the struggle for public life: Critical pedagogy in the modern age.* Minneapolis: University of Minnesota Press.

Greenfield, T.B. (1979). Organization theory as ideology. *Curriculum Inquiry*, 9(2), 97–112.

Greenfield, T.B. (1988). The decline nad fall of science in educational administration. In D. E. Griffiths, R.T. Stout, & P.B. Forsyth (Eds.), *Leaders for America's schools* (pp. 131–159). Berkeley: McCutchan.

Greenfield, W. (1987). Moral imagination and interpersonal competence: Antecedents to instructional leadership. In W. Greenfield (Ed.), *Instructional leadership: Concepts, issues, and controversies* (pp. 56–73). Boston: Allyn & Bacon.

Hauerwas, S. & Burrell, D. (1977). From system to story: An alternative pattern for rationality in ethics. In S. Hauerwas (Au.), *Truthfulness and tragedy: Further investigations into Christian ethics.* Notre Dame, IN: University of Notre Dame Press.

Heller, A. (1985). The basic question of moral philosophy. *Philosophy and Social Criticism*, 1 (11), 57–59.

Hills, J. (1978). Problems in the production and utilization of knowledge in educational administration. *Educational Administration Quarterly*, 14(1), 2.

Hodgkinson, C. (1991). *Educational leadership: The moral art.* Albany: State University of New York Press.

Kultgen, J. (1988). *Ethics and Professionalism.* Philadelphia: University of Pennsylvania Press.

MacIntyre, A. (1966). *A Short History of Ethics.* New York: Macmillan.

Mikios, E. (1990). Ministrative insight: Educational administration as pedagogic practice: An essay review of Philip Rodney Evan's dissertation. *Phenomenology and Pedagogy,* 8, 337–342.

Mitchell, B. (1990a). Loss, belonging, and becoming: Social policy themes for children and schools. In B. Mitchell and L. Cunningham, (Eds.), *Educational leadership and changing contexts in families, communities, and schools: Eighty-ninth yearbook of the National Society for the Study of Education* (pp. 19–51). Chicago: University of Chicago Press.

Mitchell, B. (1990b). Children, youth, and restructured schools: Views from the field. In B. Mitchell and L. Cunningham, (Eds.), *Educational leadership and changing contexts in families, communities, and schools: Eighty-ninth yearbook of the National Society for the Study of Education* (pp. 19–51). Chicago: University of Chicago Press.

Murdoch, I. (1970). *The sovereignty of good.* London: Routledge & Kegan Paul.

Noddings, N. (1984). *Caring: A feminine approach to ethics and moral education.* Berkeley: University of California Press.

Noddings, N. (1988a). An ethic of caring and its implications for instructional arrangements. *American Journal of Education,* 96 (3), 215–230.

Noddings, N. (1988b). Educating moral people. In M. Brabeck (Ed.), *Who cares: Theory, research, and educational implications of the ethics of care* (pp. 216–232). New York: Praeger.

Noddings, N. (1992). *The challenge to care in schools.* New York: Teachers College Press.

Pinecoffs, E. (1971). Quandary ethics. *Mind,* 80, 552–571.

Purpel, D. (1989). *The moral and spiritual crisis in education: A curriculum for justice and compassion in education.* New York: Bergin & Gervey.

Sergiovanni, T. J. (1980). A social humanities view of educational policy and administration. *Educational Administration Quarterly,* 16 (1), Winter, 1–19.

Sergiovanni, T. J. (1992). *Moral Leadership: Getting to the Heart of School Improvement.* San Francisco: Jossey-Bass.

Sergiovanni, T. J. (1993a). *Organizations or communities? Changing the metaphor changes the theory.* Invited Address, American Educational Research Association annual meeting, Atlanta, GA.

Sergiovanni, T. J. (1993b). *Building community in schools.* San Francisco: Jossey-Bass.

Starratt, R. J. (1991). Building an Ethical School: A Theory for Practice in Educational Leadership. *Educational Administration Quarterly,* 27 (2), 185–202.

Strike, K.A., Haller, E. J., & Soltis, J.F. (1988). *The ethics of school administration.* New York: Teachers College Press.

Whitehead, A.M. (1933). *Adventures of ideas.* New York: Macmillan.

The Ethics and Values of Fund Raising

Robert L. Payton

THE PRESIDENT'S SITUATION

For presidents of all sorts of institutions, fund raising is an inescapable fact of life. In an increasing number of cases, fund-raising effectiveness is the key to the office—to both getting in and staying in. Intellectual and moral leadership seem to have yielded to the effective marshalling and management of resources. The career path to the presidency is now open to those who enter it from the development function. Like it or not (and I must assume that in many respects I *don't* like it), fund raising is now at the center of the president's responsibilities.

There is a way of thinking about these grim-sounding assertions that may save the day for all of us—that is, for presidents and for the rest of us who want their leadership. While "fund raising," narrowly considered, may be a threat, "the philanthropic tradition" may provide the most effective response. In the early parts of this chapter, I will deal with the president's situation, and the extent to which fund raising and public relations influence it. In the last part, I will try to put it all in the proper context.

There is no function of the office of president that puts that party at greater risk than the development function. Not only must the president perform effectively in measurable ways—most particularly by achieving a balanced budget with the help of gifts and grants—but he or she must also guard the institution's integrity.

There are countless other actors, buffers, and shared guardians on the *academic* side: Each faculty member is expected to meet high professional

"The Ethics and Values of Fund Raising," by Robert L. Payton, in the *President and Fund Raising,* ed. James Fisher and Gary Quehl, American Council on Education and Macmillan Publishing Co., 1989.

standards. The duties to be performed are familiar to everyone. The standards of performance are very imprecise, but the lack of a clear bottom line is an accepted reality. In other words, in the academic performance of the institution, *numerous* individuals share responsibilities. But no one bears responsibility for the *ethical* standards of the institution more than its president.

The development function, in contrast, focuses responsibility *at the top.* There is no clear consensus about what spells success in fund raising, other than the funding total at the end of the year. The consensus is that fund raising is ethically ambiguous, at best. And people watch for signs that the president has strayed from the moral path in an effort to succeed at the bottom line. Although others are involved in fund raising with the president, there is little sense of shared responsibility. For fund raising the buck stops with the president, like it or not.

Success in fund raising is much more complicated and problematic than inexperienced presidents would like to believe. Simplistic bottom-line measures in dollars raised in a particular year or in a particular campaign often mask fatal damage to presidential leadership. Pyrrhic victories are common. Presidential reputation is a frequent casualty: Presidents who have been successful in meeting fund-raising goals often are denigrated for having made unacceptable compromises of personal or institutional integrity (or both) in reaching those goals.

Presidents from diverse backgrounds have come to recognize these sobering but usually tacit conditions of the office. Some abandon the idea of repeatedly serving as a college or university president because of the burdens of fundraising. For those who still believe that educational leadership is still one of the benefits of being a president, fund raising is usually looked upon as a painful but unavoidable necessity. Organizations such as CASE try to enlighten the relationship between the president and his principle development officer, and the Association of Governing Boards gives special attention to the relationship between the president and key trustees and the fund-raising volunteers. But it is the president who suffers most if fund-raising efforts fail or if fund raising is conducted in a way that detracts from the institution's dignity.

In spite of the importance of fund raising, there are important and instructive exceptions. Some presidents learn to lead the development function so effectively—carry the burden so lightly—that recognition of achievements is widely shared. The development effort is seen as a common effort in which everyone participates. Even disappointments are distributed fairly. Everyone seems to have a valued sense of making a personal contribution to a community effort—and the president receives credit for making it happen that way.

The president's situation has changed in recent years. There is too much emphasis on fund raising and other material indicators of progress and success. Presidents have been cautioned away from educational and moral leadership roles and left with a managerial assignment that no one else wants. In some cases, trustees and faculty members have been content to let the president do the work, only to second-guess performance at almost every step along the way. (A philosophy professor left his teaching role to become president of a college. When he went back to the campus to visit former colleagues, one of them asked: "John, when you become a college president, do you lose your integrity all at once or does it just dribble away?")

The most serious diminution of the office will be sacrifice of the educational and moral leadership it once called for. We can't afford that. Thus we must manage the development function in a way that lets the president put the stamp of individual ethical and overall administrative standards on the fund-raising function without becoming the chief development officer. (Chapman's Law says that under stress the executive seeks to fill the role of the person immediately below in the hierarchy.) Properly understood, fund raising rises to its rightful role of institutional development. The development function integrates with the academic objectives of the institution. It is as honorable and useful and important as any other function in achieving institutional purposes. It cannot be thought of as separate, or judged by a different (and lower) standard.

The dimension that is most critical, and yet often curiously neglected, is the ethical one.

ETHICS AND VALUES

There are several aspects of the "ethical dimension" that I should spell out. Some writers would approach the subject in terms of principles, even rules, of ethical fund raising. Other writers would emphasize the benefits to be gained by all of those affected by the fund-raising effort. Still others might write about the personal qualities called for in the effective fund raiser. More philosophers have technical terms to describe these various perspectives (and there are well-known authorities to turn to).

My own approach is shamelessly eclectic and borrows from all of these. It also places heavy emphasis on the need to talk about ethics and values in settings in which presidents and their key allies and associates can learn from their continuing shared experience. My role . . . such as it is, will be to plant questions in the reader's mind. . . .

Ethics is concerned with relationships. A moment's reflection will call to mind how diverse and numerous a president's relationships are: with trustees, faculty members, students, alumni, wealthy donors, journalists, development staff members, business leaders, legislators, foundation executives. . . . To be "ethical" means to be serious about one's concern for all of the others involved in those relationships—and to be "serious" means that lip service is not enough. We have different obligations to different others (we often use the sociologist's term "significant others" loosely to mean those people of special importance in our lives). There is also a widely varying intensity in the relationships: Some become very intimate and personal; others are arm's-length and disinterested; some are conducted by mass communication designed to seem personal and direct. At one level we speak of "constituencies" (e.g., students), while at another level we speak of "special friends of the institution."

In listing significant others we begin to appreciate that our obligations to some often conflict with our obligations to others. At times even our constituencies come into conflict. One of the reasons that ethical reflection can become compellingly interesting as well as important is that undeniably good things can be in conflict. Resolving those conflicts, as Chester Barnard wrote 50 years ago, is what the responsibility of an executive is all about.

"The president is commonly thought to be virtuous and a guide to the good life. The president is expected to be an exemplar for virtuous behavior whom young people can follow, and a person of professional integrity who provides a moral reference point for faculty and administrators." These words (made up by way of example) may sound quaint in a world where private life is distinct from public virtue, and even where words like "virtue" and terms like "the good life" are intellectually suspect. Yet I believe they still carry great weight in the common morality, and that college and university presidents are judged by them whether or not they consider this fair. I also believe that thinking about virtue and what it means to be virtuous is intellectually defensible as well as useful. As for trying to live the good life, the private lives of presidents are on constant public display. In fact, one of the reasons it is so difficult to be president is that you must be smart, efficient, decent, and honorable all at the same time—all the time.

Because development pulls the president into an arena where material values predominate, and uses the prerequisites of office to increase effectiveness, and because development activities so often are public occasions, presidential virtue most frequently is measured in that context. All those lonely, private struggles with tenure decisions and research contracts and budget compromises may in the end do little to offset the impression that the president makes as the chief development officer.

Thinking about presidents as virtuous persons has its advantages (in case this painfully high standard has made you uneasy). It requires assessment of the whole person rather than a single skill or quality. And it requires assessment over time, rather than on the basis of a single act. Because society has drifted from thinking and talking about virtue, there is a tendency to judge performance more narrowly—hence the bottom-line mentality. Among the authors contributing to this volume are some who have been very closely involved in passing judgment on presidential performance. They would agree, I think, that presidents should be judged on their character (personal and professional) over a reasonable period of time; that presidents are expected to be virtuous, but not without flaw. The recent experiences of presidential candidates Hart and Biden and others suggest that assessment of character will rest on a single act only if the act is thought to be revelatory of suspect traits of personality. The public usually is much fairer than it is generally given credit for being.

In development, the values of character given greatest weight—the prime virtues and vices—are those thought to reveal pride and humility. For instance, there are several well-known scandals of excessive expenditure for presidential residences. The lesson to learn is that the development rationale (sumptuous residences or offices are necessary to meet and entertain wealthy donors and prospects) can be stretched too far. Since we assume that Aristotle's *Ethics* is part of the cultural literacy of college presidents (whether it is or not), it is difficult to claim ignorance of the mean between magnificence and meanness. The burden for these matters rests with the trustees: Presidents should be appropriately housed and officed, but the trustees should know the difference between ostentation and good taste. If they don't, the president should err on the side of modesty and restraint.

If moderation in personal matters is important, your attitude toward others should reflect Kant's admonition that we always treat others as an end in themselves and not as a means of reaching an end. To think of donors as ends in themselves pulls you up short, because the initial reason for interest in a donor is the prospective gift rather than the donor as a person. Nonetheless, the interest of the individual must be paramount, even at the expense of the gift.

Many people see these relationships as mutually manipulative. It is better to be cynical about them, they say. Play to the pride of the donors, massage their egos, flatter and pamper them. Alas, all too often this works! In some cases, *nothing else* will work. Indeed, in some cases, only the award of an honorary degree or some other important institutional praise yields a gift. In other cases gifts become bribes: Off the record, under cover, a donor will propose a gift in exchange, say, for admitting someone to the school.

We must consider, at this point, the responsibility for weighing the integrity of the institution against its need for financial support. The taboo line to be crossed, as Kenneth Boulding warns us, is likely never to be drawn at the same place. Ethical compromises tend to be permanent. When the president is asked to make an unacceptable compromise, the institution's integrity as well as the president's is at stake.

The president needs allies in these situations. Institutional integrity is not a one-person matter. The trustees are most important, both because they are the judges of presidential performance and because they are expected to represent the public interest (that is, to be "disinterested"). Because presidential judgments of "appropriateness" of compromises often affect the heart of the institution's educational integrity (that is, admission), you should bring into the discussion faculty members considered to be people of good character.

Eventually, of course, the day comes when advisors, colleagues, and trustees cannot themselves agree, and the buck stops here—with the president. (That saying, and the advice to stay out of the kitchen if you can't stand the heat, are only two of the reasons we are indebted to Harry Truman.)

THE PRESIDENT AND THE GOOD LIFE

I've argued that the development function has come to be so important that it is perhaps the most important presidential activity. (By the way, I include legislative relations in my definition of development, however it is organized. There is nothing in this chapter that exempts the presidents of public institutions.) My second point is that the development function exposes the president to public view and assessment more dramatically than any other activity, and thus adds to presidential vulnerability. The third point is that the development function, because it is based on personal relationships between the president and so many other people, is ethically charged. Not only the president's competence but his or her character will be judged. Finally, I suggest (drawing on personal experience) that the development function can be a Slough of Despond which the president should not enter alone.

Under the circumstances, then, why would a person of good character and strong intelligence want to be a president?

In my opinion, the president has three roles to play: *manager, moral exemplar,* and *educational leader.* The first two are inescapable; the third is optional. The president as manager will be judged first on economic performance, second on academic administration. Neither task is easy. Balanced budgets achieved by careful control of expenditures as well as by effective fund raising are essential. At the end of the day, academic administration is about balancing economic and educational budgets and avoiding deficits in each.

Of course, the president is more than manager and administrator. He or she will be judged by all constituencies as a person of virtue—perhaps a person of easy virtue. There may be intellectual reasons for arguing against such judgments, but the common morality won't accept those arguments. Presidents of colleges and universities may even *survive* and *prosper* as persons of dubious personal integrity, as successful exploiters of the weaknesses of others, as clever manipulators and "con men." Some will find allies who exhibit the same qualities. But of these, many will know the truth, and many will think the truth more important than the deception.

The president as educational leader is different from both of these. The notion that educational leadership implies some national reputation is not what I have in mind. I refer only to the role of the president as a leader of the intellectual life of his or her campus community. It seems obvious that most presidents can have the first two qualities and lack this one: There are others who can pick up the slack.

The reason I give the matter such importance is that *presidents may find in the study of philanthropy itself the avenue to educational leadership.* This is the argument:

1. Presidents are immersed in development.
2. Development is one aspect of philanthropy, but not the only one. (Voluntary service and voluntary association are the others.)
3. Philanthropy is an ancient tradition, but it is little known and less understood. It is rarely taught.
4. Presidents are in an unusually good position to observe the workings of philanthropic activity in all its positive and negative aspects.
5. Presidents who become knowledgeable about the philanthropic tradition will be able to present it as a rich and complex field of intellectual inquiry.
6. Philanthropic behavior touches the lives of every constituency, every person associated with the college or university; philanthropic behavior is a common experience and a common value. It is, in fact, a major source of the common morality and of the public agenda.
7. The president who is a scholar of philanthropy as well a practitioner has an opportunity to become engaged directly in the intellectual life of the campus. The topic permeates the disciplines and professions, yet it is no one's sacred precinct.

Even preliminary study of the history of philanthropy will bring out the role of philanthropy in shaping American higher education. An excellent book by Robert Bremner on the history of American philanthropy has been issued in a new edition (see note at end of chapter). It brings out the ways in which education and other philanthropic purposes have been served by "public-private cooperation" since long before that became a political slogan. Reading such vital materials will raise important questions about your own institution's philanthropic history. And at last the names on buildings and professorships and scholarships and prizes will come alive.

Inquiry into the origins and development of philanthropic behavior and values will lead back (in the Western tradition) through classical authors to and past the Bible. The Old Testament is a rich resource: Certain of the prophets remind us that philanthropy, religion, and social reform have enjoyed a tremendously long history of cooperation. Aristotle, Cicero, Seneca, and others bring the ethical reflection central to the values we still associate with benevolent action for public purposes. Maimonides and Thomas Aquinas offer medieval summaries. (Maimonides' hierarchy of the levels of giving reveals remarkably the forces at work in benefiting others, as well as the values of anonymity.)

Study of the history of philanthropy gives evidence that some communities have held fund raising in high esteem. Many have learned that seeking resources can be an honorable activity and should not be denigrated as "begging." More commonly, in recent years we find, however, that people apologize in asking for financial support and often feel embarrassed about it. Just what is "the philanthropic relationship," and how can it be sustained at a level that protects the dignity of those involved? Psychologists and sociologists should be able to help us with this one, but thus far they haven't given it much attention. William James's *The Varieties of Religious Experience* may provide some insight into thinking about the problem. Presidents should attend very carefully to the varieties of philanthropic experience, their own and others', if they are to understand them and be sensitive to their complexity.

There is a case *against* philanthropy, of course, and American colleges and universities are in the middle of the controversy. The question of who should pay for higher education—what balance of individual, public, and philanthropic resources—appears on the front page of every campus newspaper, and often in the public media. Economists and political scientists, weak as they are on philanthropic values and practices, offer little help. Yet presidents are expected to have a grasp of the relative importance of each factor.

What is the rationale for philanthropy in the support of higher education? Where can a president read about it? There are some sources available, and more coming. For the most part, however, the resources are thin, and presidents will have the opportunity to lead the campus discussion if they can be educational leaders.

Philanthropic activity is not always placidly benign. For example, the continuing controversy over divestment illustrates the tensions arising because people presume that voluntary initiatives are for the public good. Some people would suppress student and faculty action to divest; some students and faculty members would simply bend the institution to their own political will. (In an essay published elsewhere, I have raised the question of whether corporate earnings from South Africa are "tainted" and thus rejectable when offered as philanthropic contributions.) Another example might be the conditions donors put on gifts. To what extent is the president letting outsiders determine the institution's goals when he seeks and accepts restricted gifts? If the vice president for development comes in with a prospective contribution that falls outside the goals of the institution, is it up to the president to turn it down?

The history of philanthropic support of higher education provides many illustrations of the problem, and of different solutions. The problems themselves, however, are philosophical, organizational, and managerial. They cut across the specialized disciplines. They call for reflection that combines theory, practice, and contrasting values.

Philanthropic studies might become a special field of presidential interest. No one in the institution will bring more experience to bear, so the president can speak with the authority of a practitioner. No one else will be an expert on the theory of the subject, and the president thus faces an underdeveloped field of intellectual opportunity. The president will rarely (if ever) find a better point of entry into the intellectual life of the campus. The subject is important; it is interesting, and it defies being reduced to a neat and tidy package. Philanthropic values and issues are the sort that encourage exploratory discourse. They reveal and shape the institution's character and purpose.

The development function, thought of in so small a way at the beginning of this chapter, is a threat to presidential well-being. Thought of as a powerful and often ennobling set of ideas, development can be transformed into an asset of great value.

BIBLIOGRAPHICAL NOTE

A handy starter set for an overview of the study of philanthropy would include Merle Curti's essay "Philanthropy," in the *Dictionary of the History of Ideas* (Scribner, 1973). If your library has a copy of the eleventh edition of the *Encyclopaedia Britannica* (1910), you should read Charles S. Loch's justly famous essay "Charity and Charities." Robert Bremner, now emeritus professor of history at Ohio State University, has published a second edition of his *American Philanthropy* (University of Chicago Press, 1988). Merle Curti and Roderick Nash published *Philanthropy in the Shaping of American Higher Education* in 1965 (Rutgers University Press). It is out of print but indispensable.

James Douglas's *Why Charity? The Case for a Third Sector* is a special favorite of mine.

Walter W. Powell has edited *The Non-Profit Sector* (Yale, 1986), and various essays that, among other things, add depth to one's understanding of Douglas's topic.

We are witnessing the emergence of a field of inquiry after decades of useful, sometimes brilliant, but always isolated works of scholarship. Many recent books, articles, and essays will come to your attention as you explore the subject.

Toward a Theory of Fund Raising in Higher Education

W. Bruce Cook and William F. Lasher

INTRODUCTION

In recent years, capital campaigns and other fund-raising drives have become more frequent, more elaborate and sophisticated, longer in duration, and larger in size as U.S. colleges and universities have struggled to make ends meet. One result has been that academic chief executives are increasingly expected and often required to take an active role in fund raising and resource development. However, this important role has received limited scholarly or critical interest and, for the most part, remains misunderstood and ill defined. Therefore, the purpose of a recent national study we conducted was to enhance understanding of the presidential role in fund raising and related processes.

The primary conclusions of our study were: (a) fund raising is a team effort, (b) an institution's president is typically the central player on the fund raising team, (c) presidents should focus their fund-raising attention and efforts on major gifts and administrative leadership, (d) academic quality and institutional prestige are of critical importance in higher education fund raising, and (e) fund raising is institution specific and, more importantly, context or situation specific.

REVIEW OF LITERATURE

Both fund raising and executive leadership are complex phenomena of central importance to higher education and other nonprofit organizations. For the most

"Toward a Theory of Fund Raising in Higher Education," by W. Bruce Cook and William F. Lasher, *The Review of Higher Education* 20(1) (1996): 33–51.

part, however, the presidential fund-raising role has lacked historical perspective and rigorous scientific inquiry; this lack has led to a profusion of atheoretical literature by practitioners, consultants, and journalists. Further, the vast majority of the literature on educational fund raising has been published during the last 20 years and, due to a preoccupation with fund-raising methodology, donor motivation, and economic conditions in higher education, has contributed to the false and widely held impression that educational fund raising in general and presidential fund raising in particular are new or at least recent phenomena. It is true, however, that except for such notable pioneers as Cornell University, the University of Michigan, and Indiana University, fund-raising programs in public higher education first began to appear around 1975.

According to numerous scholars, the earliest example of educational philanthropy appears to be the benefactions associated with the Academy of Socrates and Plato. The Greek philanthropist Cimon helped to finance the Academy; but Plato, through an endowment of property, also provided income which continued for some 900 years (Bakrow, 1961; Brittingham & Pezzullo, 1990; Cowley, 1980; Crawford, 1976; Fisher, 1989b; Schulze, 1991). Alexander the Great provided funds for a vast library in Alexandria, Egypt, during the fourth century B.C. and reportedly financed the Lyceum of Aristotle so generously that at one time Aristotle had a thousand men scattered throughout Asia, Egypt, and Greece, seeking data for his writings on natural history (Marts, 1953).

In regard to these early educational endeavors, Cramer (1966) also observed:

> Throughout most of the history of education, the academic head of each institution also had the responsibility for providing its financial support.
>
> Gibson noted this tendency even in the academies of early Greece when he reported, "The academies were not corporate entities, but were proprietary entities in which each scholarch named his own successor who was to be responsible for the institution and its support." (pp. 49–50)

Beyond these scanty references, the literature is largely silent regarding the early record of educational philanthropy until the rise of medieval universities in Europe. Exceptions such as cathedral schools operated by the Catholic Church, court schools sponsored by a few enlightened rulers, and private tutors employed by the rich were designed to accommodate only a small number of pupils from the elite class of society while the masses were left to their own devices or relied on vocational training available through guilds, apprenticeship, or indenture (Schachner, 1938/1962).

According to Miller (1991), collegiate fund raising began in the twelfth century:

Fund raising for higher education can be traced directly to the opening of the medieval universities in twelfth century Europe. As these institutions opened for the first time and matured, college founders were forced to take measures to secure the money and resources necessary for the college's operation, such as living arrangements for students, book acquisitions, and faculty incentives. In order to accomplish this early fund raising, the college founders and "president" [i.e., rector, principal, master, etc.] solicited businessmen, merchants, and other college supporters for cash and in-kind contributions. The concept of the chief college faculty member being responsible for fund raising was transported to the Colonial Colleges in New England, and was common at institutions such as the College at Cambridg [*sic*] (later Harvard) where head faculty members solicited, in person, gifts of brick, mortar, food, books, and cash and other valuables. (p. 4; internal references omitted)

At Bologna and several other medieval universities, a rector or rectors were elected for two-year terms to enforce statutes, decide disputes, negotiate with city officials, preside at ceremonies, and levy and collect fines. These rectors were student clerks and only the wealthiest could sustain the expense associated with the position since rectors were expected to live in grand style and entertain lavishly to uphold the honor of the university and present a favorable impression. At the universities of Paris, Oxford, and Cambridge, wealthy landowners and members of the nobility began to establish permanent endowments for individual colleges, which in turn became loosely affiliated as universities (Schachner, 1938/1962).

Collegiate fund raising in America began in 1640 with Henry Dunster, first president of Harvard College, and has continued unabated to the present (Cook, 1994b). A pattern of amalgamized, shoestring financing began with the colonial colleges (Curti & Nash, 1965; McAnear, 1952, 1955); and although many institutions now have at least some level of permanent endowment, often such resources are inadequate to provide for their needs and/or aspirations.

Educational fund raising has evolved over the centuries with presidents being assisted at various times by financial agents, trustees, senior faculty, treasurers, alumni secretaries, and development directors (Stover, 1930). Fund raising should have been the responsibility of governing boards; but since trustees are part-time volunteers—whether elected or appointed—with other interests, they have always required executive leadership to inspire, encourage, uplift, honor, and thank them, hold them accountable, and earn their confidence, trust, and respect.

Fund raising came of age at the beginning of the 20th century with the development of the intensive campaign and its accompanying techniques. Following World War I, the fund-raising consultant emerged (Cutlip, 1965). A handful of universities employed development officers beginning in the

1920s, but most fund raising was still done by the president and a variety of assistants (Flack, 1932). In the following decade, a few pioneering institutions appointed a vice president to coordinate the functions of fund raising, public relations, and alumni affairs (Jacobson, 1990).

Following World War II, as enrollments surged and campuses expanded, many colleges and universities found it advantageous to employ their own fund-raising staffs. To discuss possible ways to relieve overburdened college presidents, more than seventy presidents, trustees, advancement officers, and representatives from business, industry, and professional fund-raising and public relations organizations held a historic three-day meeting in early 1958 at the Greenbrier Hotel in White Sulphur Springs, West Virginia. The conference was underwritten by the Ford Foundation and cosponsored by the American Alumni Council and the American College Public Relations Association. Richards and Sherratt have called the Greenbrier Report "the most significant advancement document of the decade" (1981, p. 11). It recommended that the functions of public relations, fund raising, and alumni relations be integrated under the umbrella of institutional advancement, with a coordinating officer in charge, usually a vice president with status equal to chief administrators in charge of business affairs, student affairs, and academic affairs (Reck, 1976).

In 1974 the American Alumni Council and the American College Public Relations Association were merged to form the Council for Advancement and Support of Education. This organization serves as the primary professional society for all areas of institutional advancement, although many members also belong to related groups such as the Public Relations Society of America, International Association of Business Communicators, the National Society of Fund Raising Executives, and the Association for Healthcare Philanthropy (Richards & Sherratt, 1981).

Fund raising has grown more sophisticated and reached new heights in recent years, with billion-dollar campaigns planned by specialized staffs equipped with the latest computer technology and multi-million-dollar budgets. Presidents, however, are still intimately involved in the success or failure of major institution-wide fund raising efforts and historically have concentrated their efforts on cultivating and soliciting major gifts (Altizer, 1992; Panas, 1984; Winfree, 1989; Winship, 1984).

Presidents also provide fund raising leadership in many other ways for their institutions, although primary responsibility for this function usually resides with a vice president or other senior administrator. Nevertheless, presidents are involved in policy formulation, vision, strategic planning, case formulation, timing and size of campaigns, recruitment of volunteer campaign leadership, involving the campus leadership in long-term planning and needs assessment, uniting various constituencies behind the campaign, and motivating and inspiring the trustees, staff, and volunteers (Boardman, 1993; Bornstein, 1989; Brown, 1988; Cowley, 1980; Dowden, 1990; Drucker, 1990; Fisher, 1985 & 1989a; Flawn, 1990; Foote, 1986; Francis, 1975; Hardin, 1984; Hesburgh, 1988; Howe, 1991; Kohr, 1977; McGoldrick, 1989; Rodriguez, 1991; Skelly, 1991; Slinker, 1988; Smith, 1986; West, 1983; Whittier, 1980; Withers, 1986). It is obvious from the review of literature that academic CEOs have been involved in raising money for their institutions in every historical period, and that this role is not of recent origin, as some have implied. It is also obvious that, despite the advent of fund-raising consultants and professional development staffs, the presidential fund-raising role has not diminished in importance. The history of educational philanthropy and the history of the academic presidency are thus intertwined to a considerable extent (Cook, 1994b).

Further, the role of academic chief executives in fund raising has long been neglected as a topic of scholarly research and, in fact, the first formal study in this area was completed during 1988 (Hurtubise) and the first book on this subject was published in 1989 (Fisher & Quehl). Similarly, fund raising has, until recently, been neglected as a topic of serious inquiry, with most of the research in this area having been conducted during the last 20 years. Moreover, fund raising as a field of study has suffered from a lack of theoretical perspective, and it was not until 1991 that Kelly systematically addressed this issue.

The topic of presidential fund raising thus remains fertile ground for scientific inquiry and our study seeks to contribute to the growing body of research on fund raising and the academic presidency. A discussion of our research design and methodology follows.

METHODOLOGY

Our study was qualitative in nature and utilized an embedded multiple case study design, with university presidents as the primary unit of analysis and both fund raising and comprehensive campaigns as embedded units of analysis. Following an extensive literature review, data collection occurred over a 2-year period and included interviews with 50 academic leaders as well as analyses of selected documents such as campaign case statements and presidential vitae.

The central purpose of our study was to construct a theoretical model or models of presidential fund raising using the grounded theory approach of discovery, development, and provisional verification arising from systematic data collection and content analysis. We emphasized interpreting and adequately describing a central process or system and allowed emerging data to "speak" rather than forcing them into a preconceived theoretical mold.

124   *Selected Readings*

A pilot study was conducted during 1992–93, in which the presidents of 10 Texas universities (5 private, 5 public) were interviewed. The interviews were transcribed, then analyzed using grounded theory methodology. We identified 70 themes and, after sequential analysis using open coding, axial coding, and selective coding, determined that data from four provided the elements for a preliminary model of presidential fund raising. We fleshed out the details using theoretical scanning to create a model patterned after the Paradigm Model described by Strauss and Corbin (1990).

During 1993–1994, interviews were conducted with 20 respondents from a national sample of 62 presidents and former presidents at institutions which had recently conducted or were conducting a comprehensive campaign to raise $100 million or more. In addition, we interviewed a 20-member panel of experts composed of nine chief development officers, nine presidents or former presidents, and several fund raising consultants. We conducted an extensive literature review and also analyzed such documents as presidential vitae and campaign case statements.

We then followed a modified version of the data analysis process that we had used in the pilot study, beginning by (a) identifying specific themes through open coding, (b) conducting theoretical sampling to test and refine the preliminary model of presidential fund raising, and (c) further investigating cases that deviated from the general pattern once theoretical saturation had been reached. Once we had reconciled the "outlying cases," we discontinued our analyses.

RESULTS

The review of literature and comments from study participants indicated that certain key variables or prerequisites determine fund-raising outcomes, that fund raising is based on social exchange processes, and that fund raising is carried on within the context of four types of forces. (See Table 1 and Figures 1 and 2 respectively.)

Table 1 is not a weighted ranking or hierarchy since the individual elements were ordered based on the literature review and comments from study participants. Each element is therefore important for sustained fund-raising effectiveness and the absence or dilution of any single element or elements reduces the overall impact of the others.

However, few if any programs enjoy the luxury of being strong in all 12 prerequisites at any one time, particularly since items 9 through 12 are beyond the control of individual institutions. Fortunately, as Duronio and Loessin (1991) indicated, institutions can enjoy a measure of fund-raising "success" under less

Table 1   Key Prerequisites for Sustained Fund Raising in Institutions of Higher Education

1. Leadership (of president, trustees, deans, volunteers, staff and other friends). This prerequisite subsumes a host of related variables such as willingness/desire to be involved in fund raising, skill/ability/aptitude in fund raising (salesmanship), effort, commitment, integrity, effective management of the institution, fiscal viability/vitality of the institution, effective stewardship of resources, momentum, effective planning donor confidence, and appropriate gratitude and recognition for earlier donations.
2. Financial capacity/capability of constituency (wealth of donor base).
3. Clarity and strength of institutional mission.
4. Personal relationship between donors and a representative of the institution.
5. Involvement of donors in the life of the institution.
6. Prestige/reputation/image (perceived quality and strength of academic programs).
7. History/age/maturity/consistency/tradition of both the institution and the advancement program. This prerequisite includes, for example, breadth and scope of academic programs, appropriate policies and support structures, adequate budgets and staff, established habits and patterns of giving, and continuity from one president to the next, one chief development officer to the next, and one year to the next in terms of overall quality.
8. Informed and committed constituency (effective program of frequent, two-way communication between institution and donors).
9. Donor predisposition to give (philanthropic impulse in society). While this prerequisite refers more generally to the religious heritage of the nation and the fact that many donors regularly attend religious worship services, it also acknowledges that there are regional as well as community variations in willingness to give, capacity to give, and established traditions of philanthropy.
10. Continued public confidence in (the value and integrity of) higher education as well as the nonprofit sector generally.
11. State of the economy/nation.
12. Tax policy (federal and state laws encouraging or discouraging philanthropy).

than ideal or perfect conditions. In fact, the "successful" institutions in their study were strong, on average, in only 8 of the 16 variables they measured.

Similarly, in our study, all of the institutions exhibited some measure of success in fund raising, and even the institutions raising the least amounts of money were preparing to launch fairly substantial comprehensive campaigns at the time their presidents were interviewed. However, "effectiveness" differs from "success" since it includes capability and potential as well as dollar totals. Moreover, several of the institutions in our study had reached or surpassed their goals in campaigns for $100 million or more, even though their presidents did not enjoy or were not predisposed toward fund raising. Thus, the focus of Table 1 is on sustained effectiveness rather than success in fund raising.

Table 1 is linked to fig. 1 since the prerequisites make up the outer level of Circles E and H, or Short-term and Long-term Donor Response. Table 1 is also linked with fig. 2 since the top dozen prerequisites for sustained fund-raising effectiveness are made up primarily of institutional and environmental variables/factors. Certain aspects of leadership (such as salesmanship, integrity, and willingness/desire to be involved in fund raising) fall within the "personal forces" category while other aspects of leadership (such as effective management, stewardship, and donor recognition) are more institutional in nature.

Figure 1 depicts the fund-raising process at colleges and universities, and focuses on the exchange processes and relationships among donors and various institutional representatives. At the core of social exchange theory lies the concept of *interdependence,* both of individuals and organizations. According to Pfeffer and Salancik (1978), "Interdependence is a situation in which another has the discretion [power] to take actions which affect the focal organization's [or person's] interests" (p. 145). Similarly, Kelly (1991) stated, "Fund raising predominantly involves a social exchange relationship between a charitable organization and a donor, in which the power of each relative to the other determines the outcome of the exchange" (p. 199).

Figure 1 consists of a series of concentric circles and indicates that educational fund raising is driven by two forces: (a) recurrent, continuous financial need due to the nonprofit nature of higher education, and (b) competition from other nonprofits, including other colleges and universities, thus reinforcing a tendency toward prestige maximization.

Regarding the first pressure point, Harvard President Neil Rudenstine explained, "In a sense, everything we do loses money. That's the nature of a nonprofit institution" (qtd. in Flint, 1992, p. D1). As for the second, Clark Kerr (1991) stated, "All institutions, within their categories and geographical regions, compete for students, for funds, for reputation. It is, overall, the most competitive system of higher education in the world. Private fund raising by both public and private institutions has, in recent times, increasingly become a mechanism for competitive advantage" (p. 15).

This competition occurs primarily among colleges and universities of the same basic type—those serving the same market or filling the same niche—but there is also competition among educational institutions and other high status nonprofits such as museums, hospitals, and orchestras for prestige, major gifts, board members, and other scarce, valuable resources and commodities. As a result, institutions of higher education tend to follow a strategy of prestige maximization, although this pattern is less generally true of some institutional types such as community colleges and of institutions with low quality and few resources.

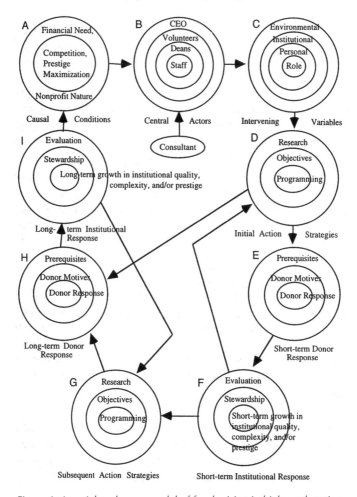

Figure 1. A social-exchange model of fund raising in higher education.

As Figure 1 indicates, the Central Actors (Circle B) in academic fund raising are the chief executive officer (usually titled president), volunteers (including trustees), deans, and fund-raising staff (including the chief development officer). All of these positions are subject to the influence of four types of intervening variables or forces: environmental, institutional, personal, and role. All of these actors (and others as appropriate, such as consultants, faculty members, and the provost) are involved in such Initial Action Strategies (Circle D) as policy formulation, prospect research, feasibility study, program development, staff training, budget analysis, internal needs assessment, strategic planning, case development, leadership recruitment, communication and public relations efforts, special events, moves management, cultivation activities, and solicitation.

Initial strategies normally focus on smaller, annual gifts with most donor prospects. These prospects then respond in one of several different ways. They may give no response, as, for instance, tossing a direct-mail letter in the trash or not returning a call from the alumni phonathon which is recorded on the answering machine. Or if they receive a direct request (they answer the phone), they may postpone or avoid by saying, "I'll have to think about it."

Obviously, some prospects respond negatively to such appeals and requests by choosing not to contribute, while other prospects make a donation for various reasons. Typically for a short-term response, donors are not as concerned with institutional prerequisites as they are for a long-term response since they are not investing as much. However, in some cases, first-time donors will make a major gift—either in cash or capital assets, or through a bequest. This type of response is represented by the arrow going from Circle D to Circle H. Such a gift may originate through the donor's own initiative or in response to a specific proposal put forth by the institution.

Other first-time donors may choose to give at the same level and frequency (i.e., a small annual gift), never maturing as a donor for a particular institution by advancing to higher giving levels. (Most people who are philanthropic give to more than one organization.) Such donor behavior forms a type of loop represented by the arrow going from Circle F to Circle D.

However, the pattern of behavior which colleges and universities try to encourage is to move donors from one level to the next in terms of the size of their gifts and the extent of their involvement in and commitment to the organization/institution. This pattern is represented by the step-wise progression from Circle D to Circle I. To encourage this donor development or progression is a common feature of most fund-raising programs, embodied in various giving "clubs" representing specific dollar levels.

Another loop is represented by the arrow going from Circle I to Circle G. In this case, the donor provides major gifts periodically, either spontaneously or in response to individualized appeals. If followed to its logical conclusion, such a pattern of behavior may culminate in a bequest or testamentary gift which will be the donor's ultimate expression of commitment to the institution.

A final type of donor response is not represented in Figure 1—the rare case where an unknown or unsolicited donor initiates a gift. Such a donor may mail a check to the president or the development office, schedule an appointment to obtain information and/or to discuss his or her interest in making a gift or in funding a certain area or activity, or have a trusted advisor such as an accountant or attorney contact the institution on his or her behalf. And of course, some donors bequeath their estate or a portion thereof to an institution which has no inkling that it is to be the recipient of such largesse until notified by an attorney or other executor upon the death of the benefactor(s).

Obviously, there are a number of variations for each type of donor response, but the primary purpose of Figure 1 is to illustrate fund raising from an institutional perspective and to document the systematic and cyclical nature of the fund-raising process. In that regard, one president whom we interviewed commented, "The idea of the university president raising money is something that if you haven't done it, tends to be a strange concept and maybe a bit of a foreign concept; but once you get into doing it, you begin to see how the whole system works" (qtd. in Cook, 1994a).

This same president also explained the social exchange on which fund raising rests:

> Really to me, fund raising is obviously trying to get some money to advance the purposes of the university, but it goes beyond that. There are people who give to universities and in a very real way benefit from the giving. So really what you're trying to do is to connect the needs of the university to the interests and the needs of potential donors, and when you do that, everybody wins. (qtd. in Cook, 1994a)

Finally, Figure 2 seeks to provide a more in-depth, detailed, and integrated explanation of presidential fund raising than the general context offered in Circles B and C of Figure 1. This amplified model shows that presidential fund raising is a developmental process with different decision or action points and with four types of intervening variables or forces impacting presidents at each stage in the process. These include environmental, institutional, personal, and role forces.

To understand this model, it is necessary to consider each decision or action point separately. First, it is obviously necessary for an individual to be selected as the CEO (president or chancellor) of a college or university. In accepting this position, an individual brings with him or her established habits, preferences, leadership styles, personality traits, administrative and educational experiences, needs, attitudes, values, beliefs, and interpersonal skills, among other qualities.

This new CEO also carries with him or her certain self-imposed or self-created role expectations for the position. In addition, others (role senders) both inside and outside the organization have role expectations associated with the presidency as well. The CEO also inherits established traditions, history, culture, norms, sanctions, taboos, rituals, rewards, and other aspects of organizational life since an institution is a complex and dynamic social organism and not a static and lifeless machine. Institutional forces also include

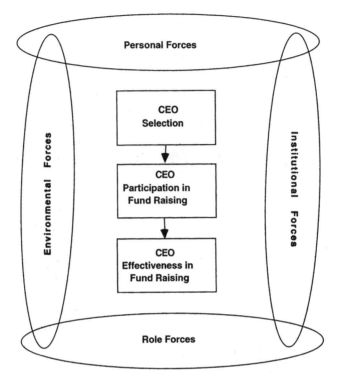

Figure 2. Four-forces model of presidential fund raising in higher education.

wealth, constituencies, capabilities, strengths and weaknesses, market position, size, maturity, prestige, and quality of the governing board, student body,
faculty, and alumni.

Finally, the new CEO inherits such environmental conditions as capacity of
the donor base; wealth and philanthropic tradition of the local community,
region, and state; susceptibility of the surrounding area to natural disasters;
unemployment rate; inflation rate; state of the economy; federal tax policy;
competition from other nonprofits; public opinion toward higher education, etc.

These four forces interact to produce the CEO's level of participation in
fund raising, which is the next step in the model. Presidential participation can
be viewed as a continuum, with one extreme being no participation in fund
raising, and the other extreme being full or total participation in fund raising.
However, very few presidents operate or function at either extreme. Instead,
the vast majority fall somewhere between these polar opposites.

One reason for these different levels of participation is that typically one of
the four forces will dominate the others, although the exact configuration will

vary from institution to institution. For example, institutional forces may be dominant or uppermost at elite, prestigious institutions, while institutions of lesser quality and prestige may be more reliant upon personal forces to stimulate fund raising.

For institutions which have lagged behind in or neglected fund raising in the past, governing boards may communicate an expectation that fund raising become a major or at least an increased emphasis of the position, and this set role may have a strong impact on the person selected to fill the office. And in the case of the Great Depression, the Arab oil embargo, changes in federal tax laws, or a natural disaster such as an earthquake, fire, flood, or tornado that damages a campus, environmental forces clearly can have a strong or even overwhelming influence that either impedes or encourages fund raising.

In reality, all four forces exert differing levels of influence on presidents and thus affect presidential decision-making and behavior in varying degrees. Presidents must therefore strive to develop a "big picture" or integrated view of these forces in order to harness the fund raising potential of their institutions and to maximize their own fund raising effectiveness.

As a president continues in office, these forces produce certain changes in the incumbent which impact his or her fund raising effectiveness. For example, over time role forces exert greater influence in the sense that presidents with longer tenure are more apt to be aware of, understand, and accept their responsibilities regarding fund raising. In support of this finding, Dyson and Kirkman (1989) reported that the percentage of time presidents of America's "best colleges" spent on fund raising and external relations increased with lengthened tenure.

Over time, presidents' commitment to their institutions also increases, their relationships with wealthy individuals deepen, and their circle of friends and acquaintances widens. For example, one CEO interviewed for our study said, "I know I was a lot more effective for [name of university] in my eighth year there than I was in my third, probably exponentially so. Now that I'm in my sixth year at [name of institution], I'm able to do things with people and to make requests and have built relationships that would have been unthinkable in the first or second year" (qtd. in Cook, 1994a).

In summary, presidents both bring with them and inherit certain realities which interact to determine how much time and energy they spend on fund raising (their level of participation), and on which parts of the fund raising process and program they focus their efforts and attention (their priorities). These same forces also determine how well presidents will perform in fund raising (their effectiveness). Consequently, there is a multiple effect, although the strength of each force changes over time and, collectively, the four forces change presidents over time as well.

IMPLICATIONS

Our study presents a number of implications. First, although the president of an academic institution is typically the central player on the fund-raising team, presidents have a limited number of cards they can play with donor prospects. Included in this "presidential hand" are: (a) the stature of the presidential office or position, (b) the quality and prestige of the institution being represented, (c) the importance of higher education to society, (d) interpersonal and human relations skills such as sales ability, the ability to listen, basic courtesy and respect, and the ability to articulate mission and vision, (e) appeals to donor motives, (f) the strength of the relationship between the donor and the institution or between the donor and institutional representatives, and (g) the stature and prestige of members of the solicitation team.

Of these, individual donors have their own priorities about which is the most powerful or important, but genuine quality is obviously a fundamental part of the fund-raising mix. The implication for presidents is that they must make sure they have something of real substance to sell to donors, whether it is a commitment to maintain quality or a commitment to achieve quality. In addition, presidents must have a sense of what is possible and desirable for their institutions, and this larger vision can come only through strategic planning in consultation with many others both internal and external to the campus (e.g., faculty, staff, alumni, trustees, students, community leaders).

Second, fund raising should be thought of and studied more as a team effort than as the responsibility of any one person or position. Similarly, fund raising should be thought of and studied as a dynamic process rather than as a set of rigid rules or a series of mechanical steps. The subtlety and complexity inherent in the fund-raising process can be fully appreciated only as a dynamic group activity involving a number of interpersonal relationships, role transactions, and social exchanges.

Third, although basic aspects of fund raising—such as types of programs and giving vehicles, methods of cultivation and/or solicitation, prospect research, and other technical aspects—are transferable from one institution to another, fund raising is situation specific and can be fully understood only in terms of a particular context. Colleges and universities differ significantly not only by institutional type, but also among institutions of the same type. Differences in culture, history, tradition, maturity, mission, number of alumni, capacity of the donor base, prestige, academic quality, commitment, effort, leadership style, and sales ability of the president and chief development officer, development budget, staff size and expertise, location, and support of the local community, among other factors, play critical roles in fund-raising outcomes. Therefore, results at one institution are not automatically replicable at another institution. However, the chances of such replication are obviously increased among programs and institutions of similar quality, prestige, maturity, mission, and tradition.

Finally, it is important to differentiate between fund-raising effectiveness and fund-raising success. The reality, however, is that both are important. Success is probably an easier concept to grasp and to quantify; it fits more readily within a short-term time frame, which is where most fund raisers and presidents have to operate. On the other hand, the long-term stability, growth, and maturity of an organization's development program are dependent upon variables and forces which may have little to do with actions and outcomes of a particular comprehensive campaign or annual fund drive. Such examples might include personnel decisions which are predicated on political reasons such as returning a favor or having the right connections, deciding to offer a new academic program in return for a corporate or civic contribution, a temporary downturn in the economy, or a fire or flood which damages the campus, etc.

Effectiveness emphasizes performance relative to fund-raising potential given present capabilities and realities, while success emphasizes performance relative to a predetermined goal in a predetermined time frame. Therefore, fund raisers and presidents need to have both a short-term and a long-term agenda for their institutions. The concept of effectiveness also carries with it a broader perspective on fund raising and encourages more focus and attention on basic prerequisites which must usually be in place before donors will consider making a major or ultimate gift to an institution.

CONCLUSION

The models we constructed from our data break important new ground in understanding academic fund raising in general and presidential fund raising in particular, and should be of interest and benefit to practitioners and scholars. Table 1 provides a comprehensive guideline to such decision makers as presidents, vice presidents for development, and governing boards about the key variables or prerequisites for sustained effectiveness in fund raising. While institutions vary widely in their individual preparedness in these areas, this list nonetheless provides administrators with a tool for assessing the relative strengths and weaknesses of their institutions regarding fund-raising potential and capability. It also offers a snapshot of those considerations that are important to major donors and major donor prospects.

Similarly, Figure 1 provides an overview of the fund-raising process at institutions of higher education. It thus focuses on a general pattern which is dynamic and changing rather than a series of discrete events which are static and predictable. Further, it portrays fund raising from an institutional and systems perspective and depicts fund raising as a social exchange which occurs between donors and institutions. The scope and complexity of such a system are enormous, especially when interaction effects are considered.

Finally, Figure 2 focuses on presidential fund raising. In this model, intervening variables include environmental, institutional, role, and personal forces. These forces interact to determine who is selected as an institution's CEO, the extent and direction of the CEO's involvement in fund raising, and the effectiveness of the CEO in fund raising. The same four forces also impact other key players on the fund raising team such as deans, trustees and other volunteers, and senior members of the fund-raising staff, including the Chief Development Officer.

These models may apply to other types of nonprofit organizations and executives as well, but that fit must be determined by future research, for example, replicating this study in a different type of nonprofit setting (hospitals, art museums, symphony orchestras, health and human service agencies, etc.) to determine the role of CEOs in fund raising. A comparison study in which university presidents are studied alongside other types of nonprofit executives would also be useful.

Replication of this study at institutions which have conducted or are conducting comprehensive campaigns for less than $100 million would also be useful for comparison purposes to see if presidential attitudes and behaviors about fund raising vary significantly from those reported in this study. A few of the CEOs on the panel of experts and several of the CEOs in the pilot study were involved in campaigns for less than $100 million; but for the most part, these officials were either at high-prestige institutions or were active in the Council for Advancement and Support of Education. A separate study is therefore needed.

Similarly, a stratified sample of institutions could also be studied, including one group of presidents at institutions with mature fund-raising programs and a high level of annual total giving matched against a second group of presidents at institutions with less effective fund-raising programs and a lower level of annual total giving. All of the institutions should be of the same basic type (i.e., Carnegie or Council for Aid to Education classification) to limit the effects of other variables related to size and mission.

Other useful types of basic qualitative studies on educational fund raising would take a holistic focus and acknowledge the complexity of the fund-raising process, the multiplicity of forces and variables involved, and the importance of situational context. Finally, additional studies are needed which seek to generate, construct, apply, and/or synthesize theories that explain or describe higher education fund raising.

W. Bruce Cook is employed in the Office of Private Investments, University of Texas Investment Management Company, and *William F. Lasher* is an Associate Professor, at The University of Texas at Austin, Department of Educational Administration. This paper was originally presented at the annual conference of the Association for Research on Nonprofit Organizations and Voluntary Action (ARNOVA) October 20–22, 1994, in Berkeley, California.

REFERENCES

Altizer, A. W. (1992). *Seeking major gifts: How 57 institutions do it.* Washington, DC: Council for Advancement and Support of Education.

Bakrow, W. (1961). *The relative effectiveness of certain procedures and practices in fund raising in selected private colleges and universities.* Unpublished doctoral dissertation, Indiana University, Bloomington.

Boardman, W. H., Jr. (1993). An effective model of a principal gift program. In R. Muir & J. May (Eds.), *Developing an effective major gift program* (pp. 79–83). Washington, DC: Council for the Advancement and Support of Education.

Bornstein, R. L. (1989). The capital campaign: Benefits and hazards. In J. L. Fisher & G. H. Quehl (Eds.), (pp. 202–211).

Brittingham, B. E., & Pezzullo, T. R. (1990.) *The campus green: Fund raising in higher education* (ASHE-ERIC Higher Education Report No. 1). Washington, DC: George Washington University.

Brown, R. W. (1988). The presidential role in financial development. In D. H. Dagley (Ed.), *Courage in mission: Presidential leadership in the church-related college* (pp. 45–55). Washington, DC: Council for Advancement and Support of Education.

Cook, W. B. (1994a). *Courting philanthropy: The role of university presidents and chancellors in fund raising.* Unpublished doctoral dissertation, The University of Texas at Austin.

Cook, W. B. (1994b). *A history of educational philanthropy and the academic presidency.* Unpublished manuscript, The University of Texas at Austin.

Cowley, W. H. (1980). *Presidents, professors, and trustees.* San Francisco: Jossey-Bass.

Cramer, R. V. (1966). *Financial development in private higher education and the effects of related variables.* Unpublished doctoral dissertation, University of Connecticut, Storrsville.

Crawford, T. R. (1976). *The role of the chief development officer as perceived by presidents and chief development officers at selected institutions of higher education.* Unpublished doctoral dissertation, Texas A&M University, College Station.

Curti, M., & Nash, R. (1965). *Philanthropy in the shaping of American higher education*. New Brunswick, NJ: Rutgers University Press.

Cutlip, S. M. (1965). *Fund raising in the United States: Its role in America's philanthropy*. New Brunswick, NJ: Rutgers University Press.

Dowden, G. B. (1990). Presidents: Effective fund raising leadership. In W. K. Willmer (Ed.), *Friends, funds, and freshmen* (pp. 21–37). Washington, DC: Christian College Coalition.

Drucker, P. (1990). *Managing the non-profit organization*. New York: HarperCollins.

Duronio, M. A., & Loessin, B. A. (1991). *Effective fund raising in higher education: Ten success stories*. San Francisco: Jossey-Bass.

Dyson, D. H., and Kirkman, R. (1989, March/April). Presidential priorities. *AGB Reports*, pp. 6–11.

Fisher, J. L. (1985). Role of the public college or university president in fund raising. In M. J. Worth (Ed.), *Public college and university development* (pp. 49–56). Washington, DC: Council for Advancement and Support of Education.

Fisher, J. L. (1989a). The historical importance of major gifts. In J. L. Fisher & G. H. Quehl (Eds.), (pp. 212–220).

Fisher, J. L. (1989b.) A history of philanthropy. In J. L. Fisher & G. H. Quehl (Eds.), (pp. 18–32).

Fisher, J. L., & Quehl, G. H. (Eds.). (1989). *The president and fund raising*. New York: American Council on Education/Macmillan.

Flack, H. (1932). History of early fund raising. In R. W. Sailor (Ed.), *An alumni fund survey* (pp. 1–9). Ithaca, N.Y.: American Alumni Council.

Flawn, P. T. (1990). *A primer for university presidents: Managing the modern university*. Austin: University of Texas Press.

Flint, A. (1992, February 9). Colleges: Do more with less. *Austin American-Statesman*, p. D1.

Foote, E. T., II. (1986). The president's role in a capital campaign. In H. G. Quigg (Ed.), *The successful capital campaign* (pp. 73–80). Washington, DC: Council for Advancement and Support of Education.

Francis, N. C. (1975). The president's management role in development. In *The president's role in development* (pp. 2–5). Washington, DC: Association of American Colleges.

Hardin, P. (1984, January). How I learned to love fund raising. *CASE Currents*, 14–18.

Hesburgh, T. M. (1988). Academic leadership. In J. L. Fisher & M. Tack (Eds.), *Leaders on leadership: The college presidency* (pp. 5–8). San Francisco: Jossey-Bass.

Howe, F. (1991). *The board member's guide to fund raising: What every trustee needs to know about raising money*. San Francisco: Jossey-Bass.

Hurtubise, M. F. (1988). *An analysis of presidential attitudes toward and participation in fund raising at select, small, independent, liberal arts colleges and universities*. Unpublished doctoral dissertation, University of San Francisco.

Jacobson, H. K. (1990). *The evolution of institutional advancement on American campuses, 1636–1989*. Oshkosh, WI: Journalism Research Bureau, University of Wisconsin-Oshkosh.

Kelly, K. S. (1991). *Fund raising and public relations: A critical analysis.* Hillsdale, NJ: Lawrence Erlbaum Associates.

Kerr, C. (1991, May/June). The new race to be Harvard or Berkeley or Stanford. *Change,* pp. 8–15.

Kohr, R. V. (1977). Capital campaigning. In A. W. Rowland (Ed.), *Handbook of institutional advancement* (pp. 236–264). San Francisco: Jossey-Bass.

Marts, A. C. (1953). *Philanthropy's role in civilization.* New York: Harper & Brothers.

McAnear, B. (1952). The raising of funds by the colonial colleges. *Mississippi Valley Historical Review, 48,* 591–612.

McAnear, B. (1955). College founding in the American colonies, 1745–1775. *Mississippi Valley Historical Review, 52,* 24–44.

McGoldrick, W. P. (1989). In J. L. Fisher & G. H. Quehl (Eds.), (pp. 160–169).

Miller, M. T. (1991). *The college president's role in fund raising.* (ERIC Document Reproduction Service No. ED 337 099).

Panas, J. (1984). *Mega gifts: Who gives them, who gets them.* Chicago: Pluribus Press.

Pfeffer, J., & Salancik, G. R. (1978). *The external control of organizations: A resource dependence perspective.* New York: Harper & Row.

Reck, W. E. (1976). *The changing world of college relations: History & philosophy, 1917–1975.* Washington, DC: Council for Advancement and Support of Education.

Richards, M. D., & Sherratt, G. R. (1981). *Institutional advancement in hard times* (AAHE-ERIC Higher Education Research Report No. 2). Washington, DC: American Association for Higher Education.

Rodriguez, C. G. (1981). *Alumni and the president: Presidential leadership behavior affecting alumni giving at small private liberal arts colleges.* Unpublished doctoral dissertation, Union Institute, Cincinnati, Ohio.

Schachner, N. (1962). *The mediaeval universities.* New York: A. S. Barnes. (Original work published 1938.)

Schulze, C. J., Jr. (1991). *The role of the community college president in successful fund raising.* Unpublished doctoral dissertation, Columbia University, New York.

Skelly, M. E. (1991, August). College presidents as fund raisers. *School and College,* 28–29.

Slinker, J. M. (1988). *The role of the college or university president in institutional advancement.* Unpublished doctoral dissertation, Northern Arizona University, Flagstaff.

Smith, G. T. (1986). The chief executive and advancement. In A. W. Rowland (Ed.), *Handbook of institutional advancement* (2nd ed., pp. 697–705). San Francisco: Jossey-Bass.

Stover, W. S. (1930). *Alumni stimulation by the American college president.* New York: Bureau of Publications, Teachers College, Columbia University.

Strauss, A., & Corbin, J. (1990). *Basics of qualitative research: Grounded theory procedures and techniques.* Newbury Park, CA: Sage.

West, D. C. (1983). The presidency of a small college. In A. J. Falander & J. C. Merson (Eds.), *Management techniques for small and specialized institutions* (pp. 11–23). San Francisco: Jossey-Bass.

Whittier, H. S., Jr. (1980). Presidential commitment to educational fund raising. In J. L. Fisher (Ed.), *Presidential leadership in advancement activities* (pp. 57–66). San Francisco: Jossey-Bass.

Winfree, W. R., III. (1989). *The role of persons other than professional development staff in the solicitation of major gifts from private individuals for senior colleges and universities.* Unpublished doctoral dissertation, University of North Texas, Denton.

Winship, A. L., II. (1984). *The quest for major gifts: A survey of 68 institutions.* Washington, DC: Council for Advancement and Support of Education.

Withers, D. C. (1986). Before the campaign begins: An internal audit. In H. G. Quigg (Ed.), *The successful capital campaign* (pp. 13–22). Washington, DC: Council for Advancement and Support of Education.

Justice and Charity

Allen Buchanan

The distinction between justice and charity is thought to be fundamental in ethical theory. Yet remarkably little has been done to develop the distinction systematically or to articulate the role it is to play in ethical theory. Four theses about the difference between justice and charity are widely held and rarely argued for: (1) Duties of justice (with the exception of those which correspond to special rights generated by promising or special relationships or reciprocal group undertakings that generate obligations of fair play) are exclusively negative duties (duties to refrain from certain actions); duties of charity are generally positive duties (duties to render aid). (2) Duties of justice may be enforced; duties of charity may not. (3) Duties of justice are perfect duties; duties of charity are imperfect. (Perfect duties are determinate both with regard to the content of what is required and with regard to the identity of the individual who is the object of the duty; duties of charity are indeterminate in both senses: the kind and amount of aid, as well as the choice of a recipient are left to the discretion of the benefactor.) (4) Justice is a matter of rights; charity is not (duties of justice have correlative rights; duties of charity do not), and what is one's right is owed to one, the lack of which gives one justified grounds for complaint that one has been wronged.

It is far from clear how claims 1–4 are supposed to be related to one another. Although all four purport to characterize differences between justice and charity, we shall see that not all are equally plausible candidates for answering the question, What makes something a duty of charity rather than a duty of justice, and vice versa? Moreover, it will become clear that some of

"Justice and Charity," by Allen Buchanan, *Ethics* 97 (1987): 558–575.

these claims are thought to be derivable from the others, although the connecting assumptions are often either not made explicit or not argued for.

By analyzing theses 1–4 and by articulating and assessing the grounds for asserting them, I shall explore the distinction between justice and charity and advance some conclusions about its importance—or lack of importance—for ethical theory. The analysis offered here not only illuminates the question of how we are to draw distinctions between duties of justice and duties of charity, it also has some rather surprising implications concerning the nature of rights and our grounds for ascribing them to individuals.

Each of the four theses refers to *duties* of charity. To some this may seem misleading, if not inaccurate. But I hasten to emphasize that 'duty' here is being used in a very broad and innocuous way, simply to refer to whatever is expressed by a moral imperative, a judgment about what ought or ought not to be done, what is in any sense morally required. In particular, it is not assumed that duties may be enforced or that they have correlative rights.[1]

I

The view that duties of justice are always negative,[2] while those of charity are (generally) positive,[3] is perhaps the least satisfactory attempt to distinguish justice from charity since it simply begs one of the most hotly disputed questions in the theory of rights, the question of whether there are positive as well as negative (general) rights.[4] Anyone who seeks enlightenment on where to draw the line between justice and charity or who wants a principled justification for drawing the line where his intuitions tell him it should be drawn is unlikely to find much solace in the claim that justice concerns only negative duties since this latter claim is as controversial and in need of justification as the very judgments about charity and justice it is supposed to support and explain. Since an adequate theoretical justification is currently lacking for the thesis that all rights are negative,[5] some who distinguish between justice and charity in the first way, like Nozick, argue in indirect fashion that all rights are negative by attempting to show that the enforcement of positive rights must lead to unacceptably frequent and severe disruptions of individuals' activities as rational planners or to intrusions that are intuitively unjust.[6]

It is clear that the establishment of certain rather ambitious positive rights—such as the right to an equal share of income or a right to be aided whenever one needs help by whomever is able to help, regardless of costs— would require frequent and severe disruptions. But it is extremely implausible, as more moderate libertarians such as Hayek have admitted, to hold that the establishment of more modest positive rights, such as a right to a "decent minimum"[7] of income or a "right to easy rescue,"[8] will always or even generally result in unacceptable intrusions into individuals' lives. As Hayek observes, well-publicized, long-standing tax laws can provide funding for a legal right to a "decent minimum" of income without shattering that stable framework of expectations which is properly valued by the champions of the individual freedom. Further, as several philosophers and legal scholars have recently noted,[9] a right to easy rescue—a limited right to be rescued from great harm—by a person who can do so without unreasonable cost or risk to herself, cannot be dismissed as either intuitively unjust or as unacceptably disruptive of individuals' expectations. And as these same writers have also pointed out, the problem of drawing a line between reasonable and unreasonable risks or costs here seems no more difficult than that of applying a "reasonableness standard" in other areas of the law, including not only the law of torts but also the law that establishes the most basic negative rights. For example, self-defense is a recognized defense in the law of homicide, and a successful defense of this sort requires that the defendant acted reasonably in the circumstances.[10] In general, the concept of reasonableness employed in limiting duties to aid seems no more a matter of degree and no more unworkable than in other areas of the law.

There is an even more basic reason for rejecting the attempt to use the distinction between positive and negative duties to draw the line between justice and charity. Until now the theorist who holds that all (general) rights are negative—that is, the libertarian—has been allowed the offensive, and arguments have been adduced to show that he has failed to undermine the hypothesis that there are positive duties which have correlative rights. The libertarian can be put on the defensive by one simple but powerful observation about what is at the heart of morality: morality is fundamentally (though not exclusively) concerned with avoiding states of affairs that are harmful for individuals. Such states of affairs, clearly, can be avoided not simply by refraining from harming but also by preventing harm. After all, a great deal of what makes harmful states of affairs a matter of moral concern is their *harmfulness,* whether or not they were the result of someone's harming. For this reason there is at least a *presumption* that there are some positive moral rights—rights to aid that prevents harm—if it is assumed that rights principles express what is central to morality and if, as the libertarian believes, there are rights not to be harmed. The burden of argument, then, lies initially on the libertarian to show that even though the harmful state may be the same, there is a right not to be harmed by another but never a right to be aided in such a way as to prevent harm.

In addition, at least part of what makes harmful states a matter of moral concern, namely, a regard for the well-being of individuals, must make beneficial states morally important as well.[11] But if this is so, then strong arguments will be needed to deny that if there are rights to be aided so as to avoid harm, there are also at least some modest rights to be benefited. None of *this proves* that there are positive rights, of course, but it does bring home the initial strangeness of the view that there are only negative rights and makes it clear that the libertarian needs powerful arguments to support his position. In sum, absent a more adequately supported theory of (exclusively) negative rights than is now available, any attempt to ground an analysis of the distinction between justice and charity in the thesis that justice is restricted to negative duties is unconvincing.

II

There are, it seems, two quite different reasons given for the thesis that duties of justice may be enforced while duties of charity may not. The first is that, since duties of justice, but not duties of charity, have correlative rights, only duties of justice may be enforced because only duties for which there are correlative rights may be enforced. The second is that duties of justice, being perfect duties, may be enforced, while duties of charity, being imperfect, cannot. Imperfect duties are indeterminate both with respect to the recipient of aid and the amount and kind of aid, and the idea is that attempts to enforce them would prove arbitrary and subject to abuse. This second reason will be taken up in Section IV; the first is criticized in the present section. In Section III I shall examine the view that duties of justice have correlative rights while duties of charity do not. But at this point in the argument I shall show that even if that view is true, thesis 2 (that duties of charity need not be enforced) must be rejected.

The thesis that only those duties having correlative rights may be enforced is a very sweeping yet too rarely questioned claim about the sole condition under which coercion is morally justified. Perhaps the most serious challenge to it rests on the recognition that enforcement is sometimes necessary to secure contributions to *collective goods,* that in some cases, at least where the collective good in question is extremely important, such enforcement seems morally justified, and that its being justified does not appear to depend upon any assumption that the individuals in question have a moral right to the good in question.[12] Enforcement of a duty to contribute is sometimes necessary for the provision of important collective goods (such as clean air, energy conservation, or national defense) owing to the fact that voluntary contribution may be blocked because some individuals attempt to take a free ride on the anticipated contributions of others. Successful collective action may also fail to occur if enough individuals refrain from contributing because they lack assurance that others will contribute, even though they have no desire to take a free ride.

It is true, of course, that collective goods[13] problems can in some cases be overcome without recourse to enforcement through the force of moral exhortation of personal example, through the assignment of property rights, or by making the process of contributing sufficiently valuable in itself (through the goods of solidarity or community, for example). Nonetheless, enforcement of a duty to contribute is sometimes the only effective means for securing some collective goods. Hence, unless one is willing to advance the very sweeping and implausible thesis that the need to achieve important collective goods *never* provides an adequate justification for enforcement of duties for which there are no correlative rights, one must conclude that it is false that only rights principles may be enforced.

It is important to emphasize not only that the need to secure certain important collective goods is widely recognized as a sound justification for enforcing positive duties of contribution but also that the force of such justification does not appear to rest either implicitly or explicitly upon the assumption that there is a right to the good in question. Once such justifications are recognized, it may be advisable, in order to provide individuals with incentives to report failures to contribute, to establish legal rights for individuals to the good in question; but this does not show that the moral justification for enforcing contribution presupposes either legal or moral rights to the collective good. Indeed, it is rather odd—perhaps somewhat hysterical—to say that by not contributing each noncontributor has thereby *violated the rights* of each potential beneficiary of a collective good, including himself.[14]

Whether or not a share of it is *owed* to each individual and regardless of whether those who fail to contribute could rightly be said to have *wronged* all potential partakers of the good, some collective goods are of sufficient importance that enforcement seems justifiable if that is what it takes to secure them. If we are *ever* justified in enforcing such non-rights principles, then we must reject any attempt to distinguish between duties of justice and duties of charity that is based on the assumption that only the need to enforce rights principles can justify coercion.

Furthermore, it is not simply that there are plausible non-rights-based arguments for enforced contributions to collective goods that do not assume antecedent moral rights to the goods in question; there are in fact plausible arguments of this sort for enforcing duties of *charity* under the certain circumstances because some important forms of charity are themselves collective goods.[15]

Without an effective enforcement mechanism, strictly voluntary compliance with duties to aid may founder due to the fact that a system of aid for the needy is a collective good. Even if rational individuals agree to a system of duties to contribute to the good, they may find it rational to defect from it so long as compliance is voluntary. The situation has an incentive structure similar to that of a many-person Prisoner's Dilemma. Each individual may reason as follows: "Either enough others will contribute to the good in question, regardless of whether I do so, or they will not. Since my contribution is a cost to me, the rational thing for me to do is not to contribute so long as I will be able to partake of the good regardless of whether I contributed."

The last condition, that noncontributors will not be excluded from partaking of the good if it is achieved, will generally be satisfied in the case of at least some important duties to aid the needy. In the case of a duty to rescue, it will not be feasible to try to determine, in situations calling for prompt action, whether a particular individual (or which individuals among a group of endangered persons) has already "contributed" to a system of mutual aid by already having performed acts of rescue. But more important, in a society in which acts of rescue are fairly infrequent, a system in which I can count on being rescued only if I have myself already established that I am a contributor by having rescued others would be vastly inferior from a strictly prudential point of view to one in which I can count on being rescued by whoever is in a position to do so, regardless of whether I have already proven that I have made my contribution. Moreover, even if there were some ready way of identifying those who either *have* aided or of predicting accurately who *will* aid those in need, it will often be impractical to attempt selective rescue of just those individuals from the midst of endangered groups. Rescue efforts, in other words, often involve externalities or "spill-over effects."

It might be replied that in fact individuals will not behave thusly (that is, will not be free riders, who defect from agreements to contribute) because their desire to maximize their own utility will be constrained by altruism. Now the extent to which individuals observe moral constraints on their individual utility-maximizing behavior is an empirical issue, but this much seems clear: since altruism is generally limited, the *scope* of duties to aid which we can expect people to fulfill voluntarily is probably considerably narrower than that of duties they would discharge if those duties were enforced.

The free-rider problem arises on the assumption that the good at which each individual aims is accurately described as 'the provision of aid to the needy.' If this is his goal, then as we have seen the individual may withhold his contribution if he believes that the needy will be provided for by others or that they will not, regardless of whether he contributes. There are several different ways in which one may benefit from the attainment of this good without having contributed to it. Some may derive satisfaction or avoid discomfort simply by knowing that the needy are provided for. Others may view the provision of aid to the needy as instrumentally good: it makes for a more stable social structure, in which those who have wealth and power may enjoy them in greater security, and increases overall productivity by enabling more people to work. Indeed it is often said that the major social welfare programs initiated in western Europe in the late nineteenth century were motivated chiefly by the latter sorts of considerations rather than by a sense of justice or a direct concern for the well-being of the needy.

However, the free-rider problem will *not* block successful collective action if a sufficient number of people desire *to provide for the needy* rather than simply desiring *that the needy be provided for.* If I regard the good to be attained as 'a system of aid to the needy *to which I contribute,*' then, of course, I cannot partake of that good without contributing to it.

Whether or not a sufficient number of people to achieve a particular goal of collective charity will be effectively motivated by the desire to be charitable (rather than simply by the desire that charity be done) is an empirical question whose answer will vary from case to case, depending upon the psychology of the individuals involved. But even if an individual does not himself wish to take a free ride on the contributions of others to a system of aid to the needy, he still may be unwilling to render aid to the needy unless he has *assurance that others* (with resources as great as or greater than his) *will also render aid* to himself or to others in similar need. He may be unwilling to contribute without assurance that others will do so for either or both of two distinct reasons. (a) He may conclude that it is better to expend his "beneficence budget" on an act of independent charity toward some particular person in need rather than risk contributing to a collective charity in which the threshold of contributions needed for success is not reached. (b) His commitment to being charitable may be limited by a requirement of fairness or reciprocity.[16] That persons who are strict individual utility-maximizers may fail to achieve systems of aid that are public goods is hardly surprising. What is striking is the more general conclusion that collective action to create and maintain systems of aid may falter even if some individuals are significantly altruistic.

Whether or not enforcement will be necessary to achieve goals of collective charity does not appear to admit of a general answer. Under certain rather strong conditions, strictly voluntary contributions may suffice. However, in the case of systems of aid that are collective goods, as with collective goods generally, there seem to be no strictly voluntary strategies which will work in all circumstances.[17] If this is so, and if enforcement is justified in *any* such case, then it is *not* the case that enforcement of a duty to contribute is justified only where there is an antecedent moral right to a share of the good in question, whether it be national defense or a system of aid.

Why does the negative-rights-only theorist, that is, the libertarian, hold that enforcement of duties to aid is justifiable only on the assumption that there is an antecedent moral right to receive aid? Perhaps the libertarian reasons as follows: "Everyone has a basic moral right against coercion (i.e., right to negative liberty). The only thing morally weighty enough to justify infringement of this right against coercion would be another moral right. Therefore, if enforced contribution is ever morally justified, then its justification presupposes that individuals have a moral right to the good in question."[18]

Elsewhere I have criticized this view in detail.[19] The claim that there is a general moral right against coercion (or to negative liberty) strong enough to rule out *all* enforced contribution to collective goods (including systems of aid) is non-question-begging only if the right in question is viewed as a presumptive moral claim (i.e., a prima facie right), not a justified moral claim (i.e., a right all things considered). In other words, if the libertarian supports his premise that there is such a strong, virtually unlimited right against coercion (or to negative liberty) merely by an appeal to our moral intuitions but views the rights as a justified moral claim rather than as a prima facie right or moral presumption, he begs the question against the nonlibertarian who maintains that in some cases duties to aid may be enforced so long as costs are not excessive and are distributed fairly. For the nonlibertarian can simply point out that his moral intuition is that a virtually unlimited moral right against coercion is simply too unlimited a right to be plausible. In other words, the nonlibertarian can say that though he finds a strong presumption against coercion to be intuitively plausible, he does not find intuitively plausible the much stronger claim that there is a moral right against coercion if this latter claim entails that the only thing morally weighty enough to justify coercion is a moral right. Yet if the libertarian admits that an appeal to our moral intuitions only supports a prima facie right against coercion, then he cannot assume that the *only* consideration morally weighty enough to defeat this presumption would be a moral right to (receive a share of the good).

Indeed, the nonlibertarian can even admit that there is a right against coercion (not just a prima facie right) but hold that so far as the existence of this right can be supported adequately merely by an appeal to intuition, its scope and content are not sharply specified. He can then argue that when it comes to specifying the scope and content of this right, one morally relevant consideration is the need to overcome barriers to successful collective action for providing certain morally important goods, such as aid to the needy, or for preventing certain morally important harms. Once the proper content and scope of the right against coercion have been determined, it may *then* be correct to say, with respect to the *specified* right, that only the need to respect another moral right could justify its infringement. But what the libertarian overlooks is the possibility that in moving from the intuitively plausible assumption that there is a moral right to negative liberty or against coercion to a specification of the scope and limits of that right, certain non-rights-based considerations—including the need to use coercion to secure certain important collective goods, and, in particular, systems of aid—may be decisive.

In sum, the premise that there is a general moral right to negative liberty, that is, against coercion, may be understood either as a claim about a prima facie right or as a claim about a right simpliciter, that is, a right all things considered. If the former, then the premise is intuitively plausible, but it does not follow from it that the only thing morally weighty enough to override the (merely prima facie) right to negative liberty is a moral right. If the latter, then it may be true that only a moral right would be weighty enough to override the (justified) moral claim to negative liberty, but the thesis that this moral right to negative liberty is broad enough to rule out *all* arguments for enforced contribution is not something which the libertarian can support simply by an appeal to intuition. It appears, then, that the libertarian cannot support his assumption that coerced contribution is justified only when there is a right to the good in question by an intuitive appeal to a right to negative liberty or against coercion.

To admit that some enforced principles requiring contributions to systems of aid or other collective goods are morally justifiable (even in the absence of a moral right to the goods in question) is not to say, however, that whenever a problem of collective action exists, enforcement is justified. First of all, since enforcement, even if not always a great evil, is never a good thing, the need to overcome the free-rider or assurance problems justifies enforcement only if the good cannot be attained by other, less undesirable means (e.g., moral exhortation, leading others to contribute by one's example, etc.). Second, and perhaps even more obviously, enforcement is not justified if the cost of enforcement surpasses the benefit of attaining the good in question. Third, even when the preceding two conditions are satisfied, further limitations may be needed to restrict the scope of collective goods arguments for enforcement simply because the class of collective goods is so large that overuse of this type of argument for enforcement may result in dangerous concentrations of coercive power.

A libertarian might raise the objection that such non-rights-based arguments for enforced contributions fail to recognize a fundamental qualification. While acknowledging that there may be some rules of social coordination, including some principles specifying obligations to contribute to important collective goods that rational individuals would wish to see enforced, even in the absence of corresponding rights, the libertarian will point out that enforcing them is permissible *only* if enforcement does not itself violate important moral rights.

This qualification is in order. However, if the qualification is to become a sound criticism either of non-rights-based, collective goods arguments in general or of the enforced charity arguments set out above, the libertarian must discharge two difficult tasks, the second of which no one has yet achieved. First, he must clearly specify *which* basic moral rights would be violated by all attempts to enforce any duties to contribute to important collective goods or to enforce duties of beneficence, even the relatively undemanding duty of easy rescue or the duty to contribute to a collective effort to provide a decent minimum of goods and services for those who cannot provide for themselves. Second, he must provide a coherent and plausible *justification* for the claim that these moral rights do exist. To rule out in principle all enforceable principles requiring contribution to collective goods and all enforceable principles of beneficence, the libertarian would have to specify and then justify either (*a*) a virtually unlimited general right of negative liberty (or against coercion) or (*b*) a virtually unlimited right to private property. The great obstacle to supporting *a*, as I noted earlier, is that he must do so without begging the question by appealing to intuitions that his nonlibertarian opponent does not share.

Similarly, even if the view that there is *some sort of* moral right to private property has considerable intuitive appeal to many people, the much stronger assertion that there is a virtually unlimited moral right to private property dashes with many persons' intuitions, as the widespread support for at least minimal welfare rights shows. So in the absence of broad consensus in intuitions, the assertion of such an extremely strong moral right to private property is just as much in need of theoretical support as an extremely strong right to negative liberty. Granted that a sound theoretical justification for a virtually unlimited right either to negative liberty or to private property is currently lacking, the burden of proof is on the libertarian to defend the sweeping hypothesis that *every* non-rights-based argument for enforced contributions to charity or to other collective goods violates important moral rights.[20]

III

Ethical theorists as diverse as Kant and Mill have shared the view that duties of justice are perfect, while duties of charity are imperfect.[21] Those who hold this view also typically offer it as a reason for the thesis that duties of justice, but not duties of charity, may be enforced. The idea is that the indeterminacy of imperfect duties (what Kant calls their "play room") makes them unsuitable for enforcement since attempts to enforce them would be afflicted by abuse and arbitrariness and would lead to highly unpredictable intrusions.[22]

In criticizing thesis 2 (the view that only obligations with correlative rights may be enforced), I presented arguments for enforcing duties to aid the needy that did not justify enforcement on the grounds that there is an antecedent moral right to the aid in question. There are two quite different ways to construe such arguments. According to the first, these non-rights-based arguments are properly described as arguments for enforcing duties of charity, and even after an appropriate enforcement mechanism is in place the duties in question remain duties of charity, without correlative moral rights. According to the second way of construing them, these non-rights-based arguments justify the establishment of institutional arrangements for fairly specifying, distributing, and enforcing duties to aid in the absence of a moral right to aid, but once such institutional arrangements are in place a revision should take place in our conception of what others have a moral right to aid. To put it rather crudely, according to both interpretations, we begin by assuming the existence of a duty, but not a right, to aid; in the first we end up with no right to aid but only an enforceable duty of charity, while in the second we end up with a right to aid. If the first way of construing the non-rights-based arguments is correct, then the view that duties of charity are imperfect is simply false. For what the arguments show, on the first interpretation, is that appropriate institutional arrangements for specifying and distributing duties to aid can eliminate the indeterminacy that is definitive of imperfect duties without altering their status as duties of charity. Such institutional arrangements can specify the amount, kind, and recipient of aid.[23]

In addition, if the first way of construing the non-rights-based arguments for enforcing duties to aid is correct, the circularity of the argument that duties of charity may not be enforced *because they are imperfect* becomes starkly apparent. If duties to aid can be made determinate by appropriate institutional arrangements, which will include provisions for enforcement, then lack of determinacy cannot itself be a reason for not enforcing them.

If, however, we view non-rights-based arguments for enforcing duties to aid according to the second interpretation—as leading to the conclusion that once the appropriate institutional arrangements are in place there is a right to receive aid—then these arguments do not contradict the view that duties of charity are imperfect. This is so because the duties in question, though no longer imperfect since they are made determinate by the institutional arrangements, are also no longer duties of charity but, rather, duties of justice. However, even though the second way of construing the non-rights-based arguments for enforced duties to aid is *consistent* with the thesis that duties of justice are perfect and those of charity are imperfect, there is a sense in which it also *trivializes* that thesis. For what those arguments show, on the second interpretation, is that the distinction between perfect and imperfect duties is in no way a fundamental distinction in ethical theory, but, rather, a shifting one which changes as our institutions change or as we move from one type of society to another. So regardless of which way we interpret the non-rights-based arguments for enforced duties to contribute to the needy, thesis 3 is of little value for understanding the distinction between justice and charity or for establishing the alleged importance of that distinction in ethical theory.

Although nothing in my argument hinges on choosing between the two interpretations, it is worth pondering for a moment the implications of the second, according to which the *existence* of certain rights can depend upon the availability of appropriate institutional arrangements for fairly specifying, distributing, and enforcing duties of aid. If this view is correct, then two rather surprising conclusions follow. First, which moral rights individuals have are not determined exclusively by the ethically relevant features *of those individuals*. On the contrary, for at least some important moral rights, whether or not an individual has the right depends not only upon whether the individual possesses certain characteristics (such as certain important interests or the capacities associated with personhood) but also upon the availability of institutional arrangements which may or may not exist in a particular society at a given time. It is important to note that the moral rights which (according to the second interpretation of the enforced charity arguments) correspond to duties to contribute to collective charity are *not* identical to any of the three types of rights usually considered to be covered by the term 'special rights.' They are not (1) rights that arise from special personal relationships (such as that of parent to child). Nor are they (2) special rights that are generated by promises or contracts. Finally, since none of the enforced charity arguments utilizes premises about fairness, they are not the same as (3) those special institutional rights that are said to be the correlative or "fair play" duties to contribute to cooperative institutions from which one benefits. But if so, then there are some moral rights that are neither special in either of these three senses nor general in the sense of being ascribable to all human beings (or all persons) regardless of the type of society in which they find themselves. Yet it has generally been assumed that the distinction between special and human (or natural) rights is exhaustive. Second, if there are some (nonspecial) moral rights whose existence depends upon the availability of social arrangements that may or may not be present, then the principles specifying these rights will in an important sense be condusory, or derivative, rather than premissory, or basic. In other words, such rights principles will not be derivable from any more basic rights principles but will require for their justification contingent premises about the existence of certain social arrangements. Thus if there are such rights, no plausible ethical theory can be exclusively *rights-based.*

IV

The fourth approach views duties of justice as having correlative rights and duties of charity as lacking them. Those who assert it take the first half of thesis 4 to be uncontroversial, and I, too, shall assume, for purposes of the argument, that all duties of justice have correlative rights. Now many who take the distinction between duties with correlative rights and those without them to be fundamental also hold that justice includes only negative duties. But if, as I have already argued, the thesis that justice includes only negative duties is unjustified, then they must argue, not assume, that only negative duties have correlative rights in order to conclude that positive duties of charity lack correlative rights.

The prevailing view is that what distinguishes duties that have correlative rights (and hence qualify as duties of justice) from those that do not is that the former, but not the latter, are *owed to* someone.[24] Thus a person's failure to perform a duty for which there is a correlative right gives one grounds for *a justified grievance* that one was *wronged*. Everything hangs, then, on *how* we are to determine what one is owed, the lack of which grounds a justified grievance or a claim that one was wronged.

B would be wronged if A failed to do his duty to aid B only if B (or B's interests or needs) is not only *the focus* but also the *source* of A's duty. If I ought to advance your interests or satisfy your needs only because doing so will advance someone else's good, then *you* are not the *source* of my obligation, though you are *the focus* of it. The distinction between the focus and the source of duties to aid is not sufficient to distinguish duties of charity from duties of justice, however. If I have a duty of charity to help Jones when he is in need, it is my duty to help him because *he* is in need, not because helping him serves others' interests.

What, then, *in addition* to the condition that B is the source, not just the focus of the duty, is needed to justify the judgment that failure to perform the duty wrongs B? One suggestion is that if A's failure to do his duty wrongs B, then A's not doing his duty itself creates a presumption that A must offer restitution or compensation to B.

The thesis that there is a connection between justice and restitution or compensation is distinct from the more general thesis, considered above, that justice may be enforced. It is true that enforcement, understood broadly as the provision of coercive sanctions, includes restitution and compensation since the prospect of being required, on pain of coercion, to compensate or provide restitution is one kind of coercive incentive. But the point of the present discussion is not to focus on the role that restitution and compensation play in enforcement. Instead, our topic here is the way in which restitution and compensation, which are always restitution *to someone* and compensation *of someone,* are supposed to give content to the idea that duties of justice, unlike duties of charity, are directed toward someone, the right bearer, in a distinctive way.

That nonfulfillment of duties with correlative rights creates a presumption for restitution or compensation may well be true, but it is of little help in deciding *whether* a duty is a duty of charity or of justice. If we already knew that A's duty toward B is a duty of justice, then the thesis that only duties of justice have correlative rights would enable us to conclude that A owes restitution or compensation for failing to do his duty. But if we are uncertain whether A's duty is a duty of justice or of charity and hence also unsure of whether B has a right to what it is A's duty to do, we are likely to be at least as hesitant about whether A owes B restitution or compensation.

The question of whether someone ought to be required to provide compensation or restitution, like the question of whether it is morally justifiable to enforce a duty, is not in general the sort of question which can be answered by an appeal to intuition, much less intuitions about what is charity and what is justice. These are highly theoretical questions: answering them will require a weighing of complex and sophisticated considerations. And in fact there has been considerable controversy in recent years over *what kinds* of factors should be taken into account in determining how or whether one should be compensated for certain sorts of acts and omissions. Much of the debate in the literature on the economic analysis of law has centered on the question of how much weight considerations of efficiency should be given in the justification of claims to compensation.[25]

If the distinction between duties of justice and duties of charity can only be made by distinguishing between duties that have correlative rights and those which do not, if we can only determine which duties have correlative rights by ascertaining whether failure to fulfill them justifies compensation, and if the justification of claims to compensation is the complex matter it seems to be, then the judgment that something is a duty of justice rather than charity is a highly derivative, theoretical statement. And if it is, then the distinction between duties of charity and duties of justice will not itself be of any use in tackling any of the issues whose resolution was presupposed in drawing the distinction. Moreover, even if, after the resolution of these complex issues in ethical theory is achieved, we can then distinguish duties of justice as those that have correlative rights and duties of charity as those that lack them, this will have rather limited significance, especially because knowing that a duty is a duty of charity will not itself settle the question of whether enforcing it is morally justifiable. At most such a judgment will serve to *sum up* the results of the various arguments that led to the conclusion that for some failures to perform duties compensation or restitution is required while for others it is not.

There is another feature associated with the concept of rights which might be thought to provide a way of distinguishing between duties of justice and duties of charity (granted the assumption that duties of justice have correlative rights and that duties of charity do not). Ronald Dworkin and others have stressed that what is distinctive of justified rights claims is that they "trump" or override mere appeals to what would maximize utility.[26] If it is true that only rights claims "trump," then it might be thought that only duties with correlative rights may be enforced at the expense of failing to maximize utility. Hence, if we knew which duties may be enforced even though enforcing them would preclude maximizing utility, then we would know which are duties of justice and which are duties of charity. However, unless one takes rights principles to be self-evident (in which case one could distinguish between justice and charity without recourse to the trumping feature), one will need arguments—perhaps very complex ones—to determine whether certain obligations ought to be enforced even at the expense of maximizing utility. Here, too, the judgment that a duty is a duty of charity rather than a duty of justice will not be a starting point for theorizing about important issues in ethical theory but, rather, a conclusory, summing up statement that rests on vigorously contested assumptions.

V

I will make no attempt to summarize the various arguments of this essay. The main conclusion of the analysis, however, can be succinctly stated: Each of the four most widely accepted theses concerning the difference between justice and charity is either unjustified or false, or it renders the distinction between justice and charity both difficult to draw and of limited significance in ethical theory.

I would like to suggest that this conclusion receives some independent confirmation from the fact that a distinction between justice and charity seems to play no role in two of the most prominent competing models for deriving basic ethical principles. It has long been known that in utilitarianism the distinction between justice and charity is not of fundamental importance: the ultimate justification for both principles of justice and principles of charity is that acting on them maximizes social utility. Principles of justice are simply those whose utility is so great as to outweigh whatever disutility attends enforcing them.[27] Thus in utilitarianism the important distinction is between those duties to aid others that may be enforced and those that may not, 'duties of charity' merely serving as a convenient label for the latter.

Similarly, the distinction between justice and charity appears to have no place in Rawlsian hypothetical contractarianism. Although Rawls suggests that this method of deriving ethical principles can accommodate the traditional distinction between justice and charity,[28] he does nothing to substantiate this claim. Moreover, the main elements of Rawls's initial choice situation that are said to determine the selection of ethical principles—namely, the veil of ignorance and the preference for primary goods—seem to ensure that the parties will simply choose a set of principles governing the distribution of expectations of primary goods without considering whether they are to be understood as principles of justice or principles of charity. Indeed, nothing in the description of the original position either reflects or seems capable of generating a distinction between principles of justice and principles of charity. The same seems true not only of Rawls's theory but of hypothetical contractarian theories generally, including, most recently, David Gauthier's.[29] Kant, as we have seen, does draw what he takes to be an important distinction between justice and charity, but it is not internal to the conception of hypothetical choice in an original position. Rather, it is anchored, quite independently and inadequately, in a distinction between perfect and imperfect duties.

The description of the choice the parties are to make could be modified, of course, so that they are to choose two different sets of distributive principles, those which are to be enforced and those which are not, and it could be stipulated that the distinction will be marked by the terms 'principles of justice' and 'principles of charity.' But here, as with utilitarianism, the real issue would be, Which principles are we morally justified in enforcing? Introducing the terms 'justice' and 'charity' would add nothing to its resolution. Though I will make no attempt to do so here, I believe that the same point can be made with respect to universalizability procedures and ideal observer theories. Across a broad spectrum of competing models for generating basic ethical principles, the distinction between justice and charity is conspicuous by its absence. If my arguments in this essay are sound, this omission is not a defect.

NOTES

I would like to thank Andrea Witte for helping me to work out the implications of the view that certain forms of beneficence, including not only the provision of a decent minimum of income but also the practice of rescuing strangers, can qualify as public goods. I am also greatly indebted to Jody Kraus, Ronald Milo, and Holly Smith for helping me to untangle a number of confusions that afflicted an earlier draft of this essay. Finally, I am also grateful for excellent comments by G. A. Cohen, Deborah Mathieu, and the [editors of this journal].

1. It might still be objected that there are some cases in which charitable acts can-

not properly be called duties because they are in no way morally required, being clearly "beyond the call of duty," as when a person rushes into a burning building to save a stranger. See, e.g., R. Epstein, "A Theory of Strict Liability," *Journal of Legal Studies* 2 (1973): 189–204. This objection is based, I believe, upon a confusion between charity, as it is ordinarily understood, and extreme generosity. It would be a case of ungrateful understatement to thank a person who rescued you from the flames for being charitable. To avoid confusion, the term 'superogation' might be usefully reserved for acts so generous that they are clearly "beyond the call of duty" in the sense that one who does not perform them is subject to no moral criticism at all.

2. Perhaps the most influential contemporary exponent of the extreme view that all (general) duties of justice are negative is Robert Nozick (*Anarchy, State, and Utopia* [New York: Basic Books, 1974]). Others who espouse this position include P. Foot ("Euthanasia," in *Medicine and Moral Philosophy,* ed. M. Cohen, T. Nagel, and T. Scanlon [Princeton, N.J.: Princeton University Press, 1981], pp. 276–303), and J. Narveson ("Equality vs. Liberty: Advantage, Liberty," *Social Philosophy and Policy* 2 [1984]: 33–60). Judith Jarvis Thomson also seems to be committed to it in her widely read article, "A Defense of Abortion," in *The Problem of Abortion,* ed. J. Feinberg (Belmont, Calif.: Wadsworth Publishing Co., 1973), pp. 121–39.

3. It may be correct to call some omissions charitable, as when one's opponent in a public debate refrains from pointing out a humiliatingly gross fallacy one has committed.

4. Henceforth I shall drop the qualifier 'general.' Throughout this essay I am concerned only with general rights and duties, not those that arise through promising or from special relationships, such as that between parent and child.

5. In this essay I make no attempt to support the claim that no adequate theoretical grounding is available for the thesis that rights are exclusively negative by canvassing the work of negative rights theorists, though I believe there is now a broad consensus that such a grounding is lacking. Like many of their opponents, negative rights theorists often rely on moral intuitions that are not as widely shared as they would like to think. It is not an accident, I think, that Robert Nozick, perhaps the most influential recent negative rights theorist, frankly acknowledges that he provides no systematic justification for the list of negative Lockean rights he espouses in *Anarchy, State, and Utopia.* For this reason, Thomas Nagel has aptly labeled Nozick's view "libertarianism without foundations" ("Libertarianism without Foundations," *Yale Law Journal* 85 [1975]: 136–49).

6. This is Nozick's aim in the famous Wilt Chamberlain example (pp. 160–62).

7. F. Hayek, *The Constitution of Liberty* (Chicago: University of Chicago Press, 1960), pp. 223–58.

8. Without attempting to list necessary and sufficient conditions for an act of aiding being an 'easy rescue,' the basic idea is intuitively clear enough and can be illustrated by a familiar example from the philosophical literature on 'Bad Samaritan' laws. Simply rising from one's poolside chair and lifting an infant's head from the water to prevent it from drowning would (for a person of normal physical abilities) be an easy rescue. An *easy* rescue is one which can be effected without significant cost to the

rescuer. The term 'rescue' implies that without aid there is a high probability that the individual will suffer great harm or death.

9. For perhaps the most thorough critical analysis of the arguments for and against a duty of easy rescue, see J. Feinberg, *Harm to Others* (New York: Oxford University Press, 1984), pp. 126–86. See also an excellent article by E. J. Weinrib entitled, "The Case for a Duty to Rescue," *Yale Law Journal* 90 (1980): 272–75.

10. T. C. Grey, *The Legal Enforcement of Morality* (New York: Alfred A. Knopf, 1983), p. 159.

11. D. Mathieu, "Individual Liberty and the Duty to Prevent Harm" (Ph.D. diss., Georgetown University, 1984), chap. 1, and "Respecting Liberty and Preventing Harm: Limitations on State Intervention in Prenatal Choices," *Harvard Journal of Law and Public Policy* 8 (1985): 19–55. A libertarian might reply that what is of moral concern is not the states of individuals but the *intrusions by* other individuals that affect those states. This reply, however, does little more than restate the negative rights only view since it seems difficult to imagine a satisfactory account of why intrusions are morally significant that would not rest on the tendency of intrusions to affect well-being in some way. Otherwise, the significance of intrusions seems mysterious. But even if intrusions can be shown to have moral significance independent of their tendency to affect well-being, this would do nothing to show that *only* this consideration is sufficiently important to ground rights and that rights do not also have a foundation in concern for well-being that is sufficiently powerful to make a prima facie case for positive rights.

12. A classic exposition of the nature and pervasiveness of problems of collective action is found in M. Olson's *The Logic of Collective Action* (Cambridge, Mass.: Harvard University Press, 1965).

13. Although coercion can solve both the free-rider and assurance problems, it is inaccurate to say that both problems are *public goods* problems. A public good problem exists only where there is an *externality* (a neighborhood or third-party effect) which encourages attempts to take a free ride on the contributions of others. The assurance problem can occur even where there is no externality and is not the result of anyone's attempt to take a free ride. Consequently, it is best to reserve the term 'public good' only in reference to the free-rider problem and the broader term 'collective good' to refer to goals of collective action that may fail to be achieved *either* because of the free-rider problem *or* the assurance problem. A collective good is simply any state of affairs whose production requires the efforts of many individuals and from which at least all who contribute will benefit.

14. It is somewhat more plausible to maintain that after the potential good is actualized, those who benefit from the contributions of others but refrain from contributing themselves wrong the contributors or violate their rights by taking unfair advantage of them, but even this will not always be so. If, as in cases of paternalism, the benefit was imposed upon one, it is far from dear that one must either try to avoid enjoying it or contribute to its provision. It might be said that even though no *individual* need have a right to the benefit (for enforcement to be justified), nevertheless, the *group* that benefits has a right to enforcement, a collective right against the *govern-*

ment. Whether or not this is so is irrelevant to my argument for two reasons. First, I am concerned to refute the assumption that enforcement is appropriate only where there are *individual* rights to the good in question. Second, my claim is that the case for enforcing contribution to collective goods is not *based upon* the assumption of a right, and the thesis that *if* there is a case for enforcement *then* the group has a right against the government to enforce does not entail that the latter right is the *basis* for enforcement. On the contrary, the collective right against the government is derivative from the argument for enforcement, not vice versa.

15. The idea that collective charity is a public good is not new. Milton Friedman floats it in *Capitalism and Freedom* (Chicago: University of Chicago Press, 1962), chap. 12. See also A. Buchanan, "Revolutionary Motivation and Rationality," *Philosophy and Public Affairs* 9 (1979): 67–68; R. Sugden, "On the Economics of Philanthropy," *Economic Journal* 92 (1982): 341–50, and "Reciprocity: The Supply of Public Goods through Voluntary Contributions," *Economic Journal* 94 (1984): 772–87; and D. Collard, *Altruism and Economy* (Bungay, Suffolk: Chaucer Press, 1978).

16. Sugden, "Reciprocity," pp. 773–74. For related work that also challenges the current emphasis on justice by taking duties of beneficence seriously, see T. D. Campbell, "Humanity before Justice," *British Journal of Political Science 4* (1974): 1–16; and B. Barry, "Humanity and Justice in Global Perspective," in *NOMOS XXIV: Ethics, Economics, and the Law,* ed. J. R. Pennock and J. Chapman (New York: New York University Press, 1982), pp. 219–52.

17. See, e.g., D. Mueller, *Public Choice* (Cambridge: Cambridge University Press, 1970), chap. 4.

18. This libertarian argument was suggested to me in conversation with Jan Narveson.

19. A. Buchanan, "What's So Special about Rights?" *Social Philosophy and Policy* 2 (1984): 71–73, and *Ethics, Efficiency, and the Market* (Totowa, NJ.: Rowman & Allanheld, 1985), chap. 3.

20. For a critical survey of arguments for a strong right to private property, see L. Becker, *Property Rights: Philosophical Foundations* (Boston: Routledge & Kegan Paul, 1977).

21. I. Kant, *The Metaphysics of Morals,* trans. J. Ellington (Indianapolis: Bobbs-Merrill Co., 1964), p. 48; and J. S. Mill, *Utilitarianism,* ed. O. Piest (Indianapolis; Bobbs-Merrill Co., 1957), p. 61.

22. Kant also holds that what he calls duties of virtue, which include those of charity, are unenforceable because they require not particular actions but, rather, the adoption of an end. If this point holds at all, it does so only with regard to the duty to *be* charitable, i.e., to have a certain disposition of character. In this paper I am concerned with duties of aid as imperatives to act, not with the development of moral character traits. Kant also attempts to provide a theoretical basis for the distinction between duties of justice and duties of virtue by claiming that the forrmer are "determined" by the "contradiction in conception" version of the Categorical Imperative's universalizability test, the latter by the "contradiction in willing" version. This way of distinguishing between justice and

charity seems unfruitful, however, because the "contradiction in the conception" test is both too strong and too weak to generate plausible moral principles. For a discussion of the problems with the "contradiction in conception test," see A. Buchanan, review of *Acting on Principle* by O. Nell, *Journal of Philosophy* 75 (1978): 332–33. Even if the "contradiction in conception" test could be salvaged, however, Kant's attempt to correlate duties of virtue with it and duties of virtue with the "contradiction in willing" test seems arbitrary and ad hoc.

23. E. Weinrib suggests this point, though he approaches the issue in terms of legal duties to aid rather than in terms of a distinction between justice and charity (p. 291).

24. R. Wasserstrom, "Rights, Human Rights, and Racial Discrimination," in *Rights,* ed. D. Lyons (Belmont, Calif.: Wadsworth Publishing Co., 1979), p. 57.

25. J. Murphy and J. Coleman, *The Philosophy of Law: An Introduction to Jurisprudence* (Totowa, N.J.: Rowman & Allanheld, 1984), chap. 5; and M. Kuperberg and C. Beitz, eds., *Law, Economics, and Philosophy* (Totowa, N.J.: Rowman & Allanheld, 1983), pt. 2.

26. R. Dworkin, *Taking Rights Seriously* (Cambridge, Mass.: Harvard University Press, 1977), pp. 184–205.

27. J. S. Mill is representative here (p. 53).

28. J. Rawls, *A Theory of Justice* (Cambridge, Mass.: Harvard University Press, 1971), p. 109.

29. D. Gauthier, *Morals by Agreement* (Oxford: Oxford University Press, 1986).

Against Philanthropy, Individual and Corporate

Neil Levy

Etymologically, "philanthropy" is the opposite of "misanthropy." The first refers to the love of humanity, the second to hatred of it. That ought to be sufficient evidence to convince anyone that philanthropy ought to be supported. How could anyone oppose such a noble activity as the love of humanity, or, more accurately, the giving which is motivated by such love? Even to contemplate opposition seems to convict one of misanthropy or worse. Moreover, to advocate such opposition is hardly rational, let alone ethical. Yet that is precisely the task I wish to undertake here: to advocate opposition to philanthropy. More precisely, I will argue that both corporate donors and individuals ought not engage in at least a certain class of philanthropic activities.

WHAT'S SO GOOD ABOUT PHILANTHROPY?

I suspect that the very question sounds strange to most people. They think that philanthropy is so obviously good that it does not require a defense. Nevertheless, in this section I enumerate the kind of reasons we might have for thinking that philanthropy is a good thing. These reasons can conveniently be divided into three classes, depending upon who or what is supposed to benefit from philanthropy. That is, we might think that philanthropy is good because it benefits the *recipient,* the *donor,* or the *community,* or some combination of these. I will give a brief overview of each justification for philanthropy, and then turn to a detailed discussion of the issues they raise.

"Against Philanthropy, Individual and Corporate," by Neil Levy, *Business & Professional Ethics Journal* 21(3/4) (2002): 95–108.

The Recipient

The most obvious reason philanthropy might be thought to be good concerns the recipient of the aid it provides. Obviously, there are many people in the world in need, many of them in desperate need. Philanthropic activity often results in these people having some of their needs met. In Australia alone, the figures are staggering. Philanthropy Australia, the peak organization for private and corporate donors in Australia, puts the total size of the sector at A$5.1 billion [all monetary figures are in Australian dollars]. Individuals in Australia donate approximately $3 billion annually and a further $1.8 billion is donated by the corporate sector.[1] It is clear that while much of this money does not reach the most needy people (these figures include sponsorships of sporting teams, for example), a great deal of it is directed at very worthy recipients. The charitable organizations with the largest incomes in Australia in 1993–4 were groups like the Australian Red Cross, the Salvation Army and World Vision, all devoted to fighting poverty and disadvantage and assisting with disaster relief.[2]

A brief glance at the figures makes it clear that these organizations are essentially involved in income redistribution, from the wealthy to the poor. According to the Australian Bureau of Statistics, the higher one's income, the more likely it is that one donates to charitable organizations and the greater one's average donation. Thus, the eighteen percent of Australian taxpayers with a taxable income below $10,000 donated to such organizations, with each such donor giving an average of seventeen dollars in 1994–96, whereas fifty-two percent of those earning over $100,000 donated, with each donor in this income bracket giving an average of $702. Philanthropy thus plays a part, albeit small, in addressing inequalities in wealth, by transferring a little of that wealth from the rich to the poor. For this reason it can be justified on straightforward consequentialist grounds. It increases the welfare (or preference satisfaction) of the poor, at small cost to the rich thanks to the diminishing marginal utility of the income it redistributes.

The Donor

Philanthropy does not benefit the recipients of aid alone; it also benefits the donors. It allows private corporations to 'give something back' to the community, thereby better integrating it into society. For individual donors, the justification of philanthropy will be on the grounds of virtue ethics. Traditional ethical theories like consequentialism focus on acts, their inherent qualities or their consequences, but virtue ethics focuses upon agents and their character. It exhorts us, not to act upon the categorical imperative or so as to maximize utility, but to exemplify the virtues—excellences of character—cultivation of which would make all of us morally good. On this analysis, regardless of its consequences, philanthropy is an activity which allows each of us to cultivate the virtues. In fact, all the major figures in the development of virtue ethics found a place for it in their catalogue of the virtues. For Aristotle, generosity is one of the paradigm virtues, a mean between parsimony and extravagance. So important was its exercise, he argued, that by itself it justified the existence of private property. The virtuous person requires private means whereby to engage in generous actions.[3] Perhaps there are corporate, and not only individual, virtues which include the virtue of philanthropy.

Moreover, engaging in philanthropy offers us a chance to exercise other important virtues. In fact, according to Mike Martin, *all* of the major virtues can be cultivated by inculcating the habit of giving.[4] Benevolence, kindness, compassion, justice, reciprocity—it is relatively easy to see how philanthropy promotes them all. Since the virtues are promoted by habituation, not by intellectual effort, providing opportunities for their exercise is an essential means of forming good characters.

The Community

Finally, philanthropy could be justified by reference to the community as a whole. The communitarian position supports this view. Communitarians typically argue that anything which promotes community cohesion and a sense of solidarity is, to that extent, good. A communitarian might hold that philanthropy is a positive force because it gives both donor and recipient a sense that they are engaged in a common project, of building a good society together. It is claimed that there are myriad benefits of such a sense of solidarity. For example, not only is income transferred relatively directly from rich to poor through philanthropy, but also the communitarian spirit helps reduce the gap between them in other ways as well. If both groups identify with the common good, then neither will be motivated solely by self-interest. The rich will be more willing to pay their fair share of taxes, and less likely to vote for parties which promote their class interests exclusively. Moreover, the community with which they identify is located physically, as well as socially. This gives the wealthy a stake in the natural and social environment which surrounds them. Rather than adopting the highly mobile life of the jet-setting elite, whose homes are as free-floating as their capital, they will invest in their local environment—in the air they share with their less-fortunate fellow-citizens, in the forests and waters of their country, and, in addition, in their urban environment, in schools, universities, roads and utilities.[5]

The poor, for their part, will be less alienated from the political process, more likely to vote, and more likely to participate at the grass-roots level.

Thus, community-oriented activities promote community participation, in what Charles Taylor calls a "virtuous circle."[6] The characteristic ills of modernity—alienation, isolation, the loss of a horizon of meaning—are thereby combatted. In these ways philanthropy can carry with it indirect benefits which go far beyond the resources it makes available to those most desperately in need. It improves the quality of life for everyone in the community, as well as carrying with it a number of more intangible benefits.

CRITICIZING PHILANTHROPY

Surely, in the face of these powerful claims, I would seem irrational to oppose philanthropy. Yet this is exactly what I propose to do. More precisely, I am not opposing *all* philanthropy. I do not claim that there is *no* place for donating money in a modern economy. What I am claiming is that a great deal of philanthropic activity, including some of the highest-profile campaigns, do not have the benefits claimed for them. On the contrary, I argue that we would be better off if many philanthropic organizations and activities did not exist.

It will be helpful for my purposes, to divide organizations which have as their primary activity the provision of philanthropic services into three broad classes:

1. Organizations that have as their aim the delivery of essential services to fellow-citizens. In Australia, organizations which fall under this heading include the Salvation Army and similar religiously-based charities, and the fund-raising arms of many organizations which are largely government-funded, such as hospitals.
2. Organizations that (i) work for political change, or (ii) provide services for fellow-citizens which are not seen as essential. Under (i) I include environmental groups, like the Australian Conservation Foundation, and advocacy groups which are funded (in part) by donation, like the Refugee Council of Australia.
3. Organizations that have as their primary purpose the provision of aid overseas—World Vision, Care, Amnesty International, and so on.

This list of classes is intended neither to be exhaustive nor exclusive. That is, there may well be organizations which do not fit comfortably under any of the three headings, and some which belong under more than one. Red Cross Australia provides services both locally and internationally, for instance, Amnesty International provides aid (of a kind) overseas at the same time that it operates locally to attempt to influence government policy. Nevertheless, I think the classification is clear enough to be able to play a role in motivating my argument. My claim is that philanthropy, which falls under the first heading—donations directed at providing essential services to our fellow-citizens—is morally problematic. While it is legitimate, praiseworthy, and perhaps even morally obligatory to donate to groups that provide overseas aid, it is far from clear that it is even permissible to donate to local charities which provide the same services.

This might seem counterintuitive. How could it be of questionable value to give to one's fellow citizens exactly the same aid that it is praiseworthy to give to foreigners? It is important to note, first, that I am not claiming that our fellow-citizens ought not to receive aid which is available to those overseas. Instead, what I am objecting to is the channel by which that aid is received. All essential services ought to be provided to our fellow-citizens by government, not by philanthropic organizations.

Stated so baldly, this claim is probably too vague to be assessable. I intend, however, to make it clearer as I defend it, and give my reasons for believing it to be true.

Why think that essential services, the kind of services which are routinely provided by philanthropic organizations (emergency accommodation, food parcels, hospital services and so on) ought to be provided by government? These services, I believe, ought to be made available to all citizens of developed countries, not on an *ad hoc* basis, but as a fundamental right. People have a right to the basic goods and services which are necessary for a complete human life, by which I mean not mere subsistence, but a life which makes possible the development of a range of human potentialities. Insofar as we aim at creating a fair system of cooperation, benefits and burdens ought to be distributed in such a manner as to compensate people for unchosen disadvantages, for, as John Rawls points out, the outcome of "the natural lottery . . . is arbitrary from a moral perspective."[7] Thus, at very least those people who are losers in this lottery have a claim on those who are better endowed.

Of course, this invocation of Rawls's political liberalism is far from constituting a defense of the claim that each has a right to compensation for unchosen disadvantages. I shall not defend that claim here, at least not directly. Instead, I defend government provision of these services against those who share with me the conviction that they ought to be delivered, but hold that this delivery should be done by voluntary organizations to the greatest extent possible. I will treat possible objections to my claim under the three headings I utilized at the beginning of this paper to sketch the apparent justifications for philanthropic organizations.

The Recipient

You will remember that the first justification of philanthropy was consequentialist. Philanthropy transfers wealth from the rich to the poor; due to the diminishing marginal utility of money, this increases welfare overall. I do not wish this redistribution of wealth to cease. Instead, I want it to be conducted by government. Rather than have the wealthy donate to charities, income and other taxes should generate the revenue to fund the services in question.

The obvious first objection to my proposal is that we already have such schemes in place. Few people deny that the government has some role in providing a "safety net," a set of services which ensure that no one need starve to death, that medical facilities are available to all regardless of ability to pay, and so on. It is simply false to think that we must choose between government provision of these services and allowing charitable organizations a role in providing them. In Australia, at present, we have both, and that is all to the good. Though we may well think that there ought to be more government provision of these services, there will always be room for private organizations as well. If employment benefits were raised, for example, the Salvation Army would not have as large a role to play as it does at present, but its services would still be needed. If government funding of hospitals increased, the fund-raising activities of, say, the Royal Children's Hospital would be less urgent, but the money raised would still be useful. A hospital will always be able to do with more funds for equipment, beds, and so on, no matter how much it receives from government. Thus, even in the most comprehensive welfare state, philanthropy will have its place.

Now, I do not deny that no matter how well funded a hospital is, it could always do with more funds, which would enable it to provide better health services. What I do deny is that encouraging philanthropy is an effective means of providing hospitals with the funds they need. The greater the contribution from the private sector, the less pressure there is on governments to maintain adequate funding levels. Recipients of aid, therefore, become reliant on private sources of funding. But these sources are subject to fluctuation for a variety of reasons, among the most important of which are the state of the economy and corporations' assessments of the value they get from such expenditure, considered as a form of advertising. This is especially the case since donors can reduce the moral pressure on themselves to donate by arguing that since the amount contributed by each particular donor does not make a great deal of difference to the extent to which the needs of the poor are met, withdrawing their donations will not cause injustice. Of course, this thought generalized across many donors will reduce contributions considerably. Thus, encouraging philanthropy will tend to reduce government provision, in favour of fluctuating private sources.

But, if we leave provision of essential services to philanthropy, then we ensure that its provision will be sporadic at best. The more philanthropy there is, the less the poor will be able to have their needs met reliably.

We can now begin to see why it is only domestic philanthropy which is subject to these strictures. For it to be the case that philanthropy reduces pressure on governments to maintain adequate funding, there must be a good chance that such pressure can be brought to bear in the first place. The recipients of aid must themselves be voters, or their plight must be capable of arousing people's sympathies to such an extent that it will influence their vote. Since, as a matter of fact, neither condition obtains at present for foreign-aid recipients, philanthropic activities directed at relieving their suffering remains necessary. Moreover, we cannot reasonably make organizations which have as a primary aim the alteration of government policy wholly financially dependent upon those very governments. There will continue to be a need for private funding of these groups as well.

With reference still to the recipient of aid, how might the defender of philanthropy respond to my claims? One argument often put forward concerns the comparative efficiency of the private sector. Private organizations are able to deliver services where they are needed quickly; being closer to the ground, they are more aware of the precise details of people's needs, and are less constrained by accountability procedures. Thus, they will be able to deliver their services more effectively and in a manner better attuned to what is required.[8]

This strikes me largely as free-market dogma. It is simply not the case that government agencies are unable to exercise discretion; they can and frequently do.[9] Governments need not define needs any more monolithically than do private organizations; flexibility can be, and often is, built into legislation. As for the claim that there are inefficiencies in large bureaucracies, that a larger proportion of resources will be consumed by administration in such bureaucracies than in smaller private organizations, this, too, is open to doubt. There are economies of scale, as well as potential inefficiencies to be weighed here.

Finally, the defender of philanthropy might claim that recipients will prefer private aid, aid with a human face, to public handouts. They will appreciate the generosity of the people who dispense it, and welcome the warmth of human contact. Aid so received, it might be claimed, will be better used than aid that is merely dispensed by an impersonal institution.

It is difficult to assess the strength of this claim. However, against it let me enter a plea for anonymity. It is not always the case that the human touch is preferable to an impersonal institution, and receiving essential services may well be one case in which it is not. It can be deeply humiliating to be the recipient of such aid; under such circumstances, one may very well prefer that the process takes place as impersonally as possible. Moreover, having donated funds delivered by volunteers might only serve to deepen the humiliation. It requires one to be grateful, and places one in debt, both to the donors and to the volunteer. It is much better to receive the government benefit one receives as a right from the government employee whose job it is to dispense it. Perhaps under these conditions my confidence—as a job seeker, for instance—will be less undermined by the experience, and the chance of my finding the work which will ensure that I no longer need the service will be that much the greater.

The Donor

Let us now assess the question from the point of view of the donor. You will recall the justification originally sketched under this head made reference to the virtues. Philanthropic activity makes possible the exercise of generosity, as well as a number of other central virtues (e.g. benevolence, kindness, compassion, justice, and so on). I think that this argument can be quickly dispensed with. If my proposal were to be implemented, one outlet for the exercise of these virtues would indeed be closed, but many others would remain open. Ample opportunities would exist for the exercise of benevolence, kindness, and so on, both in our personal lives (which is, in my opinion, the true primary locus of the virtues) and in our public lives. Moreover, there would remain many avenues for the exercise of generosity, including the donation of money and time to philanthropic organizations, both organizations that are aimed at alleviating suffering overseas and those organizations that are aimed at changing government policy. We need not fear that the scope for the exercise of the virtues will in any way be restricted.

Nevertheless, the defender of philanthropy might be able to appeal to the perspective of the donor in another way. Some philosophers—I have libertarians in mind here—claim that it is an infringement of our rights to force us to pay taxes beyond those needed to maintain the so-called minimal state.[10] Most philosophers agree that this is a wildly implausible claim, but it might, nevertheless, be thought that a greatly weakened version of it is defensible. Though it is false to think that we infringe upon the rights of the wealthy in making them pay taxes for the upkeep of the poor, is it preferable that they contribute voluntarily? One might ask: "Isn't coercion a harmful means of bringing about a certain result, which ought to be employed only when no other avenue remains open for achieving it?" Yet, here I am advocating an *increase* in coercion, since I am suggesting that services currently paid for by donations should instead be provided through taxation.[11]

I think that this objection is best discussed under our third heading that concerns how philanthropy benefits the entire community. It is to this topic that I now turn.

The Community

Perhaps the strongest reasons for retaining philanthropy, in the face of these criticisms, are communitarian. It is claimed that philanthropy strengthens the bonds of solidarity between fellow-citizens. By engaging in the common project of building a good society, we turn our society into a community, a spiritual home for all of us, rich and poor alike. It might be thought that the bonds of reciprocity are essential to this project. Thus, we need philanthropy, specifically philanthropy directed at our fellow-citizens, to build community.

Now, there is no doubt that there has been a lot of talk recently about partnership between, for instance, business and the community, with charity as the focus. I do not know whether it is true or not that this kind of partnership can build a sense of community. But there is no reason to believe that this is the only, or even the best, way of so doing. In particular, there is no reason to believe that community cannot be built when welfare is provided through government channels. While it is true that many people regard taxation as a burden imposed upon them, a burden to be avoided to the greatest extent possible, this is a contingent fact, open to change. There is no reason why people cannot come to appreciate that taxation is designed for precisely such community-building measures, amongst other things; there is no reason why people ought not to pay their taxes as willingly as they donate to charity. It is incorrect to think that having the coercive apparatus of the state backing up the tax regime detracts from its moral status, transforming it from a moral duty to a mere legal requirement. A great many of our most important moral obligations are similarly mandated by law and buttressed by a system of punishment. The fact that I will be punished if I am caught stealing does not in any way detract from the moral force of the injunction against theft. It does not transform it into a burden, to be avoided wherever possible. Similarly, the fact that the tax regime is backed by the law does not necessarily transform it into a burden whose moral point is lost upon me.

Thus, there is no reason why government-provided welfare cannot be as powerful a communitarian force as private philanthropy. In fact, I suspect that it could play this role rather better than current private charity. The fact that some corporations donate large amounts to private charities ought not to convince us that they see themselves as engaged in the long-term project of building a good society—not when this comes in the context of these same corporations doing everything possible to reduce the amount of tax they pay. It is more plausible to see their charity contributions as a form of advertising rather than as a true expression of community spirit.

Communitarians often argue that involvement in community organizations at a local level is necessary for building the bonds of solidarity. The state is too large and too distant an entity for us to be able to identify directly; by identifying ourselves with partial groupings a mediated identification with the entire society can be achieved. The state becomes an association of associations, and the benefits of community solidarity are reaped. It is not my purpose to dispute this claim. Nevertheless, and contrary to what might be thought, this claim offers more support for my proposal than it does for the supporters of philanthropy. Philanthropic organizations are not good focuses for community involvement because, by their very nature, they render a large part of the community they serve passive. Beneficiaries of their largesse cannot participate in the operations of these associations on an equal footing with those who contribute to them; thus, little is done to promote true solidarity between them.

Far better, from a communitarian point of view, for the focus of participation to be more directly political. Perhaps we cannot identify with the federal government, but we can have a voice in the running of the local branch of a political party, or on the committees of a pressure group, or in our local council. It is in and through these organizations, moreover, that we have a say in how our taxes are spent. This is, in part, what makes the problems they confront urgent, what ensures that they concern us directly. Thus, involvement at this level might be necessary to seeing government provision of essential services as part of building a society, of seeing ourselves as participants in that project. When we have a say in how our taxes are used, and we see that the government programs they fund are (largely) well-directed and useful, we might pay those taxes more willingly, with some of the spirit in which many of us currently donate to charities. Political involvement and government service provision can as easily be elements in the communitarian virtuous circle as can philanthropic activity.

I will now discuss one final objection to my proposal. It might be true that a well-designed taxation regime might be as (or more) efficient than a communitarian policy in encouraging voluntary philanthropy; but in the context in which governments must work today, there is very little such community spirit in the first place. Thus, if governments increase the tax burden on corporations, those that are able will respond by moving off-shore. Any government which took this step would, thus, find itself with shrinking revenues, and thus unable to meet the demands for its services. Hence governments cannot take this approach; instead they must attempt to attract corporations by offering a low tax environment, and then encourage—not force—them to donate as much as possible to private organizations.

Let me begin my reply to this line of criticism by pointing out that the objection itself concedes most of my argument. It points to the fact that corporations wish to minimize their outlays, thus implicitly conceding that they will want to minimize their contributions to essential services as well. Corporations simply will not voluntarily contribute the sums which a tax regime could legitimately demand of them. Nevertheless, the objection still deserves attention.

However, perhaps it is not all that serious. The level of taxation paid by corporations is just one factor they take into consideration in contemplating whether to go to the expense of relocating (or, indeed, when deciding whether to open a new branch). And among those other factors are goods which require relatively high levels of government expenditure, and therefore of taxation. Corporations seek environments which are politically stable, for instance, but political stability is more likely where the gap between rich and poor is relatively small. Many corporations also require an educated workforce, which is more likely to be found in nations with well-funded systems of public education. Though corporations have an interest in decreasing the tax burden upon them, in the short term, it may well be that over the longer term, relatively high taxing nations are more, not less, attractive to them.

In any case, even if there really is a tendency for corporations to relocate to lower tax environments, there are reasons why we ought not to give in to the pressures under which this places us. To do so speeds the turning of the vicious circle: cutting taxes places pressure on other countries to do the same. The direction of movement can at least be reversed: improving government services here at least makes it possible for governments elsewhere to contemplate following suit; the vicious circle becomes virtuous.

In any event, whatever the practical difficulties my proposal faces, its moral force remains undiminished. It remains clear to me, at least, that in a good society, and as part of building such a society, essential services ought to be provided by governments, funded by taxation. Private charities and corporations ought to have little or no role in the provision of these services, though there is much else they can legitimately do. I do not hope to have changed many minds on this question; if I have shown that philanthropy is in need of a justification at all, I will be satisfied.

NOTES

1. Figures drawn from the Philanthropy Australia website (http://www. philanthropy .org.au).

2. Figures drawn from the Australian Bureau of Statistics website (http:// www.abs.gov.au), *Report on Australian Social Trends 1997.* The figures given are a little misleading, since for many of the organizations in the ABS top ten, the major source of funding was in fact the Australian Government.

3. T. H. Irwin discusses this Aristotelian justification for the institution of private property in "Generosity and Property in Aristotle's *Politics*," in Ellen Frankel Paul, Fred D. Miller, Jr., Jeffrey Paul and John Ahrens (eds.) *Beneficence, Philanthropy and the Public Good* (Oxford: Basil Blackwell, 1987).

4. Mike W. Martin, *Virtuous Giving: Philanthropy, Voluntary Service, and Caring* (Bloomington: Indiana University Press, 1994), p. 30.

5. On the claim that the increased mobility of elites leads to a deterioration in services for everyone, see Christopher Lasch, *The Revolt of the Elites and the Betrayal of Democracy* (New York: W. W. Norton and Co., 1995).

6. In *The Ethics of Authenticity* (Cambridge, Mass.: Harvard University Press, 1991), p. 118.

7. John Rawls, *A Theory of Justice* (Oxford: Oxford University Press, 1971), p. 74.

8. Michael Novak advances this claim in his "An Essay on 'Public' and 'Private,'" in Robert Payton, Michael Novak, Brian O'Connell and Peter Dobkin Hall, *Philanthropy: Four Views* (New Brunswick: Transaction Books, 1988).

9. On the extent to which discretion can be built into governmental processes, see Jon Elster's *Local Justice* (New York: Russell Sage Foundation, 1992).

10. The best-known argument along these lines is that developed by Robert Nozick, in *Anarchy, State, and Utopia* (New York: Basic Books, 1974).

11. On the justification of philanthropy by reference to coercion, see Novak, p. 11.

CASE Statement of Ethics

Institutional advancement professionals, by virtue of their responsibilities within the academic community, represent their colleges, universities, and schools to the larger society. They have, therefore, a special duty to exemplify the best qualities of their institutions and to observe the highest standards of personal and professional conduct.

In so doing, they promote the merits of their institutions, and of education generally, without disparaging other colleges and schools.

Their words and actions embody respect for truth, fairness, free inquiry, and the opinions of others.

They respect all individuals without regard to race, color, sex, sexual orientation, marital status, creed, ethnic or national identity, handicap, or age.

They uphold the professional reputation of other advancement officers and give credit for ideas, words, or images originated by others.

They safeguard privacy rights and confidential information.

They do not grant or accept favors for personal gain, nor do they solicit or accept favors for their institutions where a higher public interest would be violated.

They avoid actual or apparent conflicts of interest and, if in doubt, seek guidance from appropriate authorities.

They follow the letter and spirit of laws and regulations affecting institutional advancement.

They observe these standards and others that apply to their professions and actively encourage colleagues to join them in supporting the highest standards of conduct.

The CASE Board of Trustees adopted this Statement of Ethics to guide and reinforce our professional conduct in all areas of institutional advancement. The statement is also intended to stimulate awareness and discussion of ethical issues that may arise in our professional activities. The Board adopted the final text in Toronto on July 11, 1982, after a year of deliberation by national and district leaders and by countless volunteers throughout the membership.

CASE Donor Bill of Rights

Philanthropy is based on voluntary action for the common good. It is a tradition of giving and sharing that is primary to the quality of life. To assure that philanthropy merits the respect and trust of the general public, and that donors and prospective donors can have full confidence in the not-for-profit organizations and causes they are asked to support, we declare that all donors have these rights:

1. To be informed of the organization's mission, of the way the organization intends to use donated resources, and of its capacity to use donations effectively for their intended purposes.
2. To be informed of the identity of those serving on the organization's governing board, and to expect the board to exercise prudent judgment in its stewardship responsibilities.
3. To have access to the organization's most recent financial statements.
4. To be assured their gifts will be used for the purposes for which they were given.
5. To receive appropriate acknowledgment and recognition.
6. To be assured that information about their donations is handled with respect and with confidentiality to the extent provided by law.
7. To expect that all relationships with individuals representing organizations of interest to the donor will be professional in nature.
8. To be informed whether those seeking donations are volunteers, employees of the organization or hired solicitors.
9. To have the opportunity for their names to be deleted from mailing lists that an organization may intend to share.

10. To feel free to ask questions when making a donation and to receive prompt, truthful and forthright answers.

The text of this statement in its entirety was developed by the American Association of Fundraising Counsel (AAFRC), Association for Healthcare Philanthropy (AHP), Council for Advancement and Support of Education (CASE), and the Association of Fundraising Professionals (AFP), and adopted in November 1993.

Bibliography

Adversity.net. "Education Quotas: Ohio thru Wyoming," 2002, http://www.adversity.net/education_3.htm (accessed 29 June 2004).

American Association of Fundraising Counsel. "About the AAFRC." http://www.aafrc.org/about_aafrc/ (accessed 3 August 2005).

American Association of University Professors. *Statement on Corporate Funding of Academic Research,* 2001, http://www.aaup.org/statements/Redbook/repcorf.htm (accessed 3 August 2005).

Argetsinger, Amy. "Fundraising Gets Tougher for Colleges," 17 June 2003, http://www.uh.edu/admin/media/topstories/2003/wpost/200306/20030617fund .html (accessed 3 August 2005).

Association of Professional Researchers for Advancement. "About APRA," 2004, http://www.aprahome.org/aboutapra/index.html (accessed 18 May 2004).

Barksdale, Joye Mercer. *CASE Board Revises Standards for Reporting Fund-Raising Results,* 30 July 2003, http://www.case.org/Content/PressRelease/Display.cfm ?CONTENTITEMID=3251 (accessed 3 August 2005).

Benioff, Mark, and Karen Southwick. *Compassionate Capitalism.* Franklin Lakes, NJ: Career Press, 2004.

Bernstein, Alison R. "Is Philanthropy Abandoning Higher Education?" *The Presidency* 6 (Fall 2003): 36–37.

Billitteri, Thomas J. "Venturing a Bet on Giving." *Chronicle of Philanthropy* (1 June 2000): 1, 7–12.

Black, Pam. "Help Your Clients—and Your Practice—with Charitable Giving." *Registered Rep,* 1 July 2003, http://www.findarticles.com/p/articles/mi_m0LFU/ is_7_27/ai_104761333 (accessed 19 May 2004).

Bowie, Norman E. "Business-University Partnerships." In *Morality, Responsibility and the University,* ed. Steven M. Cahn, 195–217. Philadelphia: Temple University Press, 1990.

"Breaking Away in the Race for Donors." *Philanthropy Matters* 10(2) (2000): 3, 10.

Brenowitz, Stephanie. "All Gifts Great & Small." *Matrix: The Magazine for Leaders in Education,* April 2001, http://www.findarticles.com/p/articles/mi_m0HJE/is_2_2/ai_79961284 (accessed 3 August 2005).

Brownstein, Andrew. "A Battle over a Name in the Land of the Sioux." *Chronicle of Higher Education* (23 February 2001): A46.

Buckley, Christopher. "Reunion Schedule." *The New Yorker,* 5 June 2000, 41.

Bulkeley, William. "Nonprofits Dig into Databases for Big Donors." *Wall Street Journal,* 8 September 1992.

Carlson, Scott. "An Oregon Philanthropist Spreads a Philosophy of Learning by Doing." *Chronicle of Higher Education* (21 January 2000): A33.

Carr, Sarah. "Sloan Foundation Turns Its Attention from Creating Programs to Promoting Them." *Chronicle of Higher Education* (2 June 2000): A49.

———. "Stanford's 1990 Graduates Didn't Wait Long to Give Back in a Big Way." *Chronicle of Higher Education* (20 October 2000): A34.

Certified Fund Raising Executive. 2004, http://cfre.org/index.php?action=website view&WebSiteID=34&WebPageID=490 (accessed 22 May 2004.)

Cohen, Jon. "Scrutinizing Special Admissions Policies." *Yale Herald* 34(9) (1 November 2002), http://www.yaleherald.com/article.php?Article=1318 (accessed 27 May 2004).

"College Tuition Hikes Outpacing Incomes." National Public Radio, 25 March 2004, http://www.npr.org/templates/story/story.php?storyId=1791294 (accessed 3 August 2005).

Cordes, Collen. "Debate Flares Over Growing Pressures on Academe for Ties With Industry." *Chronicle of Higher Education,* 16 September 1992, A26.

Council on Foundations. *Moral Obligation or Marketing Tool? Examining the Roles of Corporate Philanthropy.* Washington, DC: Council on Foundations, 1985.

Crumpton, Amy. *Secrecy in Science: Professional Ethics Report.* Washington, DC: American Association for the Advancement of Science, 1999.

Daniels, Lee A. "Potential Donors Figure in Entry to Vermont U." *New York Times,* 8 November 1989.

Depalma, Anthony. "Universities' Reliance on Companies Raises Vexing Questions for Research." *New York Times,* 17 March 1993.

Deutsch, Claudia. "Learning to Cast Bread upon the Waters, Wisely." *New York Times,* 14 March 2004.

Dunn, Katherine. "Philanthropy in a New Key." *Harvard Magazine* (May–June 2001): 39–43, 103.

Flaherty, Julie. "The Alternative Universe: A Guide." *Education Life* (25 April 2004): 30.

Florida State University. "Report from Dr. Raymond E. Bye Jr., Vice President for Research." Office of Research Annual Report, 1999, http://www.research.fsu.edu/activity/1999/vprpt.html (accessed 28 June 2004).

Frey, Donald. "University Endowment Returns Are Underspent." *Challenge* (July–August 2002), http://www.findarticles.com/cf_0/m1093/4_45/89871071 (accessed 28 March 2004).

Gifford, Gayle. "Cultivating Major Donors: Part 2." *Charity Channel* (7 May 2002), http://charitychannel.com/publish/templates/?a=592&z=0 (accessed 3 August 2005).

"Gifts Make the Grade." *Chronicle of Higher Education* (2 August 2002).

"Give & Take." *Chronicle of Higher Education* (26 April 1998): 6.

"Give and Take." *Chronicle of Higher Education* (7 December 2001): A23.

Golden, Daniel. "Buying Your Way into College: So Just How Much Do You Need To Donate To Get Your Kid In?" *Wall Street Journal,* 12 March 2003.

———. "Colleges Bend Rules to Admit Rich Applicants." *College Journal from the Wall Street Journal,* 24 February 2003, http://www.collegejournal.com/aidadmissions/newstrends/20030224-golden.html (accessed 27 May 2004).

———. "Money Talks: Many Colleges Admit Sub-Par Students Because They're Rich." *Wall Street Journal Classroom Edition,* May 2003, http://www.wsjclassroom edition.com/archive/03may/EDUC_moneytalks.htm (accessed 27 May 2004).

Grenzebach Glier & Associates, Inc. "Our Clients A–Z." http://www.grenze bachglier.com/clients/clients.htm (accessed 3 August 2005).

Grooters, Howard. E-mail "To those concerned re. the WRC, the UO, and Nike," n.d. http://darkwing.uoregon.edu/~uosenate/dirsen990/dirextra/grooters20apr00.html (accessed 29 June 2004).

Gunderson, Dan. "Ice Palace Opens at UND." *Minnesota Public Radio,* 5 October 2001), http://news.minnesota.publicradio.org/features/200110/05_gundersond_arena-m/ (accessed 3 August 2005).

Hall, Holly. "Donors Raise a Red Flag over Privacy." *Chronicle of Philanthropy* (23 March 2000): 1, 41–44.

Harkham Semas, Judith. "Planning for Planned Giving." *Matrix: The Magazine for Leaders in Education,* June 2001, http://www.findarticles.com/p/articles/mi_m0HJE/is_3_2/ai_79961312 (accessed 3 August 2005).

Herzog, Boaz. "Bearing Gift, CEO Returns to UO Fold." *The Oregonian,* 26 September 2001, A01.

"Higher Education Takes a Hit in State Funding in 2003–2004." *Educational Marketer,* 12 January 2004, http://www.findarticles.com/cf_dls/mODHM/1_35/112018933/print.jhtml (accessed 26 March 2004).

Hovey, Harold A. 1999. "Prospects for Funding Higher Education." *State Spending for Higher Education.* San Jose, CA: National Center for Public Policy and Higher Education, 1999. http://www.highereducation.org/reports/hovey/hovey5.shtml (accessed 26 March 2004).

"How It Would Be Used." *Chronicle of Higher Education* (24 March 1995): A36.

Independent Sector. "Independent Sector Survey Measures the Everyday Generosity of Americans." *Giving and Volunteering in the United States.* Signature Series, 2001. http://www.independentsector.org/programs/research/gv01main.html (accessed 29 May 2004).

———. "Robert L. Payton to Receive 2003 John W. Gardner Leadership Award." News Release, 29 May 2003, http://www.independentsector.org/media/gardner03 pr.html (accessed 29 May 2004).

Jones, Dennis. "State Shortfalls Projected throughout the Decade." *The National Center for Public Policy and Higher Education Policy Alert.* February 2003: 1–4.

Kaufman, King. "Puck Politics." Salon.com, 8 June 2002, http://dir.salon.com/news/sports/bounds/2001/03/08/north_dakota/index.html?sid=1017665 (accessed 9 September 2002).

Kellogg School of Management. "Development Update: Kellogg Corporate Partners LEnd Support." *Kellogg World Alumni Magazine* (Spring 2002), http://www.kellogg.northwestern.edu/kwo/spr02/facultynews/development.htm (accessed 28 June 2004).

King, Roland. "Painting the Wrong Picture." *CASE Currents* (January 1987): 27–30.

Krimsky, Sheldon. 2001. "Journal Policies on Conflict of Interest: If This Is the Therapy, What's the Disease?" *Psychotherapy and Psychosomatics* 70: 115–117.

Krimsky, Sheldon, and L. S. Rothenberg. "Conflict of Interest Policies in Science and Medical Journals: Editorial Practices and Author Disclosures." *Science and Engineering Ethics Journal* 7 (2001): 205–218.

Krimsky, Sheldon, L. S. Rothenberg, P. Stott, and G. Kyle. "Financial Interests of Authors in Scientific Journals: A Pilot Study of 14 Publications." *Science and Engineering Ethics Journal* 2 (1996): 396–410.

LaDuke, Winona. "Not the Fighting Sioux: The University of North Dakota's Mascot." *The Circle* 23 (3 March 2002): 12.

Leonhardt, David. "As Wealthy Fill Top Colleges, Concerns Grow over Fairness." *New York Times,* 24 April 2004.

Letts, C. W., W. Ryan, and A. Grossman. "Virtuous Capital: What Foundations Can Learn from Venture Capitalists." *Harvard Business Review* 97 (1997): 36–41.

Levine, Art, and Jo Ann Tooley. "The Hard Sell behind the Ivy." *U.S. News & World Report,* 11 April 1988, 54–55.

Lovett, Clare M. "Cracks in the Bedrock: Can U.S. Higher Education Remain Number One?" *Change* (March 2002), http://www.findarticles.com/cf_dls/m1254/2_34/83667241/p1/article.html (accessed 28 March 2004).

Mangan, Katherine S. "Company Seeks $10-Million from Scientist and University." *Chronicle of Higher Education* (17 November 2000): A50.

Marcy, Mary. "How to Reach the New Donors." *Chronicle of Higher Education* (6 July 2001): B13–14.

Martin, Robert. "Why Tuition Costs Are Rising So Quickly." *Challenge* (July–August 2002): 2.

Matthews, Anne. "Alma Maters Court Their Daughters." *New York Times Magazine,* 7 April 1991.

Melber, Ari. "Take On the Nepos." *TruthNews,* 11 July 2003, http://truthnews.com/world/2003070063.htm (accessed 6 May 2004).

Mercer, Joye. "Yale U. Returns a $20-Million Gift to Donor after Impasse Over." *Chronicle of Higher Education* (24 March 1995): A36.

Miller, Judith. "A Hands-On Generation Transforms the Landscape of Philanthropy." *New York Times,* 9 December 1997.

Misek, Marla. "Creating a New Comfort Zone." *CASE Currents* (January 2004): 23–26.

National Education Association. "Financing Higher Education: A Crisis in State Funding." http://www.nea.org/he/fiscalcrisis/ (accessed 26 March 2004).

Norris, Floyd. "Doing Well by Doing Good: Uncle Sam Can Help." *New York Times,* 9 December 1997.

Nygaard, Kathy. 2000 Excellence Fund Reaches Goals. *University of Minnesota News Forum,* 18 December 2000, http://www.umt.edu/urelations/nf/archive/121800/excell.htm (23 May 2004).

Payton, Robert L. "Giving Gets Unfashionable." *New York Times,* 21 February 1988.

Peyer, Bernd. "The Betrayal of Samson Occo." *Dartmouth Alumni Magazine,* November 1998, 32–37.

PollingReport.com. "Major Institutions." 2004, http://www.pollingreport.com/institut.htm (accessed 19 June 2004).

Porter, Michael E., and Mark R. Kramer. "The Competitive Advantage of Corporate Philanthropy." In *Compassionate Capitalism,* Mark Benioff and Karen Southwick, 128–129. Franklin Lakes, NJ: Career Press, 2004. Originally published in *Harvard Business Review* (December 2002).

Pulley, John L. "Guidelines Proposed to Tighten Reporting on Colleges' Gifts." *Chronicle of Higher Education* (19 July 2002): A27.

———. "How to Pick a 'Posse': A Foundation's Unusual Approach to Selecting Students." *Chronicle of Higher Education* (28 April 2000): A41.

Putnam, Karen. "We're Talking Triage." *Trusts & Estates* (January 2004): 38–40.

"Ralph Engelstad Arena: Home of the Fighting Sioux." http://ralphengelstadarena.com/new2/Arena_Info_Section/Arena_Info_Main.htm (accessed 3 August 2005).

Randall, Laura. "Picture This: Your Name on a . . . Flowerpot." *New York Times,* 9 November 2003.

Reed, Adolph L., Jr. "Majoring in Debt." *The Progressive* (January 2004), http://www.findarticles.com/cf_0/m1295/1_68/112247537/print.jhtml (accessed 28 March 2004).

Russo, Maria. "Cold Shoulder?" *Lingua Franca* (13–15 February 1998): 13–15.

Sager, Daryl. "Paying the Price for Offensive Mascots, Logos." *Native Voice,* 2003. http://www.naja.com/nativevoice2003/1darylcol.html (accessed 29 June 2004).

Sarver, Susan. "Proceed with Caution." *CASE Currents* (July/August 2001), http://www.case.org/currents/viewarticle.cfm?CONTENTitemid=2870, (accessed 3 August 2005).

Scripps Research Institute, The. "About TSRI: Introduction." http://www.scripps.edu/intro/intro.html. (accessed 26 June 2004).

Schmidt, Peter. "Public Universities Get Money to Attract High-Tech Industry." *Chronicle of Higher Education* (25 February 2000): A42.

Schneiter, Paul H. *The Art of Asking: How to Solicit Philanthropic Gifts,* 2d ed. Farmington Hills, MI: Taft Group, 1985.

Siebert, Mary Lou, Deni Elliott, and Marilyn Batt Dunn. Marilyn. "Handling Prospect

Research." In *The Ethics of Asking,* ed. Deni Elliott, 73–85. Baltimore: Johns Hopkins University Press, 1995.

SiouxSports.com. "The Ralph Engelstad Story." n.d., http://siouxsports.com/hockey/history/engelstad.htm (accessed 3 August 2005).

SocialFunds.com. "Nike CEO Retracts University Donation over Human Rights." 3 May 2000, http://www.socialfunds.com/news/print.cgi?sfArticleId=237 (accessed 16 May 2004).

Solla, Laura, and Researchprospects.com. "About the Guide: The Guide to Prospect Research & Prospect Management." Revised 2003 edition, http://www.researchprospects.com/generic.jhtml?pid=15 (accessed 21 May 2004).

Sommerfeld, Meg. "A Close Look at Ways to Increase Giving by Women—and to Instill the Habit in Girls." *Chronicle of Philanthropy* (5 October 2000): A12.

Spier, R. E. "Ethics and the Funding of Research and Development at Universities." *Science and Engineering Ethics* 4 (1998): 375–384.

Street, Scott. "Texas Tech Rejects a $12.5-Million Gift Leaving the Donor and Others Wondering Why." *Chronicle of Higher Education* (8 December 2000): A32.

Streisand, Betsy. "The New Philanthropy: The Tech Economy May Have Collapsed, but Tech Millionaires Are Still Giving." *U.S. News and World Report,* 11 June 2001, http://www.usnews.com/usnews/biztech/articles/010611/archive_037616.htm (accessed 24 July 2001).

Teltsch, Kathleen. "Studying Philanthropy." *New York Times,* 18 November 1986.

ThickEnvelope.com. "Hooked and Unhooked." http://www.usnews.com/usnews/biztech/articles/010611/archive_037616.htm (accessed 26 May 2004).

Toscano, Jim. "To Give . . . and To Receive: Examining the Exchange Process." *Charity Channel* (4 May 2003), http://charitychannel.com/publish/templates/?a=137&z=0 (accessed 21 May 2004).

Toward, Christopher. "Are You Ready for Donor-Advised Funds?" *Currents Online,* February 2000, http://www.case.org/Currents/freebies/Dafunds.htm (accessed 17 June 2000).

"Transforming Learning through Community Service." *CSUMB's Service Learning Prism.* Seaside, CA: California State University, Monterey Bay, n.d. http://service.csumb.edu/overview/prism2.html (accessed 18 May 2004).

UND Media Relations. "REA Sports Center Gets Approval from State Board." 26 June 2003, http://www.geocities.com/grovers50/menbball/0203news/0626arena.htm (accessed 29 June 2004).

University of North Dakota. "Opportunities for American Indians at the University of North Dakota." http://www.und.edu/newviewbook/ (accessed on 29 June 2004).

Van Der Werf, Martin. "Donor Leaves Colleges Waiting for Major Gifts Promises for Poetry Programs." *Chronicle of Higher Education* (6 April 2001): A38.

Warner, Irving. "In Their Eagerness to Perfect Techniques, Fund Raisers Lose Sight of Philanthropy." *Chronicle of Philanthropy* (5 October 1993): 43–44.

Wellman, Jane V. "Assessing State Accountability Systems." *Change* (March 2001), http://www.findarticles.com/cf_o/m1254/2_33/71966507/print.jhtml (accessed 28 March 2004).

Wentworth, Eric B. "The Ethical Landscape." In *The Ethics of Asking,* ed. Deni Elliott, 1–15. Baltimore: Johns Hopkins University Press, 1995.

Wetzel, Dale. "Engelstad Vowed to Pull Arena Funding If Controversial Indian Name Dropped." *Associated Press,* 15 January 2001, http://members.tripod.com/TopCat4/news/15jan00.txt (accessed 3 August 2005).

Winston, Gordon C. "For-Profit Higher Education: Godzilla or Chicken Little?" *Change* (January–February 1999), http://www.findarticles.com/cf_0/m1254/1_31/54051223/print.jhtml (accessed 28 March 2004).

Winter, Greg. "Rich Colleges Receiving Richest Share of U.S. Aid." *New York Times,* 9 November 2003.

Young Kreeger, Karen. "Studies Call Attention to Ethics of Industry Support." *The Scientist* 11 (1997), http://www.the-scientist.com/yr1997/mar/kreeger_pl_970331.html (accessed 28 June 2004).

Index

academic freedom, 22, 24, 66, 70, 71
accountability, 10, 14, 17, 71
admissions, 5, 11, 12
admissions officers, 17, 80–83
advancement officer, 90, 122, 171
African American, 40
Aldrich, Nelson, 62
Alfred P. Sloan Foundation, 16
Allan, George, 22
alumni, 33, 76, 77, 78, 81, 83, 84
American Alumni Council, 122
American Association for the Advance-
  ment of Science (AAAS), 66
American Association of Fundraising
  Counsel (AAFRC), 29, 31, 174
American Association of University
  Professors (AAUP), 22, 60, 68, 70,
  71, 89
American College Public Relations
  Association, 122
Anita Faye Hill Professorship of Law, 55
appropriation, 9, 13–14
Association of Fundraising Professionals
  (AFP), 33, 174
Association for Healthcare Philanthropy,
  122, 174
Association of Professional Researchers
  for Advancement (APRA), 29, 35

AT&T, 64
autonomy, 22–24

B. Dalton Booksellers, 64
Baker, Kendall, 49
Bass, Lee M., 54
Bayh-Dole Act of 1980, 63
Beck, Lynn G., 93–108
Benioff, Marc, 62
blackmail as a motivation to give,
  84
Boots/Knoll Pharmaceutical, 67
Bowie, Norman, 63, 65, 68, 71
Brown University, 67, 81
Buchanan, Allen, 139–58
business, nature of, 59
business and philanthropy, 62–63
business and philanthropy, distinctions
  between, 59–60
Bye, Raymond E. Jr., 60

California State University, Monterey
  Bay (CSUMB), 79
Cambridge University, 52
capacity, 4, 32, 125, 130
Carnegie, Andrew, 31, 62
Carr Center for Human Rights, 16
Carr, Greg, 15

CASE (Council for the Advancement
and Support of Education), 14, 21,
29, 42, 72, 85, 110, 122, 134
CASE Currents, 34, 38
CASE Donor Bill of Rights, 173–74
CASE Statement of Ethics, 171–72
Center on Philanthropy, 31
Center for Science in the Public Interest,
67
Certified Fund Raising Executive
(CFRE), 33
Chapman University, 51
charitable impulse, 29
charity, 15, 54, 139–58
Charity Channel, 34, 38
Chinese, 30
Christianity, 30
Chronicle of Higher Education, 38
Chronicle of Philanthropy, 36
City College of New York, 41
City University of New York, 31
Clifford, Thomas, 49
code, 94, 95, 100
coercion, 34, 79, 166
Cohen, Katherine, 81
Coleman, Bill and Claudia, 39
collegial governance, 22
Collins, Ronald, 67
communication, 22, 25, 26, 37, 55, 86,
89
Compassionate Capitalism, 62
confidentiality, 36, 50, 75, 78, 83, 100,
171, 173
conflict of interest, 41, 68, 69, 70,
75–80, 100, 172
consent, 78
Cook, W. Bruce, 119–38
Cornell, 31, 42
Cottey College, 52
Council of Foundation, 62
credibility, 4, 26, 61, 89
critic, 25, 36, 78

Dartmouth College, 3, 50

Davis, Evelyn Y., 52
democracy, 22
Democratic Education, 23
Desai, Ravi, 52
development admission, 81–82
development office, 81, 83, 110
development officer, 37, 39, 55, 112,
121, 127, 134
discrimination, 24–25, 86
Dr. Robert B. Pamplin Jr. School of
Business Administration, 17
Dong, Betty J., 67
donor activists, 16–17, 38
donor expectations, 4, 29, 38, 50
donor intent, 4, 37, 50, 54
donor-advised funds (DAFs), 42
Duke, 11–12, 31, 50, 80–83
duty to contribute, 142–43, 149
Dylan, Bob, 52

Eastman, 31
educational leader, 102, 110, 114–15,
Einstein, Albert, 52
endowment, 4, 11, 42–43, 54–55, 121
Engelstad, Ralph, 47–49
enticement, 34, 78
ethical behavior, 100–102
ethical concern, 4, 11, 78, 83
ethical issues, 6, 29, 41, 75–76, 85–86
ethically permitted, 25–26
ethically prohibited, 25, 34
ethically required, 4, 32
Exxon Education Foundation, 62

faculty, 61, 70–72, 84–85, 90, 109
Fair Labor Association, 51
Fighting Sioux, 47–50
financial advisor, 41
financial planner, 30, 40
Florida State University, 60
Ford Foundation, 122
for-profit institutions, 12–13
Franklin, Benjamin, 30
free rider, 71, 144–47

About the Author

Deni Elliott holds the Poynter Jamison Chair in Media Ethics and Press Policy at the University of South Florida, St. Petersburg. She is full professor in the Department of Journalism and Media Studies there. In her consulting life, Dr. Elliott serves as the part-time ethics officer for the Metropolitan Water District of Southern California. She also co-hosts a weekly two-minute radio show, Ethically Speaking, which is nationally syndicated through Public Radio Exchange (PRX). She was previously professor of philosophy and director, Practical Ethics Center, at the University of Montana (1992–2003), research associate professor of education and adjunct professor of philosophy and director, Ethics Institute, Dartmouth College (1988–1992), and associate professor, Department of Mass Communication, Utah State University (1985–1988). Dr. Elliott's doctoral degree is in Philosophy of Education from Harvard University.

Dr. Elliott has written extensively on matters in practical ethics including academic ethics, animal-human connection, journalism ethics, reproductive ethics, research ethics, transplantation ethics, and the teaching of ethics. In addition to this work, her publications include three co-produced documentaries; seven co-authored or edited books or special topic journals; and well over 100 book chapters, referred articles, and pieces for the trade and popular press.